JESUS LOST

IN THE

CHURCH

<u>Warren Litzman</u>

TABLE OF CONTENTS

Chapter   Page

1   Jesus Lost in the Church   1

2   The In-Christ Revolution   11

3   The Ignorance of the Gospel   33

4   The Gospel of the New Creation Race . . .   49

5   God's Intent and Paul's Revelation
     of That Intent   75

6   Our Glorious Teacher, the Holy Spirit . . .   107

7   Is the Christ-Life the Only Christian Life? .   125

8   The Benefits of Understanding
     Spiritual Pre-Existence   141

9   New Testament Ethics and the Christ-Life .   151

10   The Radical Basis of Christian Fellowship   177

11   The Faith of the Son of God   197

12   Living as Knowers   209

13   The Transforming Power of Christ   227

I

Treasure House
An Imprint of
Destiny Image
P.O. Box 310
Shippensburg, PA 17257

"For where your treasure is
there will your heart be also." Matthew 6:21

ISBN 1-56043-097-4

For Worldwide Distribution
Printed in the U.S.A.

First printing: 1987
Second printing: 1993

Destiny Image books are available through these fine distributors outside the United States:

Christian Growth, Inc. Jalan Kilang-Timor, Singapore 0315	Successful Christian Living Capetown, Rep. of South Africa
Lifestream Nottingham, England	Vision Resources Ponsonby, Auckland, New Zealand
Rhema Ministries Trading Randburg, South Africa	WA Buchanan Company Geebung, Queensland, Australia
Salvation Book Centre Petaling, Jaya, Malaysia	Word Alive Niverville, Manitoba, Canada

PREFACE

The ideas in this book are presented as foundational truths for what we believe is the current move of God. For believers whose interest is going on to the fullness of Christ, it is very likely the final move of God. History records that God is always moving His Church toward a fuller revelation of His ultimate intention. I believe that intention is that every born-again believer will come to the knowledge that the way God intended for human beings to live on this earth is by another Person, Christ, in them. The message in this book is straightforward and will bring a clearer understanding to the deeper things of God. I admit that there is much I do not know about the Christ-life, but for many years I have waited before the Father, listening to the Holy Spirit's teaching of Christ, that I might learn. Because Christ is literally becoming totally everything to the hungry and ongoing believer, this message of the Christ-life is filling all the vacant places in Christian living which have developed over the years.

It is my prayer that as you read and study this book, you will be convinced that there is no other place for you to look for spiritual fulfillment outside of Christ as your life. Since it is plainly stated in Colossians 1:16-17 that all things have to do with Christ, fixing that in your mind will put you in a position to allow the Holy Spirit to teach you Christ.

I sincerely urge every person to carefully search out the scriptures and the messages which are given, for by so doing you will come to know Him better as your own life, and in turn will be able to lift Him up to others. The purpose of this book is not to impress scholars but to feed and awaken the children of God. I am aware that this work, as are all human productions, is subject to endless improvement. It is my heart's desire and my prayer to God that the reader will come to see Christ as his only life and will thus enter into the ultimate intention of the Father.

I affectionately dedicate this book to Robbie, my wife, with whom I have labored for many years. Her faithful support has enabled me to give myself wholly to the Christ-life.

Warren Litzman
2nd Printing, 1993

INTRODUCTION: THE FINAL INTENTION

After Christ ascended back to heaven, the gospel to the Church was quickly perverted. Paul, in Galatians 1, warns of another gospel which had surfaced in his day. It is said that this was approximately A.D.55, just a short 20 to 25 years after the resurrection of Jesus. Virtually the entire Epistle to the Galatians deals with the distortion that had taken place so quickly in what Paul was destined to call my gospel of Jesus Christ. In Galatians 1, the Apostle makes no pretence as to what the gospel is. To him, the gospel, the certified gospel, was the revelation of Jesus Christ (Galatians 1:16). What had happened, in even so short a period of time from the vibrant ministry of Jesus of Nazareth, was that Christ had gotten lost by His followers. He actually had gotten lost in the Church, to the Church. That is, Christ had gotten lost to His body, the Church, because it had become taken up with church work, church missions, and church propaganda. Because of this, Paul spent most of his time in each of his Epistles stressing the importance of the Person of Christ over and above even the works of Christ. It is sad, but most all human beings today who have come in contact with Christ have befallen the same dilemma. The tendency is that what Jesus does is so terrific, powerful, and unusual that they get lost in this rather than coming to know who He is. It is only by knowing Him that they have life, not just in what He does.

However, as it was in the days of Paul, so it has continued through history, and is most notable in our day. Jesus Christ as the life of the believer is generally lost as the great theme and purpose of God in dealing with human beings. The end result is that in our day it is hard to find the true gospel because Christianity is faced with a virtual legion of different gospels. Yet, all these gospels are tied in some way to religion and churchianity. Every newcomer to Christianity, even when genuinely drawn by the Spirit and born

V

again, must begin the arduous task of searching for the real Jesus, who is lost in the Church. Never before in the history of religion — which I see as man's attempt to please God by his own self-effort — have there been so many voices defending their own aspect of churchianity. Consequently, there are many gospels being advocated today. All these gospels in some way look and sound like the real thing, but they all are carrying out someone's personal interpretation and desires, ignoring Christ as all and in all believers.

I am writing this book as a confirmed, unapologetic advocate and participant in the life of Christ as God's ultimate intention for every human being. All the background of my theology is died-in-the-wool evangelical and fundamental, for whatever these terms mean. But I now see that without the Holy Spirit teaching us revelation knowledge, neither I nor any other believer will become what God's intention is.

The Scriptures plainly teach that it is God's intention that man can no longer please God by living his own life, but it is in the living of the Christ-life that man is pleasing to God. My prayer for every reader of this book is, as Paul's was in Ephesians 1:17: ...praying for you that you may have "the spirit of wisdom and revelation in the knowledge of Him." Thus, the true gospel is the revelation of Jesus Christ as the life in every born-again human being. Anything less than this is not in God's intention, and anything more than this is solely human works and human wisdom.

If in reading you come to see Christ as your life, I believe you are on the journey of God's intention for your life. As you follow that journey, you will in time arrive at the ultimate destination for Christians, and that is, knowing your only life is Christ (Galatians 2:20).

Chapter 1

Jesus Lost
in the Church

Now His parents went to Jerusalem every year at the feast of the passover. And when He was twelve years old, they went up to Jerusalem after the custom of the feast. And when they had fulfilled the days, as they returned, the child Jesus tarried behind in Jerusalem; and Joseph and His mother knew not of it (Luke 2:41-43).

We are living in the most religious hour we have ever known—a day when people have a form of godliness but deny the power of God. The denial of the power of God is so great that we have a problem figuring out the mission of the church. In fact, one of the greatest arguments now is whether the church should become more involved in politics and civil rights. Recently, I read a statement made by a presidential press secretary. He said that he was very proud to see preachers getting involved in the civil rights strife because he felt that the church could have no greater mission.

Too Many Side Missions
Why has the church today become involved in so many side issues? Why are we so far away from the New Testament pattern and truth that many do not believe in men being called to the ministry, or in a message for which we lay down our lives, or in reaching the lost? It is because we have lost sight of Jesus Christ in His position as Head of the Church. He has lost His place and

His purpose. We have lost Jesus somewhere in our process of training or studying theology. Men have philosophized and analyzed so much that Christ has been lost in our intellectualism. But He hasn't lost His place in the eternal plan of God, for the Lord is still the center. He is still the Lamb of God for sinners slain. He is now, He was at Golgotha, and He will be throughout the endless ages. Christ has never ceased to be in the center of God's plan. No man can find peace, no mortal can find joy, no soul on this earth can find eternal life or salvation unless he finds it through our Lord and Savior, Jesus Christ. There is no other way, there is no other plan, there is no other purpose for living than through the Lord Jesus Christ. He is the only source of life and help there is on the face of this earth.

No Jesus Theology

Jesus is not the center of theology in these days. He is not the center of the church program, nor is He the center of the average believer's life. Because our Lord has been lost in the church, the church has become ineffectual in meeting the need of humanity. Less than five percent of our American population, it is believed, has had a born-again experience. You say, "That sounds like an outlandish statement," but it is so. If you can find five people out of a hundred living near you who are genuinely born again, you have done well. If you can find five out of a hundred working at the factory who are genuinely born again, with whom you can fellowship, despite church difference, then you have done a tremendous thing. Even in a religious city like Dallas, Texas, we have a form of godliness but not the power of God. What has happened is, the church has been outdated by the acceleration of knowledge and understanding in our modern world. I heard a theologian make the statement recently on a national telecast that the Church is not meeting the need of humanity today because the world has progressed into a modern and scientific age in which the Church is like an ox cart being driven in a generation of jet planes. Oh, how we have lost the divine purpose of God! We have lost Jesus Christ. When we lost Him out of the church, we lost the only reason and purpose the church had to exist.

The facts are much the same today as they were in the story of Jesus' getting lost in the temple nineteen hundred years ago. I want us to go on a search for Jesus as Mary and Joseph did. You will readily see the spiritual parallelisms to this message as we make the search, for Mary and Joseph are much like you and I. Even we who believe and advocate the truths of the Christ-life are prone to lose Jesus from our grasp, though talking about Him all the time. We are still in our houses of clay and must guard our hunger for Him and spend time in His Word lest we become castaways.

Lost Even in Fundamental Circles

The saddest plight of the world is not that Jesus is lost to the modernist, for the modernist has never really known what to do with the Lamb of God for sinners slain. Nor is it so sad that Jesus is lost in our theological institutions, for, in general, very few have ever been Christ-centered. But it is a sad and degrading fact that Jesus is getting lost in fundamentalist circles. Although we use His name, we doubt His vicarious nature, His suffering, His crucified life, and His dying heart that bring us into His eternal life. In the past He had a position in our circles; people lived for Him. Now His name, His person, His blood, and most of all, His cross, are only words rather than living motivations inside us.

Now, let us search these Scriptures. Mary and Joseph had come up to Jerusalem, as was the custom of the feast. They brought Jesus with them, for He had reached twelve years of age. *"And when they had fulfilled the days, as they returned, the child Jesus tarried behind in Jerusalem; and Joseph and His mother knew not of it"* (v. 43). What a sad thing this was. Jesus was doing something else while they were doing what they wanted to do. Jesus was about the Father's business while they were taken up with their own business.

In fact, Mary and Joseph were so taken up with their own lives and their own business that they did not even consider that Jesus might not be with them. They didn't intentionally leave Him out, for *"supposing Him to have been in the company,* [they] *went a day's journey"* (v. 44). They simply became preoccupied and busy. They lost Jesus because they took Him for granted. They were like Samson of old who laid his head in Delilah's lap and had all his locks shorn off. When he heard that the Philistines were upon him, he *supposed* that he had power, but when he rose, he was powerless.

This is a picture of the modern-day Christian Church. The Church supposes that because it has lifted up the name of Jesus, it has power and strength. But you cannot suppose that you have Christ.

The Church has lost Jesus Christ because it has taken Him for granted. We think that because we sing about Him, because we pray to Him, because we have Him in our poetry, because the preacher talks about Him in the sermon, and because the little children learn memory verses about Him, we have Jesus with us. But there is a vast difference between supposing that you have the Lord with you and *knowing that you are in Christ.* I asked somebody the other day whether he was born again and he replied, "Well, I think I am. I'm pretty sure I am." But you cannot suppose; you must *know* in whom you have believed. There will be many who come to the Lord in that day who will be supposing. They will say, "Surely I'm one of Your own, Lord. I've healed the sick, I've cast out devils, I've raised the dead, I've prophesied, and I've done every bit of it in Your name." The Lord is going to say, "I do not *know* you. Depart from Me. You are not one of Mine." My friend, you cannot suppose your relationship with Jesus. You cannot suppose you have received a blessing from God or that you are filled with the Holy Spirit or that you are overcoming. These are things that you *know.* You *know,* beyond a shadow of doubt, that your name is written in the Lamb's Book of Life. It is not enough to suppose these things, or to hope that you have these things; you must *know* that Christ is in you or else you may find yourself many days' journey away from Him.

Danger of Preoccupation

Preoccupation with the journey is dangerous. I am remorseful that I spent most of my life preoccupied with the journey. The first sixteen years of my ministry, I was more interested in the visible results—how big the crowd was, how large an auditorium I had, and whether I met expenses. I was more interested in the journey than in knowing where Jesus was. I know some people who are so interested in the journey that all they are doing is advocating that the believer ought to be healthy and wealthy, and that if he isn't, he's not where he ought to be with God. This is being more interested in the journey than in Jesus. I think the Lord *can* give you health and wealth, but I think it is much more important for you to know Christ than to know something He is able to do. You see, you can be many days' journey away from Jesus and still know what He is able to do, but you won't *know* Him, and that's the great difference.

Mary and Joseph were preoccupied with the journey. If you had told them that they didn't love their Son or that they weren't interested in Him, they would have been shocked. They would have quickly shown you all the provisions they had for Him on the journey—plenty of clothes and food. Besides, hadn't the journey been especially for Him since this was His first feast? But the fact remains that they were more interested in the journey than in having their Son with them. This is what has happened to us in the church. We have become so interested in the journey that we are more interested in fellowship with others along the way than we are in fellowship with Jesus. For this reason, we don't care about things that concern Jesus—reaching the masses and bringing His life to others. As a fellow in a national magazine said some time ago, "It's easier to join the country club in my city than it is to be passed by my church board for membership." We have surrounded ourselves with so many undertakings for the journey. We have all the programs and money and people we would need to reach the world, but what do we do with it all? We use it on our buildings so that the journey will be more comfortable and entertaining. We have forgotten the purpose of the journey, where we are headed and what we are supposed to be doing. Oh, may God help us! Mary and Joseph lost Jesus even though they had the journey under control. They had the trip well planned. They had enough food and water, but they didn't have Jesus. My friend, if you don't know Jesus as your life, you are missing the purpose of living and you don't really have anything.

Kinfolk Religion

There is another thing I see about Mary and Joseph here. When they missed Jesus, they immediately *"sought Him among their kinsfolk"* (v. 44). Surely He's right here where He's always been? They were bound by the system. "Yes sir, if anybody's going to have the Lord, it's our church. He's here in our constitution and bylaws, and if He isn't here, He's not anywhere." You see, that's what happened to Mary and Joseph. They were so idealistic that they thought if Jesus got lost at all, He had to be with some of the relatives. So they started looking for Him in their own camp. It won't take long to find Him. We won't lose any time on the journey. He'll be right here.

That's what I thought, too, when I started searching for Jesus and a deeper understanding of His life. Years ago I couldn't find Jesus, though my soul was craving Him. I got all kinds of advice and help, but the meetings, the speakers and the books didn't give me what I needed. Then one day I realized that I wasn't going to find Jesus among the kinfolk. I was going to have to step out in faith. I was going to have to get alone, away from the mob and the multitude. I came to the place where I was willing to go all the way back to Jerusalem to find Jesus, and I thank God that He gave me grace to go back and find Him.

No Place for Quitters

Mary and Joseph didn't find Jesus among the relatives. When they didn't find Him there, did they throw up their hands and quit? No, you can't give up easily—not if you love Him, not if you have known Him. They went looking for Him. You probably won't find Him where you are; you, too, will have to go looking for Him. The pattern is clear in God's Word. Entering into a higher relationship with God takes a period of waiting, of setting aside the usual activity. Abraham, Moses and Paul all spent time in the desert. Joseph learned the Lord in prison. The Lord may put you on a bed of affliction so that you have nothing else to do but seek Him. You will probably have to decide to move up and out to find a deeper walk with Him. It will take time and effort, but I urge you to begin seeking, begin hungering, because Jesus will be found of all who seek Him. Paul told the men of Athens that the Lord had *"determined the times before appointed...that they should seek the Lord, if haply they might feel after Him, and find Him, though He be not far from every one of us"* (Acts 17:26b-27).

It is significant that they *"turned back again to Jerusalem, seeking Him"* (v. 45). It is just a historical fact that they left the journey and went back to Jerusalem. It stands to reason that they would not have found Jesus had they looked in the wrong place. The place was of utmost importance in finding Him. In the fourth chapter of Galatians, Paul talks about two Jerusalems: the Jerusalem steeped in Mount Sinai's bondage, which he compared to Hagar, the bondwoman, and her children; and the New Jerusalem from above, which is free, which he compared to Sarah, the free woman, and her children.

Now if you are going to Jerusalem seeking Jesus, you need to be careful which Jerusalem you go to, for there are two Jerusalems. There is one on earth and there is one from above. There is a Jerusalem in God's plan and there is a Jerusalem in man's plan, a carnal Abrahamic plan that will breed bondage and death. You will have to make up your mind which one you are going to. In either one of them, you are likely to find Jesus. However, the Jesus you find in the earthly Jerusalem will not meet your need. Make sure the city you seek is that Jerusalem which is from above, where Christ is now seated at the right hand of the Father.

What Is the Right Church?

Where do you go to find Jesus? A man said to me the other day, "Preacher, it doesn't make any difference what church you go to as long as they preach about Jesus. I think *all* churches are all right." He probably thought that he was being tolerant and full of love for everybody, but he couldn't have been more mistaken. Most of the "isms" and cults talk about Jesus. For that matter, *everybody* talks about Jesus.

You see, it does make a lot of difference what kind of Christ you are seeking. Some like to go to a church where the fire falls—a place where they can *see* God. Just because you see blind eyes opened, deaf ears unstopped, and the lame walk doesn't mean that you see Jesus. You may have merely seen where He's been and what He's *done.* That isn't the Jesus of the *now.* A miracle is a by-product—a fruit of the tree; it is not the tree. There is only one way you can see Christ, and that is for the Holy Spirit to reveal Him to you. Only the Spirit can reveal Him. So you see, it makes a difference what kind of Christ you go looking for. Are you looking for something He's *done* or are you looking for *Him*? Are you just a curiosity seeker, or are you seeking Jesus? Do you want to know Christ, or simply what He'll do for you? Which Jerusalem are you headed for?

A Long Search

For two years I searched for Jesus, but I did a lot of other things on the side. I went around the world, preaching almost every morning and night. I made money, bought things...I just wasn't hungry enough to set aside any part of the journey. Paul said, *"I have suffered the loss of all things, that I might have the excellency of the knowledge of Christ Jesus, my Lord"* (Philippians 3:8).

The day I finally reckoned myself dead and said, "Litzman, you'll search the Scriptures until you find Jesus, or you'll quit the ministry," was the day my mind began to be renewed, and I saw the plan of God for the first time in sixteen years of preaching and teaching. I found Jesus, as did Mary and Joseph. I found Him right in me. Though I now know that I am a son of God, I cry with Paul,

'[Oh,] *that I may* **know** *Him, and the power of His resurrection, and the fellowship of His sufferings, being made conformable unto His death"* (Philippians 3:10). I have not attained or apprehended what He called me for, but I do hunger after Him. May God awaken such a hunger in you that you will set aside the journey and search for Jesus.

Chapter 2

The In-Christ
Revolution

The revolution is on and we are a part of it. Wonderfully and gloriously, the Father has let us be a part of it. This revolution centers on the greatest truth recorded in the Bible—the truth that we are "in Christ." It would seem that there would never need to be a revolution on such a subject—especially a revolution led by God, the Holy Spirit—but that is exactly what is happening today. It is a revolution in that the entire course of Reformation theology is destined for a radical advance into the fullness of Christ and a deeper understanding of God's eternal plan than ever before experienced.

The in-Christ truth is certainly not new. Neither is it some hidden and obscure truth. It is the most visible and oft-written truth in the entire New Testament, not to mention its vivid presence in the Old Testament. In fact, the in-Christ truth is mentioned over 200 times in the New Testament, with at least 146 of those times referring directly to the foremost doctrinal truth to be found in the entire Bible.

It may seem strange that the one truth that is the center and the circumference of the plan of God should have to be proclaimed by anyone. It should be the best known and most practiced truth of any Bible-believing saint. Yet the very opposite has been true, and this is the reason the Father has provoked a *revolution.* I believe He does this so He might direct our attention to what He is doing in the universe, as well as to what He is saying in the Word.

Most-Often-Mentioned Truth

It must be noted that without this truth being made known to the believer, there will never be a church pleasing to the Father. Satan's primary intent is to keep the believer from this truth. Satan knows that the entire plan of the Father is centered in Christ, so to confuse modern believers, he keeps them majoring in the minor issues. How ironic that this truth in Christ is mentioned more often as a doctrine than any other in the Scripture, yet many fail to see it. Perhaps that happens because many think, as I once did, that this wording alludes to Old English or to a special vernacular that was common to Paul. For whatever reason, the believer is denied an understanding of this truth. Without it, neither the Bible as a whole nor Christ as a Savior can be fully known or understood. It is a growing fact among the hungry believers of this world that, without a Spirit revelation of the in-Christ truth, the believer will never become all that the Father planned for him to be.

Now the Father, after waiting for centuries for men to turn to Him in hunger, has heard the cry of those searching ones and has provoked a move of the Spirit to reveal His liberating secret. It is called a secret because three times Paul spoke of it as being hidden in God. It was hidden from the Old Testament writers; it was not made clear in the ministry of Jesus of Nazareth, though He often spoke of it; and it was not until Paul had his revelation of Christ in Galatians 1 that the truth was made public. By this, one can see that the Father has a will to reveal His greatest truth when, and only when, He chooses. It is my feeling that the Father has once again accelerated among hungry believers the knowing of the one truth that runs the plan of God and is the only reason for the universe itself. So you can see why I call this a *revolution.* Praise God, the revolution is on as we see the Father alerting and teaching believers all over the earth His liberating secret. This move of the Spirit is not doctrinal except in the light that it is the main doctrine in the Word. This move of the Spirit is not denominational, yet people from every denomination are involved. It is not of man; nor is it a truth held by "a man," for it is God's will for all men to come to its knowing. It will be a truth that will revolutionize modern theology and be the ultimate fulfillment to the Reformation church.

Not a New Truth

The one important thing about this truth is, it has always been in the Scriptures. We certainly are not plucking out and promoting some obscure truth. It is as well known as any biblical truth. That is probably the reason that its greater essence has been so overlooked by the modern church. This is where Satan has tricked us. Because the in-Christ truth is so prevalent in the Word, many have not taken it seriously. There is a spiritual pride in most believers that surfaces when someone comes saying a thing differently than they understood it, or when someone says that emphasis should be placed in another area. This, of course, causes a revolution among believers, but as I see it, it is the only way the Father can ever bring His plan to its ultimate conclusion.

The Reason for Everything

To have a clear picture of what God is doing in His eternal plan, we must see how the in-Christ truth is the catalyst for everything He does. The incorporation of all believers in Christ is the prime work of God to correct the self-independence resident in all creatures since Satan was in the Father's house. Notably lacking was any feeling that Lucifer and the Father were one. Thus, when the Father drew up the plan for us, He in essence had to devise some way His sons could be one with Him. He is love and has always wanted love from His sons. What He wants is a union of all men with Himself, and further, a union of all men with themselves. This is His greatest desire, for one of the most singular truths in the Scriptures, in Christ, is translated 146 times to read union with God. It is further proven in that this most-often-stated truth is not just a prepositional phrase but a doctrinal truth. As a doctrinal truth, it is stated more often than any other doctrinal truth in the Word—more than faith, or power, or love, or baptism, or church. All of these doctrines are genuine, but none of them hold the importance or weight of Scripture as does the in-Christ truth.

To really get a clear picture of this truth, we need to see the truth in the Old Testament. To do this properly, we will rely upon the New Testament to explain the Old. As theologians say, "The New is hidden in the Old; the Old is revealed in the New." As I have often taught students, the Epistles explain the Gospels, and the Gospels explain the Old Testament. Therefore, to understand this great truth in the Old Testament, we must call upon Paul. For example, all creation in and before Genesis 1 is to Paul an overwhelming fact, that God's purpose is to bring the creature to a union with Him by placing the creature in Christ. This is evidenced by Paul's words in Ephesians 1:4, *"According as He hath chosen us in Him before the foundation of the world...."* Here at the foundation of the world is also stated the foundation of the greatest truth, "chosen in Him." For Paul, all of creation deals with the in-Christ truth. In Colossians 1:15-19, he states, *"[Christ] the firstborn of every creature...by Him were all things created...all things were created by Him, and for Him: And He is before all things, and by Him all things consist...that in all things He might have the pre-eminence. For it pleased the Father that in Him should all fulness dwell."*

Two Beginnings

To further seal the idea of Christ's union with the creature being the purpose of all creation, we parallel the two verses in the Word which speak the most loudly concerning the beginning. Genesis 1:1 says, *"In the beginning God created the heaven and the earth."* John 1:1 says, *"In the beginning was the Word...."* Adding these two ideas together shows that the whole creation is inseparable from Christ. But more than that, it is not just Christ born of a virgin, but Christ the Word. This is significant because the use of the term "Word" means that Christ is not only the object of the union but also that seeing Him in the Scriptures is God's means of our knowing this union. Christ is the supernatural unity of all creation and He is the unity of the supernatural work, which was God's purpose in creation. So, as the truth of the liberating secret begins in the Old Testament—that Christ is inseparable from creation itself—all the way through the Scriptures, the same theme is predominant right up to where John, in the Apocalypse, sees the New Jerusalem coming down from Heaven, adorned as a bride. Our union with Christ is the theme of it all—not just a part of it, not just some of it, but the whole of it.

Adam forfeited this union with God, both for him and for us. But this defection had been foreseen by the Father and God's plan of our oneness with Him continued to unfold. Especially was the plan of God's oneness with the creature made evident in God's dealings with Abraham. Once again, however, we must go to the New Testament and Paul to understand what happened with Abraham. The explanation is in the Epistle to the Galatians (3:8-16). Certain Jews had come into the young church and were sowing seeds of discord. They maintained that the promises made by God in the Old Testament were for Jews alone and Christians were excluded unless they submitted to circumcision. Their error is the same error being made now by some in the modern church. They are saying that, if you do not keep certain parts of the law, the promises of the covenants are nullified. Thus, some are attempting to "become Jews" by their self-efforts. They are singing Jewish songs, doing Jewish dances, wearing Jewish out-fits, and promoting a Jewish type of worship. As is the Father's custom, He allows some to go the opposite way, that all might come to His more perfect way. This is also proof of the need of the in-Christ revolution. If there is any great truth given by the Scriptures in the in-Christ message, it is that in Christ there is neither Jew, nor Gentile, nor anything out of their past, for *old things are passed away*.

Christ and Abraham

To these Jews Paul says that the Father had Jesus in mind when He made the promises to Abraham. Paul assures them that the believer in Christ is plainly in focus when he says that the promise is not made to *seeds*, but to one seed, which is Christ. He goes on to say, in verse 17 of Galatians 3, that *"...the covenant, that was confirmed before of God in Christ...."* The actual meaning of all this is, the Father made the covenant with Christ. It also means that if the sole heir of the promises to Abraham is Christ, then we are a *sole heir* also, for we are in Christ. We must see by this that the whole of what the Father did in the Old Testament is taken up with Christ. The Old Testament is concerned with Christ and with us in Christ. How we pray that those who are seeking to know God in a fuller way will not be trapped into placing anything—not even Judaism—above Christ, who is the only means by which believers become one with God.

What was present in the Old Testament in only embryonic form is fully developed in the New. It is an awesome thing that God could keep this liberating knowledge a *secret* for over four thousand years (Romans 16:25). But the fact is that, almost exclusively, the Father first gave the great truth to Paul and John. It is Paul alone who tells us first that he has received the great revelation of his union with Christ. John later on closes the Scriptures trumpeting the same truth. Thus we are able to say that the knowledge of our union with the Father and the knowledge of our in-Christ position are the same when the believer can witness to a revelation of Christ as his only life. In other words, a revelation of the Christ-life is tantamount to union. This is what is actually completed in the New Testament. The whole truth of God in us and eventually working out of us is a progression in the Scriptures. Although there is little said outright in the four Gospels concerning this truth, Christ does speak again and again in shrouded words, and sometimes in plain words, as in John 15, of the secret. It was to be the work of the Holy Spirit to make known the secret hidden from generations—that Christ in the creature was to be the only life of the creature (John 14-16).

Revealed Only by the Holy Spirit

One of the great functions seen in the four Gospels is the Person of Christ doing the will of the Father. The one great difference between the science of theology and all the other sciences is that all of its doctrines deal with a Person, not just a set of facts. It is for this reason that truth can never be derived in Christianity from the accumulation of certain facts. Facts can be translated according to any fancy. This is what great numbers of religious groups have done, with Satan's help, and have been denied the fullness of God in Christ. You can prove anything by the Scriptures, but to know Him who is the Word is to know truth. That is why the Christ-life can be revealed only by the Holy Spirit. Revelation that the believer is in Christ is the essence of the union. This Person, who is the Word, is vividly portrayed in the Gospels. It is a glorious presentation of the Word made flesh. This is Christianity alive—not just a set of doctrines, or a special set of verses from Scripture, or a fulfillment of special promises, but a life into which we have been placed (I Corinthians 12:13).

Now it is important that we see in the Gospels that the life of Jesus of Nazareth cannot be our life, for that was the Jesus who lived in a body given to Him by Mary. But we see in that Christ the Jesus who lives in our body or our clay pot (II Corinthians 4:7). The intention of the Father is not that we be Jesus of Nazareth, but that by the example of that Jesus, we would come to union with the Father (John 17). Furthermore, it is the purpose of the Gospels to show how that union comes about. The true understanding of the Christ-life is locked up in the Christ-death. From the beginning of the Gospels, we see Christ on His way to death. In fact, all of the Scriptures previous to His death clearly point to His death. But that is not all. If Christ has come into us and if He also has come to die, then it is the life of the cross that He has come to implant in our souls. Paul explained this in Second Corinthians 4:10 as he says that the dying of Christ works in us that we might manifest His life in our body. This is the strange idea that prompts Paul to call the whole truth of being in Christ the "mystery of godliness." The method by which God will work it all out is that death will bring forth life.

Simple Identification

It is with this subject of death that we must see the overwhelming truth of God's oneness with His creatures, and further, the fact that all creatures are dependent upon another for their nature. When Jesus died, every soul died in Him. The believer's identification must begin with His death. We were all in Him when He died, and He, having no sin of His own to kill Him, literally died as us. He died as us, was buried as us, was resurrected as us, and ascended as us. This union is essential to understanding the plan of God. This is also shown by Paul in his sermon on Mars Hill, directed to sinners—that even they lived and moved and had their being in Christ. This shows all the more the fact that oneness in the creature is immanent in the plan of God. On the other hand, we must not ignore the fact that Jesus said sinners were one with Satan, as in their unbelief Satan was their father (John 8).

All of this is scriptural proof that the Father, whose whole purpose in the universe is to get sons to live in His house, has chosen a plan—a method by which He shall accomplish it. He will do it by placing the only Son who pleases Him, God the Son, in every believing creature. Then He will depend upon that Son, and only on that Son, to be His love and to do His will. To bring all this about, He will cause a *birthing.* This is announced by Jesus in John 3 as He speaks to Nicodemus, *"You must be born again."* This birthing is the introduction to the mystery and is explained by the prototype example of Mary of Nazareth.

The Word Given a Body

John explains the oneness idea of the Father, expressed in the birth of Jesus, when he says, *"And the Word was made flesh, and dwelt among us... "* (John 1:14). He was wrapped in the flesh given to Him by Mary and, as such, became the total example of all who would be *born again,* for they too would be the flesh by which He would manifest Himself. Paul was to clarify it when he would say, *"...the life which I now live in the flesh... "* (Galatians 2:20) is Christ. Mary was a prototype of what the believer was to do—to bring a living Savior to a dying world. We do this by the revealed in-Christ truth. Our union with Him is a constant witness of Him as us and wherever we are, there also is He (John 12:26). He is dying in us that others might live.

It is sad that so many who love the Lord and want to serve Him have become all mixed up in their understanding of the virgin birth. To this day, one of Satan's more common tricks is to get believers arguing over the pros and cons of the birth. It should be obvious by now that my whole intent is to show that "Christ in us" was not just introduced in prototype by Mary of Nazareth, but was the entire intention of the Father from the beginning. We would never argue with the Mary situation if we could see what God's purpose is in it all.

The Word made flesh is important to the entire plan of God, and the Father's first revelation of it was at Bethlehem. We must not get lost in arguing whether or not that miracle is possible, but we must see the single plan of God—that all creatures are in Him and that He is in them. God, by the Holy Spirit, has placed, or birthed, the Son in us, and as Mary showed us that she could live her life as Him, so are we to live our lives as Christ. This is what a Christ-person is—a Christian. Aside from the importance of the virgin birth and believing in it to understand our own position with God, we must equally understand the birthing of the Father.

The Trinity and Birthing

Now, this birthing is equally argued by men untaught by the Spirit. The birthing shows so beautifully the Holy Trinity at work and may be the supreme reason why one God is manifested in three Persons. It is the dilemma of the human race to not hear clearly what the Spirit is saying to them. That is evidenced by the Spirit saying over and over again, in the Book of Revelation, *"He that hath an ear, let him hear...."* Remember, it is not so much what we think or hear others say that is important; it is what the Spirit is saying that is of great importance. Believe it or not, when the Spirit speaks, He always brings about the Father's ultimate plan, regardless of to whom He speaks. This is the way that true believers will all speak the same things. But take a look at the

Trinity at birthing. It can be simply summarized in this statement: The Father wants sons to live in His house. To get these sons, He planned from the beginning to put the only Son who ever pleased Him in every creature who believed on Him. To do that, when a creature believed, He put out the Satan nature and birthed in them His own Son. He would not just change them, He would birth a new nature—His life—in them. He would be the Father, the Holy Spirit would be the One who brought about the conception, and Christ would be the Son in them. That would bring them into perfect union with Him, and they would be called Christians. It is obvious that all of this taking place in a human being called for a miracle that simple faith—*'believ*[ing] *on the Lord Jesus Christ"*—would bring about. However, even though the miracle was God's intention from the beginning and even though Mary was a prototype, multitudes missed what the Father was doing then. They still fail, even today, to hear His Spirit. Now, how shall the Father make the mystery known?

This brings us to the one person whom God could trust with the knowledge of the mystery—the Apostle Paul. Since God plans things, it is logical to assume that He planned Paul's life from its beginning. He planned the development of a person who could explain the mystery. In time, he would be able to carry out the duties of one who was to be the Apostle to the Gentiles, who were to be part of the people of the "new creation race" reborn by the placing of another within them. Because all of the Christological Epistles have as their main theme the revelation of the mystery—the in-Christ message—there is not sufficient space here to cover it all. So it would be good to center our attention on just one portion of the Word that deals with the subject. There is no better place than Ephesians 3. Starting at the beginning of the chapter, I would like to comment on verses that are pertinent to this subject.

Ephesians, Chapter Three

Verse 1: *"For this cause I Paul, the prisoner of Jesus Christ for you Gentiles. "* Paul often uses the term *prisoner* or similar terms such as *slave*, to show that he is bound to Christ. All who see Christ as their only life readily give their all to Him, not holding any position to themselves that would show they were independent of Him. Also, the word *Gentiles* points to the fact that they are to be the new race of people—not just converted or made-over Jews.

Verse 2: *"If ye have heard of the dispensation of the grace of God which is given me to you-ward."* The word dispensation translates as "administration or stewardship." Paul says that among the gifts he was given by God was the ability to arrange things so the great truth might be made known to all believers. Certainly, this is the greatest need today in the ministry. So few are willing to give themselves to study and preparation to handle a special dispensation so needed by God's people today. The people perish and the church is spiritually destitute because so few have a special dispensation to preach the mystery.

Verse 3: *"How that by revelation He made known unto me the mystery...."* Now this is the very heart of the matter. Paul never speaks of the mystery aside from a revelation. It is well he does it this way. Since the Father hid this great truth from the likes of Abraham, Moses, David, Isaiah and Jeremiah, it certainly could not be picked up by just anyone and preached. It would take a startling revelation to make the mystery known, and Paul was the trained vessel through whom the Lord elected to do this. All mysteries must be revealed. That is the purpose of a mystery. But the mystery of the ages—the mystery hidden in God since the world began—must be made known by special revelation.

Paul made the revelation most important, and sad to say, the modern church has failed to see its importance. But thanks be to God that he has sent a move of His Spirit in which hungry hearts are receiving the revelation as never before.

Verses 3b and 4: *"(as I wrote afore in few words, whereby, when ye read, ye may understand my knowledge in the mystery of Christ.)"* The occasion Paul writes of here is found in Galatians 1:15-16, where he tells how he received a revelation of Christ. How beautifully he relates it: *"When it pleased God,* [Here he speaks of the time element necessary to spiritual growth. We come to full understanding only in the Father's timing.] *who separated me from my mother's womb* [He speaks here of his being a container, for all that mothers can do for babies is to bear them by giving them a body. The father gives the life.], *and called me by His grace* [This shows the special dispensation already mentioned.], *to reveal His Son in me* [Notice the Spirit is clear in this revelation.]. "

The revelation is not of Jesus of Nazareth, not of what Christ is doing or of what He shall do; the revelation is of the Christ that was *in Paul*. This pinpoints the move of God for today. The great revelation of the hour is God revealing the Son in believers.

Paul goes on in verse 4 of Ephesians 3 to say how important it is that all understand his knowledge in the mystery of Christ. This remark is generally unheeded by modern theologians, as they take the mystery to simply refer to how Jesus died to save us from sin. Such oversimplification has robbed the church of its greater understanding of God's plan, and certainly has thwarted the believer in his search for God's fullness. Paul plainly said that he wanted to be understood concerning the in-Christ truth. Our prayer is that all who hunger will come to understand Paul.

Waiting on the Lord

Verse 5: *"Which in other ages was not made known unto the sons of men, as it is now revealed unto His holy apostles and prophets by the Spirit."* For four thousand years, from the foundation of the world to Calvary, God had the liberating secret waiting. His plan was to get a new race of sons—not angels, not Jews, not Gentiles—but a new creation, with Christ as its life and God as its nature. Notice that Paul said that the revelation was now available to the apostles and prophets. All who preach the Word could have the liberating truth, but alas, few there are who want it, and few there are who even know about it. The one major reason so few are making the revelation known is, it comes only by the Spirit. Far too few are waiting upon the Lord these days; few there are who are hearing what the Spirit says. Books, tapes, church services and worship, radio and television, can never take the place of the revelation *by the Spirit.* The revelation is more than head knowledge of union. It is more than the taking of a "step of faith." It is God, in all His power and splendor, revealing the liberating secret that He, Himself, by the Son, is the only life of the believer.

Verse 6: *"That the Gentiles should be fellowheirs, and of the same body, and partakers of His promise in Christ by the gospel."* The Gentiles became a chosen people of God that they might be admitted into the family. The Jews had rejected the king who was to rule over their kingdom, so the Father set aside their kingdom until later and opened the new program, new for the world but certainly not new in His planning, for it was designed before the foundation of the world (Ephesians 1:4). Notice the language of verse 6. The Father does nothing that does not have, at its center, the in-Christ truth. Even the promises of God, which are for the new creation people, are in Christ. Finally, the verse says that this message is to be called *the gospel.* Today the true gospel, with its core of truth in Christ, is generally lost. Multitudes who are sincerely seeking God are on a hopeless treadmill of religion because of this lacking in truth. The born-again believer has no other life, or hope, or truth, other than that which is in Christ. He is not a Jew. The earthly promises made to Israel do not apply to him. He is not saved by keeping covenants or by doing anything on his own. He is saved only by grace. He has no place in the Old Testament, no place in its promises, no place in its people; he is a stranger and a sojourner in a weary land. He has a place in the whole plan of the Father only as he sees Jesus. Jesus alone is his attachment to God. Gloriously, he sees Jesus in the Old Testament and, by that, draws life—Christ's life—but he knows he is not of an earthly people. He knows he is strictly a heavenly creature, reborn into a new race. Now, when the modern Church and theology denies this believer his rightful place in the plan of God by forcing him into all sorts of erroneous doctrines and methods of worship, he becomes frustrated and defeated and eventually wants to quit religion. He is a heavenly creature, seated with

Christ, and cannot fit into any other role. The only gospel that will feed his spirit and seal his relationship with the Father is the revelation of Christ as his only life.

A Soul Set Free

Verse 8: *"Unto me, who am less than the least of all saints, is this grace given, that I should preach among the Gentiles the unsearchable riches of Christ."* How wonderful to see the expression of a soul set free from the self-effort of religion! Paul knows that his only life is Christ and that in Christ he has everything necessary to enjoy life eternal. Thus, he can constantly decrease in his own self-works that the Jesus he is might increase. It becomes easy to say, *"I am the least of all saints."* Modern believers, trapped by their own efforts, cannot afford to demoralize their thinking processes for fear that they will lose faith. Of course, Paul calls this attitude a *grace,* and this grace is a benefit of his in-Christ knowledge. The product of this *grace* was his preaching of the Christ-life. It produced a whole new gospel which was centered solely in Christ. It was so powerful that Paul said the riches in Christ were *unsearchable.* Again, I must say that this is the gospel being denied our generation. Provoked by our ignorance of the true gospel, we have limited God to dealing with us as if we were an earthly people, like Israel, demanding earthly blessings, temporal blessings, body blessings, and material blessings. We have become so duped by Satan that many say to God, "If You don't keep Your Word to us, You cease to be God." The Word we want kept is based on the promises made to an earthly people, and the new creation believer, born again into the family, is not earthly. By this, religion denies believers the unsearchable riches in Christ Jesus. So this is the gospel that must be preached.

Nothing else will fit the new race. It has in it all the benefits that God gave to Israel. It has in it all the blessings that are in any Old Testament covenant. It has in it all the personal benefits, such as health and wealth, but none of these things need be preached because they are not blessings aside from Him. They are the benefits of Him—not just from Him. This is why Paul was eventually made to say that he was determined to know nothing among men other than Christ and Him crucified. He had learned the true gospel. He knew that we were a whole different race of people, bound by a new covenant, in Christ.

To every hungry, weary, sick and frustrated believer, let me encourage you. You trusted Christ for your salvation; you can trust Him for your life. You actually do not have any other life than His, and to pervert that is to be deceived by Satan. The riches in Christ are unsearchable.

The Fellowship of the Mystery

Verse 9: *"And to make all men see what is the fellowship of the mystery, which from the beginning of the world hath been hid in God, who created all things by Jesus Christ."* Here is Paul's apostolic commission plainly stated—to make all men see the mystery. Strong are the words "to make." They imply two things: First, that the church of his day had difficulty seeing Jesus as its all and in all. This is how it is today and is why the gospel of the mystery must be preached. Second, it means that a "holy boldness" must come upon the modern ministry to preach the truth. Multitudes have been denied a fellowship in the mystery long enough. God has graciously sent a move of the Spirit to remedy this. There is a new anointing to those who would dare to be God's and say the things of God.

Next, Paul says that there is a literal *fellowship* in the mystery. We are only now beginning to see this fellowship. For years every hungry heart has pondered a relationship with other believers where there was no strife, no hate, and no confusion. To my knowledge, such a fellowship has never been produced effectively by religion because of the lacking of the knowledge of the mystery. There is a fellowship of the mystery that produces a relationship between believers and the Father hitherto unknown. We are beginning to see the fellowship these days, and the root of it is believers who see Christ as their only life. They are beginning to realize that the "new race" is to know no man after the flesh (II Corinthians 5:16). It is a fellowship of Christ-persons who know that there is no need for struggling, fretting or worrying over things that are already under Christ's dominion. They are a people who know their love is His, their power is His, their works are His, their all is His. This is the fellowship of the mystery.

The Nature of God

Paul goes on to state the imperativeness of his mission. It lay in the fact that the mystery was hidden in God from the beginning, not a new truth, not a new idea, not a man-made message— it was hidden in God from the beginning. The essence of this fact must not be ignored. It means several things. It means that the in-Christ message is predominant to the world itself. It was before the world; thus, all that is in the universe is secondary and subservient to the mystery. It also means that the very idea of the mystery is an intricate part of God and, in effect, is the very nature of God. In comparison, it means that the way that God dealt with Adam, with Abraham, with Moses, with Israel, with David, and with all the prophets, was not His full nature at work. It means that the only time God actually was doing what was true to His nature was when He planted His seed in the believer and birthed the Son, Christ.

No other gospel can possibly take the place of this. It is astounding, overwhelming, unbelievable, and absolutely necessary to Christianity. It is why Paul said that if anyone preached any other gospel than his, let him be accursed (Galatians 1:8-9). It is also why God said that this gospel could be known and preached only *"by the revelation of Jesus Christ"* (Galatians 1:11-12).

Next, Paul says that God created all things by Jesus Christ. This is further proof that the universe is secondary to the in-Christ truth. God planned that all things would deal with His Son from the beginning, and when He created the world, all of the creation dealt with Christ. This simply means that all created things are but "converging powers" to push the creature to Christ. It is the literal fulfillment of Romans 8:28; Second Corinthians 4:15; and Second Corinthians 5:18. The strongest evidence for the creation of the world is that God made it as a place to train sons. The world is no more than a schoolhouse to bring us to Christ. The Father built into the world all the things necessary to teach us the Spirit of His dear Son. It is not Satan's world; he usurped it. Men made him the god of this world—the Father didn't. When a believer sees this, he can for the first time function in the world as God intended. The next verse plainly shows this.

Satan Is a Defeated Foe

Verse 10: *"To the intent that now unto the principalities and powers in heavenly places might be known by the church the manifold wisdom of God."* Principalities and powers relate to Satan's work. Notice that the work of Satan in this instance is in the heavenlies. That is where the true believer, in Christ, is seated; so that is where the battle is waged by Satan. How strange that Satan knows where the true believer is, while the modern church fights him on earth in the temporal realm. True, he is there also, but I hear Paul saying that Satan's greater interest is with the believer already in union with Christ. Also, Paul wanted the devil to know that the church had the revealed wisdom of God. What a thought! The true Church has the power to defeat Satan by its very knowledge. Of course, this is not secular, religious or theological knowledge, but Spirit-taught knowledge. Furthermore, Paul says that this knowledge—this wisdom—can come to the believer only by Jesus Christ, for whom all things are created. It means that creation cannot be separated from Christ and that the believer living in this world, having received a revelation of Christ, sees Christ in all things.

Verse 11: *"According to the eternal purpose which He purposed in Christ Jesus our Lord."* This seals the ultimate truth. It was in God Himself, by the personality of the God-Son, that this glorious eternal plan should come about. It means that the Father wanted sons in His house like Himself, God the Son; therefore, everything He did centered in the Son. If this seems difficult for you to grasp, you are now being faced with the necessity of the revelation of Jesus Christ. Without this revelation, as Paul taught it, your union with Christ is nothing more than head knowledge and will deny you the ultimate fellowship which is yours in Christ. This is the work of the Holy Spirit, and it must be asked for and sought after. A renewed mind is essential to the revelation and this is where the Spirit will work.

There is no end to the commentary we could make on these verses, but I feel enough time has been given presently.

In our day, there are many writers and commentators who would substitute other terminology for *in Christ* because they do not have the revelation of Christ planted in them by the Holy Spirit. The Holy Spirit will never confuse the original language, but will, in fact, more purely describe it. We must believe that Paul, by the revelation of Christ, was able to base his entire theology on the original wisdom of God. This means that the wonderful truths presented in the Old Testament could point only to Christ. Finally, knowing Christ as the life of the believer must hinge on a special revelation. That is why Paul prayed for believers to receive a *"revelation in the knowledge of Him"* (Ephesians 1:17). Without this knowledge, no believer can ever go beyond his Old Testament knowledge or his head knowledge. Today, many of the new translations of the Bible are so full of sense knowledge that the believer is left without a spirit to know God. Religion is a "thing of the head" rather than a revelation. In fact, many of the newer translations cut out numerous statements of the in-Christ message, supposing that they were redundant, or cliche, or unnecessary. This not only denies the Father the making of a son in the believer, but denies the believer a work of the Holy Spirit necessary to his fitting into God's plan and Christ's world.

Christ in Us—Not Just for Us

We must be careful not to substitute other wording for the in-Christ truth. Some say that we are "within Christ." Some say that Christ is "for" us rather than in us. These changes and many others which are being made show that Satan's major work is to blind the believer to who he is in Christ by deceitfully and minutely changing Spirit-language into carnal language.

True believers will not be tricked by this change. Many believers are buying good Greek lexicons and learning to use them, realizing that they can no longer depend on even the most godly-appearing writers for their Word. It is obvious that depending upon man has brought about thousands of different gospel beliefs, all of which disagree with each other. Praise God, the revelation of Jesus Christ in believers is making a true fellowship of the mystery—a fellowship that will be soundly rejected by those whose interpretation of the Scriptures is based on sense knowledge.

One important reason for the modern church's rejection of Paul's revelation of the Christ-life is that the *revelation* denotes and requires a supernatural work of the Holy Spirit. In every place in the Scriptures where the revelation is alluded to, the Holy Spirit is at His basic work. His main office is to reveal Christ as the Son in the believer. Any work of the Holy Spirit is supernatural. Sad to say, some believers have so fought modern-day miracles that they have denied the miraculous work of the Spirit also. It is a supernatural work of the Spirit when one is saved, is filled with the Spirit, or receives a revelation of Christ. If you reject the supernatural, you limit yourself to head knowledge. That is where the modern church is today. Believers are forced to go about looking for "another Christ" rather than the one they are. How sad! Christ is already in them, and they don't know it and cannot live like it. How limited they are! Finally, this believer must turn to the outer things such as health and wealth messages to feel like God is working at all. The treasure within him, Christ, is locked up by his religion and he lives, as Paul said, like the other Gentiles, as if he were not in Christ.

Seeking the Lord

This miracle of the revelation of Christ is accessible to all who hunger. Paul said that when he wanted to know Christ, he did not go to the other brethren, he went into the desert. This is real hunger. Paul said in Philippians 3 that when he wanted to know Christ, he was willing to suffer the loss of all things that made him what he was for the *"excellency of the knowledge"* (v. 8). This is real hunger! Some may see this kind of "seeking after God" as self-effort. I must give a warning here. When I seek after God, it is not my seeking, but He in me. I, within myself, can do nothing; I cannot even desire God within myself. That is the reason the Father put another in us. It is Christ in me who seeks to please the Father. It is Christ in me who wants to do only the will of the Father. This is truly me as Him, and Him as me. This is not human effort, but self-effort with Christ as my only self. Christ in me needs my mind—*"Let this mind be in you..."* (Philippians 2:5). The mind of Christ wants only the things of the Father. Thus it was with Paul. Christ, as me, seeks after the Father and wants to know Him and to be only His.

The modern Church and its preachers will have to seek after God to know the mystery. It will not fall on them. They will not pick it up from some book. It will not come out of the present seminaries or Bible colleges. It will not come by great efforts in soul-winning or miracles. It will not come through seminars or conferences. It can come only when a Christ-created hunger comes and the believer cannot continue without it. It will come when the believer shuts himself up with God, as did Paul, who went into the Arabian desert. It will come only when a believer has gotten sick and tired of being sick and tired of religion. It will happen only when the believer shuts off all other attachments, as did Paul, who would not go to the brethren at Jerusalem for help. It will happen only when all the believer wants to know is Christ and when he is willing to pay the price of the desert, of the loneliness, of the loss of self-independence, and of being separated from all the past and all that makes him a person. When these ideas begin to work in the believer, the miracle has begun.

The Point of Separation
Finally, once the believer sees Christ as his all, the union is in effect. From then on he grows in Christ until all he does is Christ. It is Paul saying that the life he now lives is Christ—not like His, but literally His. This is where the revolution is. It is here that

carnal religion and the in-Christ message part. It is here that the knowing believer and those who reject the Christ-life differ. This is the heart of the revolution. God could not bring about His ultimate plan without there being confusion and strife among those already giving their lives to religion. They will fight, they will ridicule, they will become embittered, and they will, unto death, seek to defend their message. But in the end, this is the "negative" of God working in them that will, in time, bring many of them to fullness. Already we see this; many who fiercely fought the Christ-life have, by that fighting, come to see Christ.

Seeing that there is no other Christ to the believer, other than the Christ in him and in his brother, is the essence of the mystery. It is seeing that he has no other life—no more Satan life, for Satan is out at Calvary; no more life of his own, for he is crucified with Christ; no more nature of his own, for he never had a human nature. Our nature is the nature of the one lives in us. First we had by Adam a sin (Satan) nature, (Ephesians 2:3, John 8:41-44). Now by Christ we have a God nature (II Peter 1:4). Believing this and all the other things the Spirit has yet to teach us will undoubtedly provoke the greatest revolution ever known to the Reformation church. But, praise be to God, it is happening! This move of the Spirit cannot and will not be stopped and will continue throughout eternity. It is God, Himself, at His best. It is God above religion. It is God over all man-made truth. It is God as all and in all. We welcome you to the fellowship of the mystery!

Chapter 3

The Ignorance
of the Gospel

Ignorance is one of the principal weapons Satan uses to attack and destroy the Church of Jesus Christ. To make matters worse, it is often the ignorance of essential things rather than that of peripheral things. This is certainly true in the evangelical and Spirit-filled church of today.

The Apostle Paul asserted that the gospel is the power of God (Romans 1:16). Paul was alluding to the gospel being more than some written pages. He was saying that the gospel is power and that all power is Christ (Matthew 28:18), and he was unashamed of proclaiming it in the great Roman metropolis. This confidence, I fear, is woefully lacking in the church today. The modern church hears far more *promotion* than *preaching*. Our churches are filled with people who may not have a genuine conversion; they live a lifetime in church and never know the difference. It is possible, today, to arrive at being a full-time believer without ever having been born again. That is because of the high-powered promotion used to keep the church program going. The pursuit for new people and the constant demand on the preacher to keep things moving seem to make it possible for souls to be assimilated into the program rather than birthed into Christ. As a result, many are saved *from* something, but not saved *to* anything.

This is due to an ignorance of what the true gospel is. The ignorance of the gospel in much of the Church today is threefold: theological, ethical and existential.

We so often refer to the gospel of Jesus Christ, but it is more than a gospel "of Him." He *is* the gospel. This is not a play on words; it is the deep difference between *who* He is and *what* He does. Herein lies the great ignorance concerning Christ. By seeing only what He does, we never really get to know Him. His doing things may be for us, but His being in us is the essence of our very life. For too long the church has been obsessed with what Christ can do; we have looked for signs, wonders and miracles. Miracles have become a cure-all for our problems. Much like Israel of old in the wilderness, the believer of today looks for and expects a miracle just to live, yet is ignorant of or in disobedience to the will of God to go on into the life of victory.

This is the theological ignorance that is destroying us. Our problem is not simply failing to see Jesus as our life; it goes deeper. It also is not seeing Him as the *Word*. It is by a miracle of grace that we come to the Christ-life, but we still lack a mind—the mind of Christ—to make it all work. This is where we cannot see Jesus only as our life; we also must see that the Scriptures testify of Him. This is where we get His mind to make our life in Him work. Thus, the root of our ignorance lies in the nature and essence of Christ, the Word.

Three Levels of Mental Renewal

In order to see our theological ignorance, we need to understand at least three means by which a believer comes to knowledge. The first is philosophy. The Scriptures are clear on the ignorance in philosophy. Let us look at some self-defining verses. Speaking to the scribes and Pharisees, Jesus said in Matthew 15:9, *"But in vain they do worship Me, teaching for doctrines the commandments of men."* Then in Mark 7:13 Jesus said, *"Making the word of God of none effect through your tradition, which ye have delivered: and many such like things do ye."* Also, Paul said in Colossians 2:8, *"Beware lest any man spoil you through philosophy and vain deceit, after the tradition of men, after the rudiments of the world, and not after Christ."*

The Holy Spirit makes it plain that ignorance is bred when we take what man says as the truth. To make sure the traditions of men do not worm their way into our doctrines, we must join the believers in Berea, who searched the Scriptures to see whether or not the things they were being taught were of God (Acts 17:11). Philosophical teaching is a very learned discipline and has always been very attractive to many people; yet, there is no life in philosophy or in man's interpretation of the Scriptures.

The second is the use of the Scriptures themselves as a means of mental renewal. There is nothing more precious than the Scriptures; they are holy and God-inspired. Yet the Scriptures within themselves fall short of bringing life to the believer and actually can add to his ignorance. The ordeal that Jesus had with the Jews in the fifth chapter of John points out this fact. He said that they searched the Scriptures, believing they gave eternal life, but the Jews themselves did not have eternal life—His life—because they did not see Him in the Scriptures that they were searching (John 5:39-40). Jesus said that the very Scriptures they were searching testified of Him, and in saying this, Jesus laid down the greatest principle of Spirit-knowledge—that as we see Christ in the Scriptures, we have true knowledge, but more than that, we have life—His life.

Every cult and any spurious religion makes liberal use of Scriptures. Some even claim to be 100 percent scriptural. Also, much of the philosophical teachings of the day come directly from the Scriptures. Great numbers of believers put the Scriptures together to prove certain points, which often leads to the separation of verses from their context and essentially nullifies them as truth.

The third and final level of understanding is the *Word.* This level is not dealing with the Scriptures alone, but gives us a deeper dimension. That is the dimension of a person, Christ, as is beautifully shown by John in the first chapter of his Gospel: *"In the* beginning was the Word, and the Word was with God, and the Word was God" (John 1:1). God saw that man would twist and turn the Scriptures to his own liking and that the cure for that was to give the Scriptures personality—*His* personality, in the form of His Son. So He made Christ "the Word." He made the Word flesh that He might dwell among men and be seen and heard—not just as words, but as a life that all men could see, hear and live. God fixed it so that when a believer saw Jesus in the Scriptures as the believer's only life, there could be no human interpretation, human philosophy, or human knowledge that could do away with the truth there is in the Person of Christ.

Truth is not something we come to or see within ourselves. Truth is a Person (John 14:6). How uniquely the Father fixed the knowing of His plan and purpose. He did not merely write it; He demonstrated the writing by a Person—Christ, the Word. It is this knowledge—Christ, the Word—that finally brings the believer to the purpose of God. This is wonderfully declared by Paul in Second Corinthians 3:18: *"But we all, with open face beholding as in a glass the glory of the Lord, are changed into the same image from glory to glory, even as by the Spirit of the Lord."* This is such an enlightening verse that we should see it paraphrased. All believers, with their whole hearts, should look into the Word and see Him who is the essence of the plan of God; by so looking at Jesus, they will be changed into that same image, going from one aspect of the plan of God to another, with the help of the divine Teacher, the Holy Spirit.

We see by this that the Father did not leave the knowing of Jesus as the believer's life to the interpretations of man. He had only one Son and planned that one Son to be the total life of believers. In studying the Scriptures, many have not seen that the life they now live is Christ. But when people see that it is the Word that brings the Christ-life, then do they enter into that life.

This brings us to the heart of this teaching. The true gospel is a Person, and that Person is Christ; thus, the gospel is Christ, the Word.

The Historical Aspect of Christ the Word

First, Christ the Word is a past-tense happening. His work and obligation as the Father's Lamb is a finished work (John 19 and 20). God acted once and for all in His Son. Nothing in the present or in the future can be equated with the work Christ did at Calvary. This is not to say that the Father, through Christ, cannot do glorious things today. But we are simply saying that nothing done today is equal to the finished work at Calvary. It is important to fix that truth in our minds, for a true theological premise can be formed only by seeing the very things the Father saw. Seeing Christ as ourselves is the essence of the Word coming in our flesh. Our identification in His death, burial, resurrection and ascension is imperative to our entering into oneness with Him now.

Second, the gospel, Christ the Word, is not only a past event, it is also an historical event. Christ, the Word incarnate dwelling in flesh, is as historically significant as George Washington crossing the Delaware, or Franklin discovering electricity, or World War II. Believers often think Christ's becoming their life is some mysterious fantasy which has no foundation. Far from it! Just as Christ took our places at Calvary to do away with our sin, He takes His place in us to be our life. On God's part, this act is just as real as any event in history. Placing Christ in us as our life at conversion is just as real to the Father as Christ's death on the cross. Your receiving Christ as your Savior and the revelation that He is in you as your life is just as great an historical event as has ever happened. As C.S. Lewis once put it, God has invaded our planet. More than that, He has invaded our lives! As an historical fact, Christ the Word must be viewed as a finished work. This gospel of the Christ-life can be declared, proclaimed, announced, praised, feared and believed in, but it cannot be commanded. It cannot be commanded to work or function. What we command is law—not gospel.

Third, the gospel of Christ the Word is not only a past historical event, but also the message of and about a Person. This fact separates the gospel from all other historical writings. The gospel is a Person, but we must carefully denote who that Person is. He is neither the first Person of the Godhead nor the third Person; neither is He a combination of these. A part of the gospel is the birth, life, death, resurrection and ascension of One, Jesus (Romans 1:1-4). It is from these historical facts of what a single Person did that we have a gospel that is the power of God unto our salvation.

All of these events that comprise the historical facts concern Jesus of Nazareth, in whom the Father bases His right to claim sons as His. However, it is not this Jesus of Nazareth who is our life. It is the same spirit that was in Jesus of Nazareth that is in the believer today (Romans 8:9). But we boldly state that the Christ in the believer today is not Jesus of Nazareth. Jesus of Nazareth was the Christ living in a body given to Him by Mary. The One who is in us is the Christ living in our bodies which were given to us by our mothers. We often hear of someone trying to be Jesus of Nazareth. For such people, the Christ-life becomes the things we must do to appease God. Some might even suggest that it is possible to live the same life now that He lived. No, that was Jesus living through the flesh of a Nazarene. Today, it is the same Jesus, but He lives through the flesh of each of us as we are (Galatians 2:20). It is indeed the same Christ, but He expresses Himself through us as we are in our flesh. We believe the Bible is quite clear on this point.

Our Great Need Today

The great need today among evangelical and Spirit-filled preachers is the ability to preach and teach the gospel from virtually any passage in the entire Bible. It appears that our desire to defend the inspiration and authority of the Scriptures may be our guilty conscience at work, because we have forsaken the true authority of the Bible—Christ the Word. The true gospel is an awesome power! We are tempted to resort to psychological manipulations, techniques, and sometimes, infantile gimmicks. It is as if Christ the Word can no longer convert sinners and must have our help. We ignore Christ's Word when we become committed to get souls into our programs at all costs. Paul says the gospel is the power of God to convert sinners. Once in a while someone says to me that the Christ-life message is solely for the believer wanting to dig deep into the things of God. Far from it. We are seeing sinners come to the Father more and more as the Word is preached. Men do not see truth because it is explained; they know the truth by the teaching of the Holy Spirit (I Corinthians 2:12). We have witnessed the fact that the Holy Spirit readily uses the gospel to draw all men unto Christ.

It might be good to reflect for a moment on the word "salvation." Salvation has a past, present and future reference in the Word. Hence, when Paul says that the gospel is the power of God for salvation, he means that the gospel is the power of God at the initial point of conversion, throughout the period of continuing conversion (the Christ-life), and at the point of our final, total completion in Christ. This makes the gospel, Christ the Word, the most powerful force to be known by the believer.

Galatians 2:20 is not often understood to refer to justification, but to a believer's higher or additional act of commitment. Likewise, Second Corinthians 5:17, which states that all things are new for those who are in Christ, becomes a legalistic stick to beat believers into guilty paranoia. This is dishonoring to the Father, who paid the price by the slaying of the Lamb so He could make all things new. He is not interested in the believer's veneer of piety.

The rediscovery of the gospel of Christ the Word will greatly help to de-jargonize our language. The heart of the gospel is Christ dying and Christ in the believer; seeing that truth is the greatest need in our training schools today. We should use the language of the gospel. Over 200 times, the term *in Christ* is used in the New Testament, and over 146 of those times, it refers directly to the fact that Christ, the Word, is the life of the believer. Yet the term *in Christ* is seldom used by the modern believer.

It was this rediscovery of the gospel as Christ that prompted us to see Jesus as life, and to come to the true gospel language, such as knowing that the Christ in you is the real you to the

Father. So only as we begin to speak meaningfully about the Christ who is in us will we ever make an impact on the world around us.

An Ethical Ignorance of the Gospel

The gospel of Christ in us has important ramifications in the area of ethics. Let's begin by looking at the general role of experience in the evangelical church. The modern believer finds expression in the emotional or feeling aspects of his life. Sin, repentance, forgiveness and worship are not intellectual theories or just mental processes. They are personal acts accompanied by fear, regret and deep resolve. However, despite the presence of such feelings as repentance, it is not biblically true to say that repentance is a feeling. As far as the Word is concerned, repentance and guilt, along with forgiveness, have their basis in God and, therefore, represent far more than our feelings or emotions.

A growing major problem in popular church circles is that almost all basic relationships with the Father are being identified with feelings and experiences. Guilt becomes a feeling of guilt; God's forgiveness exists only as the believer feels forgiven; worship means experiences in a certain context. Too many of God's preachers have forgotten that Jesus Christ and God's justification, through His Lambship, are more important than the believer's feelings or emotions.

For example, true repentance involves hearing objective facts from the Word concerning Jesus of Nazareth and what He did as the sinbearer at Calvary, and grasping with the mind the claims and promises relating thereto. Great ignorance is evolving in church circles today, as feelings are substituted for Bible facts.

It Doesn't Really Matter

With consistent practice, the believer begins to expect certain feelings in every relationship with the Father. Then, instead of the Word being the center, experience becomes paramount. A good example of this is in the general worship service we see today. We no longer give God His glory as God and as the Father; instead we seek for a worshipful experience. In the crucial matter of salvation, the receiving of God's pardon has become a feeling of well-being that is to help us stop worrying about what God thinks of us. In all of this, the essence of the word *gospel* is being lost.

Too many believers are saved from things that hurt them, giving them a great new feeling; but they never come to the knowledge that God put another Person in them, who is their new life. This is not to say that the Christ-life does not have joy and wonderful feelings. They may come; they may not come. *It really doesn't matter!*

What does matter is that the believer must know in whom he has believed. He cannot depend on anything or anyone other than Christ in him. If feelings and emotions lead in his faith, it is unlikely that the ultimate intention of the Father will ever materialize.

Although emotions are a valid aspect of Christ being in you as your life, such things as cheer, mirth, praise, rejoicing and merry-making are the by-products of a concentration on the mighty acts of God's saving and redeeming a people for Himself. The modern church is absolutely sick unto death as it substitutes psychology for gospel facts. It is not that such psychological entities are exchanged for the gospel; rather, they have become the norm by which our relationship to God is measured. *Success* has become spirituality. *Things* have become the test of one's faith, with *receiving* them the proof of faith. *Results,* regardless of how they are achieved, are proof of God's blessings. A good conversion is one that can be dynamically promoted.

The greatest worship service is one where there is great liberty and anointing, and perhaps no preaching. Prayer has become a tool for getting what we need from God, and simple communion of a son with his Father is long lost. Music is no longer just a joy of the soul set free; it too is a tool to appeal to the senses and carnal drives of the believer.

The Old Satan Nature Affinity

In many places, believers ask us why there has not been a witness in their area for the Christ-life—especially if the Holy Spirit is the Revealer. The answer is not always simple; but, technically and theoretically, we see that the issue we are presently addressing is the major cause. The old Satan nature that the believer possessed had a real affinity with the psychological aspects of man. Experiences of any kind were the aim of the sin-life. "Do your thing; have a fling" was the keynote of sin.

Now, even though there is the new nature of Christ in the believer, the old house, the body, still has yearnings and drives leaning toward the old experience-centered life. This is the dilemma in the modern church. These drives and pulls of the flesh are now being satisfied by religion, and the church has lost and is losing its power—the power of God unto salvation—as a result.

It is an ethical mind-set that has elevated experience above the realities of Christ the Word. As a result, the work of the Holy Spirit is being severely restricted. Jesus plainly said in chapters 14, 15 and 16 of the Gospel of John that the major work of the Holy Spirit is to teach the believer the life of Christ. When religion places the experiences of the believer above the teachings of the Holy Spirit, the plan of God suffers, and so does the believer.

We are seeing a reversion to the pre-Reformation days, when the work of the Holy Spirit was taken over by the Church and all experiences and forms of worship were handled and dictated by the Church. Believers then were told they could "buy a blessing," and we border on this today. We are told that personal indulgences dictated by men will bring prosperity and health.

It is not these surface matters that are the greatest problem; it is the loss of the understanding that the Father never looks to our faith, but depends on the faith of Christ. He never determines our walk with Him by our acquisitions or possessions; He depends on the Treasure we hold in us. He never judges our standing with Him by what we do for Him, but depends solely on what Christ is in us. Satan's greatest attack will be on the issue of all believers being perfect in their standing before God. It simply means that God is able to place another in us and depend on that One in us to be our sole salvation because we are justified by Christ's finished work at Calvary. When our experiences become the issue, we have fallen into Satan's most subtle trap.

Guilt Will Set In

Finally, what happens as a result of all this emotionalism is, the Father and His plan are reworked according to our sinful energies. Soon we have a God who is angry if we do not do something like He told us to do it. This leads the believer into the greatest trap of all—*guilt*. The believer then thinks he no longer has the abiding Christ in him expressing Himself through him, so he resorts to self-effort, which works to the spiritual death of the believer. He now must pray without ceasing; he must confess ritualistically; he must plant seeds daily if he is to receive; he must love everybody; he must fight Satan daily; and, in fact, if anyone comes up with something else that *must* be done, he will try to do it. All because guilt will set in if it is not.

The local church has become an institution of "good feelings." Is it not possible that the local church could also be a place of deep prophetic unrest and discomfort? Is there not a place for believers to groan that they might be delivered from this earthen vessel? Is there not a place to *glory in our tribulations?* Is there not a place for a *thorn in the flesh?* Should a believer always receive a revelation from God? Is there not a place for believers to simply give to God and His work without making some kind of an investment to get more back? Is there not a place to be comforted by the thought that we will get out of the schoolhouse one day with the return of Christ? For the truly hungry believer, the current status quo will never satisfy.

The Christ in Us Does Not Sin

We now look to the matter of Christian virtues in modern religion. The general approach to virtues in the ethical thinking of today's believers usually is neither informed nor guarded by the gospel. It is not surprising that believers who are unclear on the nature of the gospel are also unclear on the nature of Christian virtues. Nothing shows us our sin more than the consciousness that the life in us is Christ. Also, this same Jesus is Christ the Word, and He, by the gospel, constantly shows us that sin is a work of Satan and is the continued manifestation of Satan's rebellion.

The crucified and risen Christ at God's right hand, ever interceding on behalf of the saints, is a constant reminder that all of our thoughts, words and actions stand in need of the sweet fragrance of the righteousness of Christ. The Scriptures, as well as our best theologians, have testified to the inherent sinfulness of all our actions as Christians. Augustine, Pascal, Luther, Calvin, Wesley, Kierkegaard and many others have testified to man that he is a continuing sinner this side of the Father's house. Of course, it is not the believer who sins, but sin that dwelleth in his body (Romans 7:17-20). As John said, *"Whosoever is born of God doth not commit sin"* (I John 3:9a); and the real Person now in the believer is Christ. He does not commit sin. So if there is sin, it is sin that dwells in our bodies—bodies which are not saved now, but which will be on the resurrection morning (Romans 8:23). Our bodies sin when they are fed by a carnal mind. But praise the Lord, John gives liberty even here, for all we need to do, or can do, is go to *our Father,* ask for forgiveness and go on living in that forgiveness. Bodies will not be sinless or changed until the resurrection (I Corinthians 15:54).

It is hard to realize this fact when we look at the ethical mind-set of today's believers. The popular idealism built on the possibility of human perfection dies hard. Too many of us believers have an implicitly perfectionistic approach to our thoughts and actions. We are so often convinced, and try to convince others, that our motives are pure and right and that we are really behaving with no thought of ourselves, yet our living and speaking belie what God has definitively revealed in Christ the Word. Christ's righteousness is now, and always will be, what the Father sees, and *this* is our perfection. We cannot handle our sins of the flesh ourselves, but they are swallowed up by the Christ in us, who is daily moving into new areas of our lives to perfect us as Christ-persons (Christians).

Satan's Misuse of Self

Fundamental Christianity has long shouted that the believer must live for God and others and not for self. Most commentators and teachers loosely throw out the challenge that the believer should crucify self. The error here is not in self. True, to be selfish or self-*independent* is contrary to the gospel, but self is not the problem; the problem is Satan's misuse of our selves. The Father has gloriously chosen to put Christ's nature in our *selves.* Christ could not operate as me without a *me,* and *that* me is my self. More gloriously, the Father elected to place Christ in me with all my body problems and sins of the flesh. This was grace personified to me. The Christ in me is not getting rid of my self, but is swamping and overwhelming the sins of my flesh, my rights, my independence, in order that He can use me to be Him.

It is impossible for us to live or to become selfless. Many believers try to do this on their own; such unselfish acts, more often than not, bring misery to those who are served. C.S. Lewis had a comment about this concerning one of his characters he called Mrs. Fidget. *"She was the sort of woman who lived for others; you could always tell the others by the hunted look on their faces."*

We are to do good, but the *do*-er and the *be*-er are not us; it is Christ in us—Christ using our *selves* as Himself.

An Existential Ignorance of the Gospel

The modern evangelical believer is being destroyed by an ignorance of the gospel and its implication for the believer's life of victory. For example, the life of victory has become an obsession in most circles. The idea that the successful believer is to be a getter and that God is basically a good God-the-giver is rampant. The heart of this self-effort gospel seems to be what we will call the "positive thinking syndrome." This syndrome, or sickness, came into the modern church, as well as we can ascertain, at the close of World War II. It came about through the great evangelistic campaigns which started about that time. It teaches that you can, within yourself, do anything. You can raise your self-values; you can get faith; you can be somebody. Through the years it has grown until, today, all who hear it want to become all it implies. This error is a trap of Satan. You cannot work, labor, fast and pray, confess or do anything within yourself to become what you already are in Christ. Satan is ever keeping that believer from a life of victory by making him think that working brings victory.

Ignorance of the truth of justification is the cause. As far as Christ the Word is concerned, it is impossible to be justified and not be sanctified. The Word never speaks of a believer who has been set free from sin's guilt but not from sin's power.

Failure to understand Christ the Word as our only means of spiritual existence is stunting many believers' growth. Believers are confused by a well-meaning but unbiblical theology that they must have victory. The believer becomes eaten up with thoughts of himself, and this is selfishness at its most base. The Christ already in the believer is the believer's total victory to the Father. The believer needs only to begin to rest in the finished work of Christ and hear the Holy Spirit who teaches and reveals that Christ is already in him. Then, equipped with the knowledge of who he is in Christ, he need only begin living as Him—as His wife, His vessel, His branch or His house. This is the knowledge of the renewed mind, and that knowledge working in you is victory. You are victorious, not by doing something, but by knowing Someone as your life.

The Problem of Rewards

Ignorance exists also in the issue of rewards. Rewards in the Bible are not evidence that our works here on earth as Christians are meritorious. The gospel recognizes *no merit* in *any works* before or after our conversion. Neither do rewards mean that there will be graduations in glory.

What we receive at the end of the world is as much a matter of grace as our entrance into the Kingdom in the first place. Many passages are concerned with rewards for works done (Matthew 16:27; 25:34; John 5:29; Romans 2:9-10; I Corinthians 3:11-14; II Corinthians 5:10). These passages indicate an *order of sequence* rather than *cause and effect.* God leads His chosen into salvation by mercy, alone, but He leads them to it via the desire to do good. They are not saved *because of* their good works, but *through* their good works. Works of our own are *never* effectual causes for our salvation.

It Is Time for a New Communion

Calvin speaks of rewards as inheritance. That is borne out in Matthew 25:34-36; Galatians 4:7,30; and Ephesians 1:18. The Lord rewards the works of believers with the same benefits He gave them before they contemplated any works (cf. Genesis 15:5; 17:1 with 18:18; 22:16-18 for an illustration from Abraham). God rewarded Abraham's works with what He gave to Abraham before Abraham did any works. Again, in Matthew 20, the idea of merit from any good work is totally excluded. This parable shows that the reward, or payment of works, is a matter of the gift of grace. Those who had worked longer hours did not get higher status in the Kingdom.

Our salvation is mentioned in a multitude of ways in the Word: *possess the Kingdom, receive a crown, enter into rest, treasure in Heaven,* etc. These differences of word expressions do not represent differences of reality. The reward of the believer is nothing other than his enjoying being a co-laborer and co-doer with the Christ who is his life, experiencing eternal life in Him now, and knowing that he already is an heir of God.

These things, and many more not mentioned, show the need for the true gospel, Christ the Word, to come to the present church. The Church, already sick, can be healed only by revelation knowledge. The greatest move of God ever is now started. It is time for all hungry believers to begin a new communion with Him.

Chapter 4

The Gospel of the New Creation Race

$\mathbf{A}$ new gospel? Is this what is needed in our world today? Has the "grand old gospel" failed us? These are questions that hungry, sincere believers are asking today. We see different gospels preached everywhere that seem contrary to the way the Spirit is leading truly hungry hearts. In fact, there seems to be a different gospel for every ministry, and multitudes are being deceived by them. There can be only one true gospel from our Father. There can be only one true message brought by the Holy Spirit. Yet, those who claim to hear from God seem to say different things. Hungry hearts are left to discern on their own what truths they are to follow, as if the Scriptures never give a distinct sound or bring a clear message. The other day a minister said to me that the Spirit had told him there would be a worldwide revival which would swamp all other truth in existence and bring about a new order. Another believer said to me that the Church was coming into a new day in which all the promises of the Scriptures would come alive, and by manifestation of them, all the needy and sick and suffering would be delivered. He saw believers going into hospitals and healing all the sick and even going to cemeteries and raising the dead. Although these are beautiful works, to advocate them as being the essence of the gospel is perversion. All of this smacks of man-made gospel. Sad to say, man-made gospel is all most believers in Christianity have ever had.

The Old-Time Gospel Has Not Failed

It is not a new gospel that we need. The grand old gospel has not failed us. In fact, most believers do not even know what the grand old gospel is. The Bible, which has been the most read book in history and is the very lifeline of every true believer, still holds the basic truth of the gospel.

The fact that the average believer is oblivious to its message is astonishing. Modern believers are constantly diverted from the truth of God's message by seeking in the Bible for "their" answers instead of God's purpose. Although God's Word is dedicated to meeting human need, its far greater purpose is showing forth God's purpose in mankind. God's purpose in mankind is for Him to find a people to fill His house and to train those people in His kind of love. So it is not a great revival that we need. It is not the winning of more souls that we need. It is not human success with God that is important. The problem of Christianity is much more acute than this. The real problem is in the gospel we preach.

Now, most of all, the true gospel must be based on God's ultimate intention for man. The first chronological mention of man in the Scriptures is in Ephesians 1:4, where Paul says that man was chosen to be in Christ before the foundation of the world. Thus, the first thought God ever had concerning mankind, as far as we know, was that believers would be in Christ.

I see this as God's prime and ultimate intention for man. To ignore the importance of this is to pervert the gospel, which is what man has done today. If you do not start with this "God-idea," every other place where you start to understand God will be lacking. The believer chosen in Christ is the only foundation that the Father and the Scriptures build upon. Most in religion have failed to do that. To keep believers from understanding that is Satan's main objective.

The Filling of the House Is a "God-Idea"

Unless this eternal plan of God is in focus, the true gospel will never be known. It is the Father's eternal plan for having sons in

His house, such as Jesus, that is the substance of the true gospel. All creation, all creatures, including Satan, and all things, including evil, deal with the Father's plan of sons being in Christ. In fact, there is nothing in existence separate from God's intention of filling His house with Christ-sons (*Christians*). To preach a gospel that does not embrace this God-idea of Him filling His house with sons is to preach a perverted gospel. This perverted gospel now fills the church world and is the reason multitudes of hungry hearts are bewildered, wondering why God does not minister to them in a greater way.

To be able to get to the true gospel, one must first see how the Father conceived and worked out His plan for sons. He saw that creating and bringing sons to His house would not serve His need. His great need, as a God of love, was to receive love from His sons. It was already proven to Him that merely having created sons in His house would never bring about reciprocal love. He had had this with Lucifer in His house. Created sons would never do. So He saw that He would have to "birth" the sons Himself. In order for the sons to be as Him, He would have to birth them by placing His own seed in them and giving them His own nature. It is with these God-thoughts that we begin to see the true gospel.

When Jesus met Nicodemus as described in the third chapter of John's Gospel, He boldly told Nicodemus that he must be *born again.* Now this was the first time in the Scriptures that such a thing had ever been said. It was so devastating to Nicodemus that his only thought was that a person would have to enter his mother's womb again and be reborn. It is interesting to note that Jesus answered Nicodemus with a mystery, saying that the wind blows where it wishes and you cannot tell where it is coming from or where it is going. Why would Jesus not answer Nicodemus? Why did He give a mystery? To understand this, you must go to Paul. It is interesting that Paul never uses the term born again. I can see his purpose in not doing so. He saw that the truth of God's plan was so far beyond man's ability to understand it that it was truly a mystery. It was indeed a mystery that all the sons would be in Christ. It was indeed a mystery that all the sons would be born again. Paul knew mysteries must be revealed by another, that one could not come to the understanding of a mystery within himself. He also saw that this was God's intention. He saw this so plainly that in First Corinthians, Chapter 2, he says the true gospel is foolishness to natural man and can be revealed only by the Holy Spirit (v. 14). The modern church has veered away from this God-idea. Today, men seek to make the gospel a "simple gospel," robbing it of all its divine essence. Therefore, there are multitudes of born-again believers who have no concept of God's plan for them, for the world, or for the Church.

The Correlation Between Natural and Spirit Birthing

Let us look much closer at the way these sons would be born again. The next time the term born again is used in the Scriptures is in First Peter 1:23: *"Being born again, not of corruptible seed, but of incorruptible, by the word of God, which liveth and abideth for ever."* Notice that we are introduced here to the method by which the Father would birth the sons. Rather than create them, as He did with Lucifer, He would birth them Himself by becoming their Father. To do that, He would invest His own seed in them, just as an earthly father puts his seed in a woman and she conceives a child.

It is here that we are introduced to the heart of the true gospel. Salvation is not just a gift or a thing. Salvation is a Person (Romans 5:10). When God put His seed in the believer, there was conceived a Person—a Person called the Son, and that Son is Christ. This birthing fulfilled the ultimate intention of God—that the believer would be "in Christ." This is why they were "called Christians [Christ-persons] first in Antioch." God put His seed in the believer and that seed was Christ—God the Son. That is what makes believers into sons of God. This means that the believer, to be saved, must have another father. Salvation is not only getting a new life, Christ; it is also getting a new Father. Peter emphatically states this concept in this same verse when he says, *"not of corruptible seed"* (I Peter 1:23). The corruptible seed comes from our earthly father, direct from Satan. Peter stressed that to show that our natural birthing by our natural father cannot suffice for salvation. The verse says that we cannot change the corruptible seed into a good seed. It strongly says that salvation is not a change in one's lifestyle, but rather an exchange of fathers. Unless believers see that there has been an exchange in fathers, from Satan (John 8:44) to God, they can never know the true gospel.

The Believer Has the Very Genetics of the Father

The Father intended that this birthing would produce the son who would be pleasing to Him. He would not have to wait on the son to be like Him; the birthing itself would give the son His nature. Peter goes on in his second Epistle to show this. He says that the believer has received the very *nature* of God by this incorruptible seed and escapes the corruption which came by the seed of our former father (II Peter 1:4). This means that every believer has the very *genetics* of Father God in him. This was God's intention. That seed, Christ in the believer, was to be the wisdom, righteousness, sanctification and redemption of the believer (I Corinthians 1:30). Never again would the Father need to depend upon a creature to be someone who pleased Him; the creature now has the very nature of God, with all His attributes. To make all of this work, the Father instituted the awesome works of Calvary. It all would come about by the Son. The Son is the ultimate life, the only seed and the Father's only love.

Now these factors, the ultimate intention of the Father, the birthing of the Father, and the placing of that birthing, laid the perfect foundation for the true gospel. But still the *whole gospel* is not in focus. To get focused, we must carefully analyze Second Corinthians 5:17, *"Therefore if any man be in Christ, he is a new creature: old things are passed away; behold, all things are become new."* It is plain to see that the in-Christ message is clearly stated, but the real focus of truth in this verse is on the believer. The believer has had something unbelievable happen to him. This verse says that the believer is a new creature. This is the way the King James Version puts it. Still stronger is the Amplified translation, which goes further than *new creature* and says *"a new creation."* But better yet is the translation by Johnson that says the in-Christ believer is a *"new race."* Now, this "new race" translation fits all the rest of the Scriptures, and it is the part of the modern gospel generally missing from today's theology. God's plan of salvation has created an entirely new race of people. They are not made-over people; they are not earthly people anymore; they are not "just natural" people anymore. They are a new *race*. There has never before been anything like them on the face of the earth. They are a people who have given up their old lives that were from the corruptible seed and entered a new and living way of life. For them *old things are passed away*—their old father, their old mind, and their old purpose.

An "Outward People" No Longer Considered

To see this new race of people, we need to hear Paul as he says they are in Christ, *"where there is neither Greek nor Jew, circumcision nor uncircumcision, Barbarian, Scythian, bond nor free: but Christ is all, and in all"* (Colossians 3:11). This means that when we are born again, we no longer retain our previous backgrounds, for in Christ there are no nationalities—no Germans, no Mexicans, no Irishmen, and no Scotsmen. A new race of people was formed at Calvary and nothing that meant anything to them previously, matters anymore (Philippians 3:1-9). Paul goes so far as to say that in the Spirit there is not even male or female in Christ.

Two things are very obvious at this point. Paul is saying some things that are not generally preached in our day because we have not really understood what he was saying. Our problem has been that we tried to make the mystery Paul writes of "a simple gospel," while he has repeatedly said that these things must be revealed to us by His Spirit (I Corinthians 2:7,9,10). What has happened to modern theology is that Christ as the life of the believer has been denied in preaching, while everything the believer can get from or by Christ has been over-promoted. The end result is the new creation race not having any gospel.

These people who have hungered to know God have had to use a gospel that is not the whole truth and the end result has been frustration. They are a people who go to church and wonder why. They are a people who know that the modern servants of God could wait before God and get greater truths, but they see no waiting or greater truths. They are a people who cannot quit God, though tempted to at times because of their frustration with religion, because they know they are in Christ and that Christ is their all. They are the people whom the Father is dealing with these days and they are the foundation stones for the present move of God. These are the people to whom the Father is ready to reveal Christ in His fullness, and these people will be the bearers of the new creation race gospel.

Paul Has the Gospel of the New Creation Race

The question that must be answered at this point is, "What is the difference between the gospel we now hear and the gospel for a new creation race?" It is to the Apostle Paul that we must go for the answer. It is to the Apostle Paul alone that the message of the new creation race was first given. It was over four thousand years of our time from when the Father chose the sons to be in Christ to the time when He gave a gospel for this truth. What an awesome thought!

It is also important that we see the way the Father brought about His messenger for this gospel. Acts 9 tells the thrilling story of how the Father arrested Saul of Tarsus on the road to Damascus by knocking him down, striking him blind, and shouting out of Heaven to him. Indeed it was a tremendous event—an event Paul was to relate many times. It was by these unusual means, however, that the Father got the right preacher for the new creation race gospel. But first, Paul himself had to experience this new-race gospel. Some time after his conversion, when he had a deep yearning to know Christ in His fullness, he went into Arabia and after three years was able to say that he had had Christ revealed in him. Then, by this revelation he was able to give the new-race gospel to the Church. Receiving this gospel did not come easily to him. He had no help from any other, and as a result, said plainly that no man could teach the Christ he had had revealed. He specifically said that he did not go to the brethren in Jerusalem who knew Christ before him. He let it be known that this gospel of the new-race people came straight from the Father by the Holy Spirit.

Two Kinds of Gospels

At this same time, a breach of fellowship was growing between Peter and Paul over this new-race gospel. Peter had not received, at that time, the revelation Paul had of the Christ-life, for Peter knew Jesus only in the flesh, the Jesus of Nazareth (II Corinthians 5:16). Later on, when Peter wrote his Epistle, it is evident that he had come to the same revelation. But when Paul's Epistles were written and read in the churches, there was a schism between the two men. It was finally decided that these two preachers would preach different gospels. Peter would preach the gospel of circumcision, which was man's effort to please God by keeping a law, and Paul would preach the gospel of uncircumcision, which was Christ in the believer as the only salvation. Peter's gospel was based on what men do. Paul's gospel was based on what God has done.

The issues of the gospel are the same today. Most believers are bound by a gospel which demands that they do something rather than trust the finished work of Christ. Men today, to be saved, must be baptized a certain way or they must join a particular church or they must adhere to a certain doctrine. On and on goes the "doers" religion. Now some of the acts are not only scriptural, but also are done by every believer as an act of love. However, none of these things saves or brings the believer to the fullness of Christ because, to be a believer, one must be "born again." This is the birthing act, and it is total in itself.

Once one is "birthed," that is all that can be done to make a Christ-person. There is no such thing as a "little bit of birthing or pregnancy." When you are born again, you have all of God and all of Christ you will ever have. A total Person, Christ, is in you. It is this total birthing idea that is being denied the believer today. That denial comes in the message of the circumcision, Peter's message—a message which says that you can do something yourself to make it all work. So multitudes of hungry believers have given themselves such a message, only to fall defeated, crying that they still want to know God.

Paul Distinguished the True Gospel

The great difference between Peter and Paul's messages is Paul saw that the new creation race was a whole new group of people who were birthed to be the way they were. Paul alone gives a gospel for these people, and it is that gospel the hungry believers today are seeing. Paul goes on to say in Second Corinthians 5:17 that old things are passed away, meaning that the corruptible seed given by our former father is gone and all things are now operated by the new seed. There is no more trying to change the believer. God is not in the business of just changing people. His business is that of the Father: inhabiting people. He births the sons and gives them His perfect, unchangeable and eternal nature. This is Paul's message and is the gospel of the new race. We see this difference between the two gospels even more vividly as Paul was forced to make a distinction in Romans 2:16 by calling it, *"my gospel."* It appears that it was necessary for him to distinguish what he preached from what Peter preached. It was also stated in the same way in Romans 16:25, where he says, *"my gospel."* Of course, the gospel he preached came by the revelation of the Holy Spirit, and that would make it very personal to him. This is the great lacking factor in modern preaching. Few preachers stress the fact that the gospel they preach came to them by the revelation of the Holy Spirit. Until the Spirit is able to reveal the Son in the messengers, there will be no gospel for those who are of the new creation race.

Presently the most frequently preached gospel in the church is what I call a conglomerate gospel. It is preached as if Paul had no revelation of the Christ-life. Men preach from Genesis to Revelation as if God had not birthed a special group of people in between. The conglomerate gospel preaches Abraham as a knower of the truth. Abraham had no concept of Christ in him or of the birthing. Although we can see Jesus in Abraham as we look back—for Christ said that all of the Scriptures testified of Him (John 5:39)—there is no life in Abraham for us. Nowhere in Abraham's story, nor in the rest of the Old Testament (though Jesus is alive there), is there any message for the new creation race. That message comes only by the revelation of Christ as the believer's life. The abounding ignorance of the Christ-life has brought about a mixture of gospel preaching that is deceiving multitudes. One preacher says that God can do anything if we believe and then tells the people that if they don't give him money he can't continue. If God can do anything, can He not supply the preacher's need too? This is a mixture of truth. Hungry believers cannot grow on such a gospel. Another preacher lives a lifestyle of the rich and famous, yet preaches that Jesus was humble, meek and lowly. This is the mixture gospel.

Some Important Ideas for a New-Race Gospel

Aside from all of that, however, the Father has sent a move of the Spirit to His hungry people and they are seeing and hearing a gospel for the new creation race. They are a people who will never again imbibe the juice of carnal religion. They are knowers; they know in whom they have believed. They are through with philosophers and promoters. But exactly what are the real issues denoting the new creation race gospel? I believe there are several ideas with which the hungry believer can start to renew himself to seeing Jesus as his all and in all. Here are some ideas leading to a gospel of the new creation race.

I. Salvation is a Person. Although this concept has been previously mentioned, I feel that much more attention should be given to it. I feel that the modern church has generally missed the essence of God's plan by not seeing this truth. There can be no firm foundation in any believer without the knowledge that led the Father to save mankind in this way. Before the foundation of the world was laid, the Father had already faced the issue that to create a free moral agent able to make a decision was not enough to get what He wanted.

What He really wanted was a son to make a *free decision* to love Him as Father. His past experience was with Lucifer, who had miserably failed even though he lived right in the presence of God and had full liberty to do as he pleased. He did as he pleased, and it was the opposite of God's intention. What developed out of this experience was the fact that a son is not made by creation. A created son will never have the spirit of the family. There had to be another way to get true sons and yet leave the creature a way to make free moral decisions. This was when the Father chose the sons in Christ (Ephesians 1:4). But to *get* the sons in Christ would be the heart of God's plan. He would birth them by putting His own seed in the creature. That seed and the way that He would put it in the creature would be the great "mystery of godliness." His seed would be that part of Himself known as God the Son, the only Son who ever pleased Him. By placing that Son in the creature, He would have His own nature (His life and Spirit) ever working in them.

Salvation Is a Very Personal Act of God

He would depend on that nature, Christ in us, as the means of saving us. This was the most important thing the Father ever did. Saving mankind by placing another Person in him was to accomplish the two greatest demands of God's justice. The creature was to remain a free moral person to make an open decision for God, and at the same time God would, upon the creature's decision for God, place the kind of nature in him that He could depend on. That nature, or spirit, or life, that He would place in us would be a Person—Christ. It would be the birthing of that Son in us that would be our salvation. Thus, salvation would never become a "thing." Salvation was to be a Person, a new Person, operating out of the creature for the glory of God. God never intended that salvation be incorporated into other things to make it complete. It was to be a personal act by God, who would place His own seed in the believer and by it conceive another Person as that believer. All of the rites and doctrines of man, whether baptism, acts of righteousness, affiliations, or good works, would have to follow this initial act of birthing.

Sad to say, these works of man were destined to take over the birthing to the extent that multitudes today are churched, sanctified, and even in a ministry, without the understanding that they are saved by a Person in them, and *only* by that Person in them. All the other things the church or preacher or doctrines may do must be secondary to this God-kind of salvation. The people of the new creation race no longer will tolerate a watered-down gospel that denies the bulk of the Scriptures; these people are consistently dedicated to God's eternal plan of salvation by another Person. All over the earth, it is as if the Father has said that a time is at hand when the Church will have a people who see the ultimate of God. We are a part of that people and have no reservations about boldly declaring the whole gospel.

II. Faith is of Christ. If Christ is the only life in the believer, it is natural that as He becomes to the believer all that the Father intended, then all the virtues and all the personality traits of Christ will surface and will be the only life of the believer. This does not hinder the free moral decisions of the believer. He still must make the decision to be the Christ that he is to God. He must decide in the first place to accept Christ. This is saving faith at work.

Saving Faith Is the "Measure of Faith"

This saving faith is of the Father, for He has given to every man the *"measure of faith"* in order that, when he hears the gospel, he will have the ability to believe. Then, after the new birth, the believer grows in the Lord. That growth is basically growing out of his self-independence into the Christ-life. As that takes place, all of the personality traits of the Christ within begin to surface. The act on the believer's part that makes this possible is love.

The love of God working in and through the believer places more and more responsibility on the Christ within until finally everything the believer does is Christ. The great asset of "faith" eventually is seen by the believer to be the faith of Christ.

This concept, of course, is almost opposite to religion's idea of faith. That is because Satan, who works through religion, wants to keep the believer separate from the Christ within. There is no area where Satan accomplishes that more greatly than with faith. The believer who is always seeking faith, always going to some faith-building meeting, always trusting some man of faith, always believing that his own faith is weak, is a tool for Satan's work of separatism.

Not only does this place the believer in a vulnerable place of potential defeat, it also denies him the rest which resides in knowing that the only life he has is Christ. I have long believed that the misuse of faith is the most crippling aspect in all religion. So many believers are trapped by an erroneous gospel which says "We can be something," or "We can believe for something aside from the Christ within." This is where the growth of the believer must reach Galatians 2:20.

The Faith of the Son

Finally, when the believer sees that he is crucified with Christ, his self-independence killed at Calvary, he is ready to enter into the sonship the Father intended with the birthing. He is ready now to say with Paul in Galatians, "The life which I now live in the flesh I live by the faith of the Son of God" (2:20). What a glorious position to be in, no longer depending only upon self, no longer groping outside of one's Christ-life for an answer, no longer going to and fro for help; but living by the faith of the Son of God. It is a very natural thing now for the Christ within to do all the loving, the hoping, the working, and most of all, the believing. It is not our faith now, nor has it ever been our faith. We, the crucified with Christ, have given our selves to Him to use as Himself; therefore, we have no life of our own, no faith of our own, but the faith of the Son of God. We will see this truth more clearly in another chapter.

The new creation race seeks only that gospel which spells out this truth in every sermon, in every book, by every preacher, for there is no other gospel from the Word.

III. Simple eschatological truths. It is important to make the point in this writing that the Apostle Paul is the first and major propagator of the Christ-life. No one who knows the chronology of God's dealings with mankind, especially in the scriptural record, could possibly deny this. He alone gives the Christian the basic truths of the life we now live in Christ. He is the major author of the new creation race gospel. Yet, when we look at the essentials of Paul's teaching, we see very little mention of end-time doctrines. For a long time I found that hard to accept, even though the record plainly verified it. There had to be some important reason for this apparent lack. Even though I did not know the reason for Paul's manner of treatment of eschatology at the time, the Christ in me was working.

Through the years, I was connected with two different Bible colleges and was able to direct the curriculum that was to be taught at each. After weighing the issues presented by others as to what degree we would teach end-time truths, or the Book of Daniel and John's Revelation, my decision was always based on the Spirit of Christ in me. Like a well of water springing up within me, the knowledge would come that most of the things dealt with in these books and on this subject simply did not matter to the Christ-person. I practiced this idea, even though I did not see at the time Paul's attitude on the subject. I already knew, for instance, that the most divisive teaching in all theology was connected with the doctrines of eschatology. Whole denominations operate because of their interpretation of Daniel and Revelation. As a college president dedicated to training youth to evangelize the world, I was constrained by the Christ in me not to enter into the many divisions men had made over their doctrines. I knew that the sinner could not care less and that hungry believers certainly offered no more interest. In time, however, the Holy Spirit taught me the reason the Christ within was oblivious to most of the man-made, end-time doctrines. The Holy Spirit opened up Paul's teaching on the new creation race as the answer.

A Special People to Fill the Father's House

When the revelation came to Paul of the Father's intention that the life we now live is Christ, it meant that everything that had ever happened on earth and everything that was to happen in the future was to center on a new race of people. Everything related to them was premised on their being in Christ and Christ being their all. They were not to be an Old Testament people merely saved by grace. They were not to be Jews or Gentiles. There was nothing that ever took place in history to identify these people. They were a special people to fill the Father's house by being the only Son who pleased Him. They were not to be a covenant people, as was Israel. It was God's intention to set Israel aside because of their rejection of the Messiah, and not to deal with Israel in the covenants until the time of "Jacob's trouble" in the end-time. It was the Father's intention, when He set Israel aside, to get for Himself a new people who would please Him totally. These are the people in whom He placed His dear Son as their life. Only His Son could please Him totally. To get this special people, He created a whole new race—a new race not connected to anything or anybody who had ever served God by the law or self-effort, a race that was totally dependent upon Another in them as their only life. This new race of people would not serve God in respect to any past covenants given to Israel, but would be all the Father wanted sons to be by the Son who was in them.

Eschatology embraces the fulfillment of these covenants of Israel as its means of scriptural interpretation. Paul comes giving the true gospel for this new race, saying that all of the end-time fulfillments for Israel will not apply to these people because they are not to be saved by the keeping of the covenants or by anything that they themselves do. They are saved by Another, Christ in them, and there is no expectation on God's part for them to be "doers." In fact, God's great plan of salvation is flouted whenever any believer tries to save himself or do anything that adds to his salvation. In our day, religion is constantly basing its program on man's doing something to add to God's salvation.

A Perfect Church

Some teach that the new race will go through the tribulation period. It is taught that man and the Church can do something which will appreciate the plan of God. It ignores the new race created by Christ as being the only life the Father approves. Christ is perfect to the Father, the Church is perfect to the Father, and that perfection is already in the believer by the birthing of the Father.

Paul does deal, however, with an essential part of eschatology. In First Thessalonians 4:13-18, he gives to the new creation race the means by which their life on earth is to be consummated. He speaks of the believer being *"caught up...to meet the Lord in the air"* (v. 17). This verse speaks of the heart of the Father's plan, for it was the Father's plan to save for Himself sons on the basis of the one Son who pleased Him and nothing else. For man to teach that there is something else that saves or that there is something else that a believer can do to add to this salvation is to totally annul the plan of God and salvation by Christ. Therefore, Paul separates himself from the teaching of eschatology that has the believer becoming anything within himself. These verses in First Thessalonians end by telling the new race that they are to *"comfort one another with these words,"* that Jesus is coming back and will receive them unto Himself and so they will ever live in the Father's house.

With this in mind, it is plain to see why the Spirit does not allow the new creation race to get involved in end-time doctrines beyond what is necessary to reach those who are chosen to be in Christ from the foundation of the world. Our mission is to go *"into all the world, and preach the gospel."* It also means the world will rock along as the Father planned from the beginning, without destruction, for the purpose of the world is to be the schoolhouse

page 64

in which to train the sons. When He has all the sons He chose from the foundation of the world, and when all Israel finally has salvation (Christ) offered to it, then will the Father throw away this world. With His new race at home and Israel saved, time as we know it will be no more. We will have entered into the joy of the Lord.

Condemnation Is the "Oil" That Runs Religion

The modern church denies itself the rest and peace there is in Christ by using the doctrines of eschatology, which belong mostly to Israel, to perfect the believer. These doctrines are one of the major sources of condemnation that keep the believer striving to be what he already is in Christ. This condemnation is the major source of oil for the wheels of religion. But thanks be to God, believers are awakening to the truth. Everywhere saints are seeing Christ as their life and are standing in that liberty alone, free from religious entanglement.

IV. The baptism in the Holy Spirit. There is no area of doctrine where Satan has hindered the growth of the believer any more than this area. The baptism in the Holy Spirit was intended by the Father to be a precious ministry to cause the believer to know and become all that he is in Christ. But the simplicity that there is in Christ was thwarted by religion's separating this marvelous act of grace from the Christ in the believer. In fact, in many places in religion there is the teaching that the Person of the Holy Spirit is Christ—that when a believer is saved he receives the Holy Spirit, and that is the life of Christ. To teach this is to annul the Christ who was birthed by the Father. The Holy Spirit was never intended by the Father to push Christ out of the believer or in any way to take over from the Christ within. God has already made the Christ within all that is pleasing to the Father (I Corinthians 1:30). This great error of teaching has been perpetuated because Satan has blinded so many to the truth of the new birth. Many go on to teach that the baptism in the Holy Spirit is to help the believer to live the life—that it is the Holy Spirit who lives the life. There is partial truth to this in that the

Holy Spirit is a comforter, a paraclete (one who goes alongside and comforts and instructs), thus helping the believer to become one with the Christ in him. But to teach in any way that the Holy Spirit is the life or the giver of life is error. The new creation race sees this and is demanding a gospel that teaches it.

The Operation of the Godhead

Now, exactly where does the baptism of the Holy Spirit fit into the new race? To really understand that we must hear what Christ Himself has to say about the coming of the Holy Spirit. He sets the stage properly when, in John 16:7, He tells of how He must go away or the Holy Spirit cannot come. By this He tells more about the plan of God in that He cannot be present when the Spirit comes. This means two things. First, it means that from the beginning of time there has been only one Person of the Godhead operating on earth at a time. In the Old Testament it was Jehovah God, the Father. For three and a half years of the Christ-life on earth it was Christ. Now, since the Day of Pentecost, the operating member has been the Holy Spirit. Second, as long as Christ is on earth in the flesh, it is impossible for men to experience the reality of the Holy Spirit's ministry. That ministry is to reveal Christ in them. Jesus knew that as long as men could see Him in the flesh, there would be no way they could ever come to a revelation by the Holy Spirit that Christ was in them. That is the best introduction I could possibly give to the true ministry of the Holy Spirit. Although the Holy Spirit was to do many things to work out the plan of God, His prime mission was vividly spoken of by Christ in three chapters of John's Gospel, Chapters 14-16. In these three chapters, Jesus says at least seven times that the Holy Spirit is a teacher. This also is dealt with in another chapter.

Now, the Holy Spirit is an essential part of God's plan. The Father has created a new race of people. He has birthed in them His only Son. But the understanding of what He has done cannot come from natural man. What He has done must be taught by God Himself—God the Holy Spirit. Beautifully, there was a thing in God that wanted His creatures to know He had placed another in them so that they might be pleasing unto Him, and that thing in God was manifested as God the Holy Spirit.

The Holy Spirit began His work in the believer at regeneration. It was He who actually placed Christ in us and us in Christ (I Corinthians 12:13). Then, along the way He continued His teaching ministry until real hunger gripped our hearts and we were faced with a crisis experience with the Holy Spirit. This experience the Scriptures call the baptism into the Holy Spirit and it was to accentuate the believer's knowledge of the in-Christ position as nothing else could. It was to be the ultimate mind renewal necessary to living daily and being the Christ-persons we are.

The Essence of John 14:20

This verse vividly pinpoints the purpose of the Day of Pentecost. Once again we hear Jesus explaining the purpose of the Holy Spirit by saying what was to happen on that day. In John 14:20, Jesus focuses the entire plan of God on the believer receiving the Holy Spirit and anchors it all to the happenings on that day. Jesus says that on that day—the Day of Pentecost—the believer will *know something*. Now here is where the new creation race is demanding the true gospel. Jesus did not say that the believer would simply receive something or that the believer would receive power or that the believer would become someone within himself. He plainly says that the believer will come to *know* something. It is so sad that so many who claim to experience a baptism have never come to this knowing. But look further. Jesus said that the thing believers would *know* is that as He was in the Father, so would they *know* that He was in them and that they were in Him.

What a revolutionary statement! It's a statement that religion generally has kept away from most believers. The modern church has not really understood Pentecost and the Father's purpose on that day, and the result is a world without the true gospel. Jesus plainly says that the essence of the Pentecostal experience is a believer coming to the revelation that Christ is his only life. The new creation race will not be denied this part of the gospel any longer. There is only one work of grace—the birthing of the

Father. The strategic ministry of the Holy Spirit is to make that birthing continuous and ever-growing in knowledge.

V. The Church. The true Church of Jesus Christ is a formidable weapon of God against the forces of Satan. In fact, I see the Church as the major force to perpetuate and make known the Word of God. It is because of this that Satan's major attack, aside from the individual believer, is against the Church. Satan works at causing division, bringing schisms, confusing the Word that is preached, and finally, making the Church a laughingstock.

There is little wonder that there are probably more saints, those truly born again, outside the church buildings in America than inside them. Notice that I said "church buildings." Sad to say, many believers have come to believe that a building is the church. In fact, so many are being deprived of the true gospel so much that, through the erroneous preaching of the day, buildings have become a spiritual criterion. Preacher after preacher has made a new building, or the next building to build, the essence of the gospel.

The Modern Ministry Needs a Transfiguration

This transfiguration was an important issue with the Father and He worked it out in a beautiful way. One day He had Jesus take Peter, James and John up to the Mount of Transfiguration. There He miraculously had Moses, Elijah and Jesus appear all together. The first reaction of the three preachers, when they saw this great sight, was the desire to *build a tabernacle* for each of them. The Father knew that there was a very carnal strain in human beings that would take a glorious moment and want to institutionalize it by building buildings. Then the Father brought a cloud that swallowed up Moses and Elijah, and *"they saw...Jesus only."* His purpose in the whole event was to break that carnal tendency in them that made something they could do a spiritual act.

You see, this is what is happening in our day. Buildings have become images of spirituality. Most successful preachers have a building in their plans. But the message of God is that whatever we see that makes us want to do something for God must give way to seeing no one but *"Jesus only."*

Now, we must get it out of our mind that buildings are the true Church. As we see bigger and bigger buildings being built, they become nothing but warehouses where believers are stored and the preacher, instead of being one who would lay down his life for his sheep, is simply a warehouse manager. This is a far cry from the true gospel, and hungry believers everywhere are rebelling. The Church is the Body of Christ. Whether it is two thousand or two or three individuals present, in Christ that is the Church. Numbers do not make the local Body of Christ in any place more important. Numbers may accelerate the growth of the purpose of that body, but *quantity* never replaces *quality* in Christ.

With so many of God's new race turned off from buildings these days, there is a deep restoration of divine truth as to what the Church really is. Some believers, who live in a very lonely and sparsely settled place, said to me some time ago that there were only three of them present at their worship meetings, but that Christ was there. Others have said to me that even though they live in a great city, the churches have become promoters, constantly reaching out to bigger and greater things, leaving the hungry no place to worship. Thus, these people were gathering in a front room of a home and seeing Christ as their all and in all. What is happening these days and what will continue happening until a gospel is preached for the new creation race is the Father allowing more and more of His children to meet in small groups which constitute Christ in that place. Jesus said that if just two or three gathered in His name, then was He there (Matthew 18:20). Until the modern church can once again see that Christ is a body and not a building, and when preachers see that their responsibility is to preach a gospel for a new race, the Father will continue to allow multitudes to be deceived.

The Dying Seed Brings Forth Much Fruit

The true, new-race believer knows that he is a dying seed. He knows that it is not the things he does that reproduce souls, but rather, who he is. Jesus said in John 12:24 that out of His death, life would come automatically. It is that way with us today. The true Church is being built by those who, as dying seeds, see the glory of God flow out of them automatically. The modern church has little dying in it. As a result, there are many weak and sickly believers. Our hope for them is to preach a new-race gospel.

VI. The mind of Christ. It is a most logical conclusion that if the creature is given new life, then there must of a necessity be a place where the Father works out His need of love. That place is the *mind* of the believer. In the tripartite man of body, soul and spirit, we see a very unique thing happen with the apostle of the new creation race. In the area of the soul, Paul makes a radical change in his terminology. All through the Scriptures the word *soul* is used to denote any mental aspect of man. It is here that Paul sees something different. He sees that the whole plan of God hinges on the believer's mind. Knowing that the soulish part of the human relates to the intellect, the will, and the emotions, Paul sees that it is always a *mind* and *heart* function for which the Father is looking. So instead of using the term *soul,* he relates all knowing and all spiritual growth to a "mind function." As it was with the body, in that there was not to be any regeneration, so it was with the mind. Regeneration would be only in the spirit. Although the body would never be regenerated, the mind would have progressive growth as we come into full stature or *"grow up into Him."* With regeneration of the spirit total and without regeneration of the body, the only place left for the progressive growth of a believer is in the mind.

The Plan Centers Upon a "Mind Function"

It is also important to see that the whole of God's plan, as far as the believer is concerned, centers upon a mind function. Adam's test in the garden was a mind function. Would he believe God or Satan? He was made to make a *choice.* Love—the kind of love that the Father wanted—must come from a free moral agent well able to make that choice. Furthermore, we see that the issues in the garden were ones dealing with knowledge. All choices are based on whatever knowledge the human has. God had given ample information to Adam to run or operate the world. The Father made His ultimate test to involve a *"tree of the knowledge of good and evil."* Had God made Adam with a degree of mentality any less than was necessary to make such an ominous decision, God would have been unfair. Adam was perfectly fitted by the Father to handle the issue. It was all up to Adam as to the outcome. It was a mind issue, and by the choice that Adam would make, he would determine what nature or life would be in him. Satan was destined to put into Adam's mind his ideas, along with what the Father had taught. When Adam believed what Satan said, there was birthed in him his new nature. By his decision, he got his Satan spirit. Thus, as Jesus said in John's eighth chapter, all sinners have the spirit of their father in them, the spirit of Satan.

It is the spirit of Satan as the death-life of the human that necessitates our being born again. It is most interesting to note that the same "mind battle" that Adam had is what every believer has today. Notice how a sinner is born again. The Scriptures say, *"Believe on the Lord Jesus Christ, and thou shalt be saved"* (Acts 16:31). To believe is a mind-heart function. Adam believed what Satan said, and that produced Satan's nature. Peter says in First Peter 1:23, *"Being born again...by the word of God."* How is one born again? By believing the Word of God. That is what Adam did not do in the garden. But God demands the same today from every creature. Then again in Second Peter 1:4, Peter says that those who are *"partakers of the divine nature"* are those who have taken hold of *"exceeding great and precious promises."* All spirit birthing comes by believing, and believing is a mind function.

Three Important Mind Verses

Paul gives us three potent verses which show the essence of the mind in the plan of God. In Philippians 2:5, he says, *"Let this mind be in you, which was also in Christ Jesus."* It means to allow the ideas of Christ to be in us. Truth is not automatic to the believer, for the "untruth" is equally available. For love to emote from the believer, there must first be *contrast,* and with contrast there follows *choice.* So we are to allow the same mind to come to us which was in Christ. Where do we get that mind? From Him who is the Word. We look into the face of the Word, Jesus, and are changed into His image. It is a free, moral mind function.

Then again in First Corinthians 2:16b Paul says, *"But we have the mind of Christ."* A stronger rendering of the line would say that we have the mind of Christ available to us. This means that ever available is the information that causes the grace of God to abound in every believer. The Word and the Spirit are always working to show forth the knowledge of the Lord in the believer.

Also, in Romans 12:2, Paul speaks of the real issues of love as he says that the believer should not conform to the world, noting the ever-present contact allowed by the Father, *"but be ye transformed by the renewing of your mind."* This mind growth, demanded by love, is the constancy invaluable to the hungry believer. The carnal soon become taken up with conformation to the world, but the hungry and the loving seek those opportunities to renounce the world as an act of love to the Father.

The Battle for the Mind

The new creation race is a people who see that the real battle is for the mind. They are a people who demand that the preaching and teaching of the Scriptures center on the Word, Christ, and they will not be deceived by man's philosophy any longer. They will demand Scripture and verse for every idea man presents. They will turn off the worldly influences, even though they know that the evil one cannot touch them. Their minds are still the only place where Satan can do any real harm. They know that all faith and believing is a mind function, and they will *give* that mind to Christ who is the real person they are, rather than do what the unregenerated body desires. By this, their whole being—body, soul and spirit—will be supervised by the knowledge of the Lord.

Finally, Peter says in First Peter 4:1, *"Forasmuch then as Christ hath suffered for us in the flesh, **arm** yourselves likewise with the same **mind**: for he that hath suffered in the flesh hath **ceased** from* *sin.* "Now, there could not be a stronger admonition than this. All spiritual growth centers on the mind. All overcoming of sin centers on the mind. Our thinking and our understanding must never become automatic. We must always be open to the Teacher, the Holy Spirit, whose greater ministry is to teach us Christ. Sin will be set into the believer's life, even unknown to that believer, if the Holy Spirit does not teach us the Father's *ways.* The new creation race cannot be duped any longer. For too long have they walked with a "mindless Christ" in them. *No longer!* They will give to the Christ in them a mind, their mind, and by that mind of Christ, they will operate as Christ-persons.

VII. Our union with Christ. This is the ultimate truth of the new creation race. It is only by an understanding of this truth that a believer will ever come to know God. It is only by living daily this truth that a believer will ever live the true life of a Christian. It was never God's intention to save the creature for the creature's self. Rather, the creature was to be saved by *Another,* Christ, for *Another,* the Father. There was never any intention on the Father's part of saving creatures, aside from His plan. It was Satan's idea that the creature be an independent self; God's plan called for the creature to be in Christ from the beginning (Ephesians 1:4). To renew men's minds to this truth, the Father, in the Scriptures, made the statement *"in Christ"* over 200 times, and 146 of those times translate *union with Christ.* Religion has too long taught that man is the center of God's plan. No! A thousand times, no! *Christ is God's everything!* From the beginning it was man in Christ, a union that settled, once and for all, what kind of son the Father would have in His house. The union meant that the Father would have a true, obedient Son, Christ, in a human container, and that the union would become so perfect that it would be Christ operating in and as that believer. This is, in fact, what a Christian (a Christ-person) is—one who no longer operates as a self for self, but as a Jesus-self. Actually, this very idea upsets carnal believers, but the only way the Christ in any believer can express Himself

page 73

is *as* that believer. The new creation race people will no longer tolerate this ignorance, but will boldly speak the truth in love.

Trying to "Be Like Jesus" Is to Fail

The truth is, whether others see it or not, the believer is a Christian who expresses the life in him. If you do not think Christ is in you, then you will struggle to be *like* Jesus of Nazareth and will be an utter failure. When the Father placed Christ in a body called Mary of Nazareth, a union was formed between that body and Christ for the Father's will to be perfectly done. Now the Father places Jesus in you and by that placing (birthing) you are able, for the first time, to be free of your self-independence and be Him. That is what the Scriptures mean—you are a Christ-person in your human form, and Christ is the *"fulness of the God-head"* in you. Thus, the Father, from the beginning, wanted every son to be as Jesus. Yet He wanted a free moral creature who could make a choice to be what He planned. The choice was the essence of love, and love was the whole of what God needed. The idea of union solved this. When He put Christ in the believer, He no longer needed to look to that believer for anything, but He could now trust Christ in him to do and to be the Father's desire.

Chapter 5

God's Intent and Paul's Revelation of That Intent

And Elisha came again to Gilgal: and there was a dearth in the land; and the sons of the prophets were sitting before him: and he said unto his servant, Set on the great pot, and seethe pottage for the sons of the prophets. And one went out into the field to gather herbs, and found a wild vine, and gathered thereof wild gourds his lap full, and came and shred them into the pot of pottage: for they knew them not. So they poured out for the men to eat. And it came to pass, as they were eating of the pottage, that they cried out, and said, O thou man of God, there is death in the pot. And they could not eat thereof. But he said, Then bring meal. And he cast it into the pot; and he said, Pour out for the people, that they may eat. And there was no harm in the pot (II Kings 4:38-41).

The Corruption of Civilization

It is very obvious that there is a great dearth in our land. It is our experience that men and women are hungering for the Word of God as never before. The great pot, the Bible, has been set before them; but sad to say, some of the enthusiastic translators have inadvertently shred wild gourds in the pottage. Millions who feast upon this poison, hoping to find life eternal, are finding very little life and not living any eternal existence at all.

It is my prayer that this message will reach not only the multitudes who sit in darkness waiting to see a great light, but also those who handle the Word of God, that they be careful where they get their Scriptures, how they translate the Word of God, and what they feed the hungry hearts. It is as declared in the text from Second Kings that even in this day there is greatly needed those who can bring "meal" to the pot and actually feed the people the fresh bread that comes down from God out of Heaven.

The Christ-life strongly proclaims that that bread is Christ, and only Christ. God set up unbelievable miraculous events at the Transfiguration, and the cloud came down upon Moses, Elijah and Christ. When the cloud lifted, the Scripture says there was standing only Jesus as their life, and this is the "meal" we feel that must be brought to the hungry in order for them to be fed. There is no doubt that we are entering into the closing moments of this dispensation We are becoming more and more conscious of the approaching end. Something is bound to happen. Our population is increasing at the rate of 55 million souls a year. Our natural resources are diminishing. We have no idea how long oil will be available to this society. Our forests are disappearing. Animals are dying out. Our rivers, lakes and cities are becoming polluted. Crime and immorality are increasing on every hand. There are new methods of wholesale destruction of life and property being discovered every day. Even nature itself appears to be warring against humanity as we see an increase in cyclones and floods, famines, earthquakes, pestilences and other disasters. Yet the Word of God has plainly declared that these things would take place.

The Father Is Raising Up a Hungry People

The Bible also warns us that the Judgment Day is coming and that Christ will be the only one worthy to judge those who stand before Him. We hear the ominous words from Revelation 22:11, *"He that is unjust, let him be unjust still: and he which is filthy, let him be filthy still: and he that is righteous, let him be righteous still: and he that is holy, let him be holy still."*

Although these seem to be ominous words aimed right at our generation, in the midst of it all God has seen fit to bring a *"meal"* to hungry people where they are seeing only Christ as their life, and by this are able to stand righteous and perfect before God. Thus, all of the dreadfulness of the hour and the devastation that appears to be upon the face of the earth is made of no avail to this believer who is eating the perfect fruit that comes down from God. Converging powers are a part of God's plan. In the Christ-life we have seen that, even though all of these devastating things will take place in our day, they are but tools of the Father to push us closer to Christ and to press us into living the only nature we have. The one thing that is happening these days as never before is the bringing forth of the Christ-like character and personality to the hungry people on earth. Obviously, this could not happen unless the proper food were being fed them.

We are gloriously involved in this move of the Spirit now, whereby the true Bread that comes down from God out of Heaven is feeding hungry hearts. They are beginning to grow up in Him and are seeing their very lives—their very personalities—overwhelmed by One who has gloriously been placed within. The message for this day is clear. To escape the destruction soon to come upon this earth, we must move into a deeper and more powerful relationship with God. This relationship with God actually has already been given to every born-again believer, for God the Father, Himself, has birthed in the believer the only life that He has—His life, His nature (II Peter 1:4). It is necessary now that this son who has had the birthing take place come to knowledge and understanding of what has happened to him. This is the essence of the current move of God. This is not a new truth. It has been an ever-existing truth since the days of the Apostle Paul, who was the first to write of the revelation of Christ as the hope of the believer. As it has been through the centuries (a truth much maligned and much fought by Satan), so it is today. As a consequence, Satan, by his use of religion, has done all he could to put poison in the pot and to change the intent of the heavenly Father who seeks sons to live in His house. He did it through the multitude of translations of the Scriptures.

The Scriptures Are Pure to the Intent of God

Although it is not our purpose here to simply pick at everything men do, what they are doing is seemingly in disagreement with what we do. It is a truth that must be borne out; the renewed mind comes only from the Scriptures, and if the Scriptures are not pure concerning the intent of God in their translation, then there will be death in the pot. As we have watched the various and sundry translations of the Scriptures come forth in recent years, we have seen an increasing attempt to make the truths of God so simple and plain to natural man that the ultimate work of the Holy Spirit in revealing Christ has been shut out. As a result, few people seek to know God and few hunger and thirst after righteousness. Religion has been made so simple and plain that it has become head knowledge. So the true revelation knowledge brought by our glorious Teacher, the Holy Spirit, is seldom sought after. Of course, Satan would do all within his power to keep the believer from seeing the Christ in himself. This is very often shown by the mistranslation of the Scriptures. We are increasingly made aware that as new translations come about—many which conceal or hide the Christ-life truth—more and more they demand of the believer something he must do to be pleasing to God. This has long been the effect of religion in our world. *Religion* as a term means self-effort, or man's effort to please God. If anything is clearly taught in the ultimate intention of God, and especially in the new creation gospel which Paul gives us, it is that man cannot, by anything that he does, please God.

God's Intention Must Take Place

Man's unfaithfulness springs from his ignorance of who and what he is in Christ. Man's unbelief comes because his mind has not been renewed with God's plan and God's purpose. As Paul says in Romans 12:1-2: *"I beseech you therefore, brethren, by the mercies of God, that ye present your bodies a living sacrifice, holy, acceptable unto God, which is your reasonable service. And be not conformed to this world: but be ye transformed by the renewing of your mind, that ye may prove what is that good, and acceptable, and perfect, will of God."*

The believer must not conform to the world, for if he does, his mind will not be renewed. To place the whole of God's intent upon man's doing something is a literal conforming to the world, for that is the natural, material and worldly way of doing things. Thus, it becomes absolutely necessary that the believer in his understanding of the Scriptures sees what is God's intention from the beginning, as well as what is the revelation of that intention to be found in the Scriptures. It is our viewpoint from the Christ-life that, very simply, the Father's original intention is to fill up His house with sons who have the very same nature He has. The giving of this nature is to be in the form of an incorruptible seed, Jesus Christ, who is placed in every believer (I Peter 1:23).

Ephesians 1:4 plainly states that all believers were chosen in Christ before the foundation of the world. This is the heart of the initial intention of God. The revelation of this intention of God is clearly brought to us by the Apostle Paul, who says to us in such places as Romans 16 and Ephesians 3 that there is a Father who has placed His own seed in the human being, causing God the Son to be birthed in him. Though such knowledge has been hidden for generations, it is now revealed by the Holy Spirit to hungry hearts. In the Christ-life, we believe this is the essence of the gospel and that all translations of the Scriptures and all understanding of the Bible must hinge on this union between the human being and the Christ God has placed within him.

Several Factors for Consideration

As we look into the Scriptures, there are several factors we should consider if we are to determine how we look at the plan and purpose for mankind.

page 79

1. We must clearly see in everything we study from the Bible that God has a plan and that His plan is materializing and working out according to His will, whether or not men can see it or understand it. It is a fact that the New Testament brings to us a new and vivid insight into the original plan of God—one which was determined before the world ever started. Furthermore, the Apostle Paul introduces a new righteousness and a new sanctification that are, in fact, not entities at all, but demonstrations and expressions of a Person—a Person whom God births in us in the born-again experience. Thus, we must begin our understanding of the Scriptures by seeing that through what Christ did, God was able to bring about a whole new way of living and establish a new people—a new creation race—which had never before been in existence. This new race of people was not one of converted Jews or lawkeepers, but a people who were saved by Another, Christ in them.

2. We must never equate the law with Jesus Christ as our life. It is not our purpose, in the Christ-life, to just separate the law from the gospel because the law is our schoolmaster to bring us to Christ. But as it is in everyday living, the schoolhouse carries an imperative position in our lives. Once we have finished its training, it no longer holds an imperative position and, in fact, is only a memory. It has no daily operation in our lives.

Christ-Life Not a Part of Law

The law's purpose is to give us a schooling that brings us to Christ. Once we see Christ who is all and in all, we come to the understanding of the new creation race.

3. It is imperative in our searching of the Scriptures that we see Christ as our life in an entirely different form than anyone in the Old Testament or even in the four Gospels saw Him. Throughout the Old Testament and the four Gospels, the message was to be faithful to God and that if we are unfaithful, we must offer a sacrifice to atone for our sins or we will not be acceptable to God. The death of Jesus Christ did away with this sort of operation, for God knew that no man could live the law by whatever degree of strength and power he might manifest. Thus, God set into operation what He had planned before He ever created any man. All were to be His children by being birthed; they would be in Christ, and the only faithfulness they would have would be the faithfulness of Christ.

The responsibility of the believer would be, as Paul plainly admonishes in the new creation race gospel, that he must grow up into Christ, come into full stature, and cease to be his independent self. Unless the believer is able to take hold of these facts and cause them to help him see these Scriptures in this light, he cannot grow up in Christ as he should.

4. Grace is the all-consuming word for the new creation race gospel. There are many who read the Scriptures seeking only justice. Sad to say, there are many who accept grace and justice in the same light and who, in doing so, have frustrated the gospel. This was a major fight that Paul had in the teaching of the gospel, for there were many Judaizers in his day who had a mixture of grace and justice. This mixture literally was between the teaching that God does it all and that man does it by himself when it comes to salvation. Certainly, the four thousand years of history in the Old Testament is plainly written to show that men could never please God by anything they do. Thus, the manifestation of grace is God doing it all and believers growing up into that by seeing their responsibility in the renewing of their minds. It is not through their doing, but through what God has already done.

5. We must come to an understanding of the Scriptures that teach eternal life is right now within the believer. The Apostle John has made this most clear in his first Epistle. His dynamic word is *"Beloved, now are we the sons of God."* The believer who is born again is not earning eternal life, working for eternal life, or hoping to receive eternal life. If he has been birthed, it is total and complete. If he has not been birthed, there is no hope. Thus Jesus came saying, *"Ye must be born again."* When one is born again, he has the nature, the life, and the Spirit of God within him. This spirit within him overwhelms every other part of the believer in soul and body and is the operating spirit in him and, as such, manifests God's true Son. This is not something the believer earns; this is an unconditional gift. This is the bringing about of the Kingdom of God inside every believer, for now the Kingdom is within us. To see any other thing is to pervert the gospel which God has sent to those who hunger. This is the gospel that constitutes the true meal and is the eating and drinking of Him who comes down from God out of Heaven. The only way the believer ever has the power of God is by the power and the life within him. The only way the believer can ever be faithful is by the faithfulness of Christ. It is Paul saying in Galatians 2:20, *"The life which I now live in the flesh I live by the faith of the Son of God."* Also, the only way the believer ever has true Christian character is by the expression of the one and only true character, Christ, from within.

The Latter Explains the First

6. All translations of the Bible are literally a combination of the work of God and the work of man, for man has done all he could under the inspiration of the Holy Spirit. If he has failed to see what is God's main theme—that of filling up His house with sons—all of the translations of the Scriptures may fall short. Very often the Scriptures are translated as if the understanding of God's program starts with creation. However, most Bible scholars know the simple fact that to understand what God is doing, one cannot start in Genesis.

First the believer begins with the study of the Epistles for the progression of God-knowledge. Bible students know that the Epistles must be understood before the four Gospels can be understood, and the four Gospels must be understood before the Old Testament can be understood. As I have often told students, the first book in the Bible very likely should have been one of Paul's first-written Epistles, for the Epistles explain the purpose of Christ in human form. Following the Epistles should be the four Gospels. Then should come the Old Testament, which covers a period of forty-three hundred years of God's dealing with mankind, proving that mankind could never do what God said to do.

So, as God's original intention was the final believer in Christ, we come to understand why the Old Testament was written. God, who is a just God and working out His own plan, required forty-three hundred years of proof that man, without another in him, could never be pleasing to God. Then, finally, God took seventeen hundred years of dealing with Israel to show that when a distinct and formally written law was given to mankind, man still fell short of God's intention. All of this was necessary to show that the essence of salvation was not man's saving himself or doing his own works. But by trusting another, God might eventually have His house filled with sons who not only had His nature, but who also bore His characteristics through the Son He had birthed in them.

The Hope of the Mystery of Godliness

7. It is here that the new creation gospel given by the Apostle Paul developed the very people planned in the mind of God before the foundation of the world. Until this gospel is seen, believed and lived, there cannot be a true believer. Unless the Scriptures we read point out this belief and point out this new race of people created by another Being in them, there can be no hope that the Bible will produce the one people pleasing to God. The mystery of godliness is simply that God has the power and the ability to take the only Son He has and place that one Son in every human being who trusts Him. This is by no effort on the part of the human being; it is by grace. Salvation is the gift of God, and the gift of God is literally a Person.

Now that that Person has come to the believer as his only life, the mind of that believer must be renewed. Here is where the Scriptures come in as this believer is told by the preaching of the gospel that he is in Christ. He will, by learning to love the Jesus in him, form a *union,* and as this *union* begins to form, the Scriptures become imperative to his growth. He will literally be transformed in his mind into that glorious Kingdom within him.

All Scripture Testifies of Him

It is for this reason that we are so strong in stressing how you read the Scriptures. The *searching of the Scriptures* is the only means for renewing the mind. There are multitudes today who fall into the same category as the Jews whom Jesus spoke of in Chapter 5 of the Gospel of John, where they searched the Scriptures to find life, but of course did not find that life because they looked for it in the things they did. Jesus said, *"They are they which testify of Me. And ye will not come to Me, that ye might have life"* (vv. 39-40). So it is with us today when we search the Scriptures. If we see not Christ, we have no life. Furthermore, as we see Christ in the Scriptures, we see the same thing Jesus said is in us, for God has only one Son. As we begin to grow up into this one Son, we are radically changed into His likeness and image so that our personalities are swamped and overwhelmed by His very character. Thus, we manifest His fruit of the Spirit, which is love, joy, peace, longsuffering, temperance, etc. (Galatians 5:22-23).

It becomes important that we see faithfulness on the believer's part as the fruit of His faith working through us. If the life we now live, we live by the faith of the Son of God, that constitutes faithfulness. To put it simply, none of us is faithful; nor can we ever be faithful. When we are faithful, it is His faithfulness that is being expressed. Obedience, on the other hand, is the fruit of love. Once again, it is not our love; it is His love shed abroad in us that works out through us in the expression of obedience. In the Book of Revelation, faithfulness is presented as the criterion of the New Testament believer. That is Christ operating His faith through us. Throughout the entire Bible, obedience is given to us as an act of love and as the only thing that pleases God. The Old Testament declared, *"To obey is better than sacrifice."*

That is God saying, "I am not interested in any of your work and your efforts which constitute your sacrifice." So often there are those who want to take us back under the Law of Moses, where men were forced by God, by their own doing, to please Him. All of this, in time, showed that none of it did please Him and finally made necessary His birthing Christ in us as our only hope of glory. Obedience is the fruit of His love working through us. I found out, as a believer, that I could not within myself be obedient to God. It was then that I became one with Him who is obedient, and by this union of Him and me, I began to express obedience. This means that there is a whole new righteousness for today's believer. That new righteousness is not the believer's working toward God; it is God's working out of the believer's everyday living. Today there is a new method that comes from seeing in the Scriptures that God's initial plan is the believer being saved by Another. Salvation is not a piece of paper, or a baptism, or a joining of the church, or a keeping of the law. Salvation is a Person. Unless we read the Scriptures and see this Christ, we shall be like the Jews in John's fifth chapter. They had no life because they failed to see the Scriptures that testify of Jesus. So it is today. Multitudes of people read their Bibles and do not see that salvation is a Person. Therefore, they do not grow up into Him who is life. They then fall short of the peace and rest that belong to every believer in Christ.

There are many who are quick to say that God's only standard of righteousness is the Ten Commandments which Moses received at Sinai. True, these commandments were a revelation of the character of God, but from their very inception mankind has had great difficulty with them. Moses, himself, in anger threw down the original tablets and broke them.

All Men Failed to Live the Law

From that time on, for the next seventeen hundred years, no man could live by those commandments, although many strived to do so unto their very death. These commandments were a revelation of the character of God, but men lost sight of becoming godly in their vain attempts to live by the commandments. Thus, it is only by the coming of Jesus Christ, birthed of a virgin, that man has ever seen the character of God in operation. By the coming of the Son, God began to be demonstrated, for Jesus said, *"He that hath seen Me hath seen the Father"* (John 14:9). This was an absolute imperative in the introduction to the Christ-life, for later on Paul was to say that this one Son is now in every believer. As Christ had said, "I am an expresser of God the Father," so now the believer, by Christ in him, could say that he, too, is an expresser of God. As such, whatever he expresses is the character of God according to his level of understanding. In this way, God had completed His plan.

The Old Testament proved that Another would be needed to express the character of God. Now Jesus, as the true Manifestor of the character of God, is placed in every born-again believer, expressing His character by His nature in them. Thus, there was a new salvation and a new righteousness that was to bring to mankind, once and for all, finally and ultimately, what is necessary for man to please God and, most of all, to be in His family and to live in His house. The apostle was destined to state finally that Christ came not to destroy the law, but to fulfill it. How did He fulfill it? He fulfilled it as the only sinless One who could keep the law. Therefore, God's ultimate intention was to place that Christ, who perfectly fulfilled every aspect of His character, in the believer.

There is one thing that is very obvious in the study of the Old Testament: God could not give us His righteousness by our works. It is plainly established that over the forty-three-hundred-year period, all the way from Adam to John the Baptist, it was nearly impossible for God to impart righteousness to man. He did everything He could to give man His righteousness.

He gave him every opportunity to win it, to work for it, to strive toward it, and to build that righteousness in himself. But from Adam to Noah to Abraham to David to Isaiah and finally to John the Baptist, in the end all men failed. They all sinned, and through all five Old Testament dispensations, it is proven by God that whatever method and means He gave, man still failed on every count.

God Proved His Plan

This was God's justification in operation. For Him to be justified in placing Another in the creature, One on whom He could depend to save, He must go through this process. He proved to Himself and to all mankind that there was no possible way for man to receive righteousness on his own. It would take Another, totally righteous, in him to be his righteousness. This is the work of Calvary. This is the ultimate of grace. When man comes to the point where he sees Christ as his only life, after the revelation of Jesus Christ has taken place, he is able to look back in the Old Testament and see that all Scripture did point to Christ's being the only salvation.

It means that, first, man must have the revelation of Christ (I Corinthians 2:9-10) before he can possibly understand the Old Testament. He also must come to see that the New Testament, and especially Paul's Epistles, are not a new gospel because Paul plainly says in Ephesians 1:4 that the believer was chosen to be in Christ *before the foundation of the world was laid.* That actually means that the Christ-life truth is older than any other truth in the entire Bible. It literally means that the in-Christ message and our union with Christ were planned by God before creation, before Adam, before Noah, before Abraham, before Moses, before any of the tribes of Israel, or David, or Isaiah, or John the Baptist.

From the very beginning, the plan of God for us was to place Another in us. This is the message of the New Testament and the Epistles. The New Testament is not a new gospel. God does not change. His thinking from the very beginning was that the believer would be saved solely by the life of Another, as expressed in Peter's First Epistle, and Revelation 13:8, that the Lamb was slain before the foundation of the world. So, just as it was imperative that God place Another in the creature, the means by which He would accomplish this was the death of His own Son. The death of His own Son took place in His mind before the foundation of the world and before anything was created. It is unthinkable that the believer of the new creation race gospel can ever have the feeling that he is establishing any new principles of truth or retranslating any of the Word of God to suit his purpose.

The new creation race believer knows beyond any shadow of a doubt that what he has become in Christ is what God intended to happen to every creature before the world was ever created. Thus, we are able to establish that there are definite new creation race truths given to us in the Scriptures that are absolute to the believer's growth.

Five Important Truths

Truth Number 1. The entire Bible establishes the fact that, in order for one to live forever, he must have the only life that is eternal placed within him. That one life is Christ. Christ in us is the essence of eternal life.

Truth Number 2. This character of the Person of Christ, who is in the believer, is transferable. The whole of the plan of God hinges on Christ being in the believer not only as his only life, but also becoming his only expression. God gives to all born-again creatures His very righteousness. In order for this Christ-righteousness to operate in the believer, his mind must be renewed by the Word of God as he grows in his love for the Christ in him.

Truth Number 3. The whole Bible affirmatively teaches that this Christ-life is obtained simply by believing what God says. The original sin in the garden took place because Adam and Eve did not believe what God had said, but what Satan had said. In order for a human being to enter into the fullness of God's plan, all he needs to do is simply believe on the Lord Jesus Christ and he shall be saved (Acts 16:31).

Truth Number 4. The Bible clearly teaches that the purpose of grace is for God to give to a human being what the human being cannot get by himself. The grace of God is most greatly emphasized by the gift of His own dear Son to be the life of the believer. The only way any believer can ever become God's pleasure and God's purpose is for the Christ in him to swamp and overwhelm him until the only life he lives is Christ.

page 88

Truth Number 5. This grace of God is available to every hungry, needy heart on the simple condition that he senses he cannot save himself and must have another to save him. How pleased the heavenly Father is when any soul comes to Him, saying, "I have tried, by my own effort, by the keeping of the law, and by the doing of what is right to be saved, and I have failed. Now I want Your plan, Your way, and Your Son." Grace is more powerful than sin at this point, and he who has been a sinner is suddenly overwhelmed by marvelous grace. The moment this person believes on the Lord Jesus Christ, a birth takes place; Satan is put out and Christ is put in.

If these five principles are firmly established in the believer's mind, the Scriptures will open up a whole new world to him.

God's Intent

One of the most marvelous things we see in the Christ-life is how the Bible becomes a brand-new book to the believer when he is released from the self-effort of saving himself by some law. For so long a time, so many have read the Scriptures according to some man's law, only to find that when the two major themes—God's intent and Paul's revelation of that intent—were united, they were destined to have a brand-new Bible. Certainly, this is not by the creation of some new truth through the twisting of Scripture, but by seeing that the whole of the Scriptures is for the believer to come to the knowledge of God's intent. The question then arises as to why there are so many who have not seen this truth or who have begun operating out of this truth.

There are three things to be said about this. First, we must mention that many who preach the truth, being only human and thus motivated by the old man syndrome of the knowledge of good and evil, love popularity more than truth. Their audiences are delighted to hear the message that there is something they can do. This confirms a belief wrought by Satan in all human beings—that they will be as God if they eat of the forbidden truth. But this is a deceiving lie, for when men eat of the illicit fruit of the idea that man is something within himself, they are deceived, for it doesn't work. *No man becomes God.* Thus, Satan's lie continues to deceive multitudes, and his method of doing so is through those who preach the gospel without having God's intent in focus.

Salvation is free. This is the gospel that must be preached. It is not joining the church, or some baptism, or some work, or giving, or trying to live a holy life, that brings salvation. Salvation is a gift of God. It is bought without money, without price; it comes from the finished work of Christ at Calvary. Those who continue to preach that there is something man can and must do to please God are unfaithful servants and are deceiving the audiences who listen to them.

Imputed and Expressed Righteousness

There is another group that is very honest, but fails to distinguish clearly between *the righteousness that is imputed* and *the righteousness that is expressed.* There are many who fail to see the difference between Christ's responsibility in being the life and the believer's responsibility of expressing that life. The only righteousness that can ever be manifested by any believer is Christ's righteousness.

The Bible clearly states that all our righteousness is as filthy rags (Isaiah 64:6). The mystery of godliness taught in the new creation race gospel plainly says that we become the righteousness of Christ because we are the righteousness of Christ. In time, the knowing believer can shout out literally, "I am the righteousness of Christ." This is a gift of God. This is imputed righteousness. This is what God sees when He looks at every believer, even if the believer is manifesting his own works—works of the flesh. By the birthing that has taken place, God still sees the righteousness of Christ in him. No believer can enter into rest without Christ's righteousness, for he will kill himself in works if he attempts to bring about righteousness by his own efforts. That is why so many in the modern religious circles have never entered into the rest that was given to us by the Father even before anything in creation came about (Hebrews 4:3). The believer who is dedicated to doing his own works in his own way will never enter into that rest and will always be striving and working, first to please himself, second to please others, and last, to please God. Sad to say, this is the chronology of a working believer, for he works by Satan's devices to better himself and last of all to please God.

Learning From the Glorious Teacher

Now, expressed righteousness is the righteousness of Christ that comes from the believer who has been sitting at the feet of the Teacher, the Holy Spirit. This expressed righteousness comes forth from the believer who has understood that he is in a schoolhouse called the world, and by the circumstances and situations God has arranged for him in the world, expresses the Christ in him. This expression is never perfect at first and often begins in a negative way, but as the believer learns of the Spirit, he gives his total mind to the Christ within him and thereby forces the outer expression through the body. The very character of God becomes our own character as we practice obedience to His Word.

The law of love—Christ manifesting himself through us—brings about this perfect obedience. By this we express the imputed righteousness, although others may have great difficulty in seeing a radical change in our living at first. We come to rest by realizing that we are fully accepted by the Father on the basis of the Son in us. This is the only way mankind could ever be free to love and worship God the Father. It all comes about because man is relieved of the horrendous self-effort that has made of him a failure rather than a spiritual success.

Faulty Translations

Another reason there are many who do not teach the truth is their faulty interpretations of the Scriptures. Many times we look at certain verses and, not seeing Christ in the verses, heap upon ourselves a personal effort to live the verses. Take, for example, First Corinthians 15:57. This verse reads, *"But thanks be to God, which giveth us the victory through our Lord Jesus Christ."* It is plain to see that the only way Paul felt that the believer had victory was by Jesus Christ. The verse says, *"[He] giveth us the victory through* our Lord Jesus Christ.'' There is no inference in this verse that the believer earns victory or has worked for it because that would be reverting back to the old unsuccessful way of doing things—literally, the old man syndrome that Paul speaks of. That way of doing things was crucified at Calvary, and now it is not God giving *us* the victory, but the victory coming through our Lord Jesus Christ. This is consistent with the two main themes of the Scripture, *God's full intent and Paul's revelation of that intent.*

Another word of warning should be given to those who use even the original manuscripts or Greek lexicons or analytical concordances; unless it is known that it is the original manuscripts that are being directly translated from, even certain Greek translations can pull the believer away from seeing Jesus as all. It is so important, therefore, for any hungry believer to depend upon the teaching of the Holy Spirit. He reveals the theme of the Scriptures: Christ, and Him crucified. The Holy Spirit helps us see how it was God's intention to declare that it was His faithfulness working through the believer, rather than man's becoming faithful within himself. Several verses of Scripture bear this out. First, it is very important to see that the greatest attribute of God is His faithfulness. God is faithful so that He does not fail in any promises made; nor does He fail any of His people. His children can depend upon His faithfulness in His dealings with men. On one occasion David said to Saul, *''The Lord render to every man His righteousness and His faithfulness''* (I Samuel 26:23). The Hebrew word for faithfulness is *emunah.* In some versions of the Scripture, this word is given in the Greek as *pistis.* Both times they mean God's faithfulness or the faithfulness of the Son of God.

David's Song

Many times in the Book of Psalms, David sang of the Lord's faithfulness. *''Thy faithfulness reacheth unto the clouds''* (36:5); *''I have declared Thy faithfulness and Thy salvation''* (40:10); *''Shall Thy lovingkindness be declared in the grave? or Thy faithfulness in destruction?''* (88:11); *''I will sing of the mercies of the Lord for ever: with my mouth will I make known Thy faithfulness to all generations"* (89:1); *"Thy faithfulness shalt Thou establish in the very heavens"* (89:2); *"And the heavens shall praise Thy wonders, O Lord: Thy faithfulness also in the congregation of the saints"* (89:5); *"O Lord God of hosts, who is a strong Lord like unto Thee? or to Thy faithfulness round about Thee?"* (89:8); *"But My* [the Lord's] *faithfulness and My mercy shall be with him"* (89:24); *"Nevertheless My lovingkindness will I not utterly take from him, nor suffer My* [the Lord's] *faithfulness to fail"* (89:33); *"It is a good thing...to shew forth Thy loving-kindness in the morning, and Thy faithfulness every night"* (92:1-2); *"I know, O Lord, that Thy judgments are right, and that Thou in faithfulness has afflicted me"* (119:75); *"Thy faithfulness is unto all generations: Thou hast established the earth, and it abideth"* (119:90).

Then we read from Isaiah, *"And righteousness shall be the girdle of His loins, and faithfulness the girdle of His reins"* (11:5); *"Thy counsels of old are faithfulness and truth"* (25:1). Jeremiah writes, *"It is of the Lord's mercies that we are not consumed....great is Thy faithfulness"* (Lamentations 3:22-23). Now, in all of the quoted verses, the faithfulness that is referred to is that of God. This is literally the faithfulness of Christ manifested through Old Testament writers because it was God's plan that Christ should be the life of the believer from the very beginning. Obviously, the Holy Spirit would have godly men of old to write on numerous occasions the facts that would fulfill that one and only life that pleased God. Thus, even in the Old Testament when writers wrote, they wrote not of their faithfulness, but of the faithfulness of God.

God Is Loyal to Principles

Now, the faithfulness of God cannot be separated from the love of God. It is His loyalty to the principles that He has set forth that are comparable to His nature. Since it is His plan that every one of His sons bear the character of His nature which He placed in them by the incorruptible seed, it is His will that His righteousness and His truth be expressed by the believer. Of course, it is His purpose in creating man in the first place that man would be like Him, made in His image, and possessing His very faithfulness, His love and His life. This was all brought about whenever He, to justify Himself in doing this tremendous thing, offered His own sacrifice, the Lamb. This is the work of Calvary. At Calvary not only are we saved by the death of Another, but the Father, by the offering of that sacrifice, was also able to place His faithfulness in every creature.

In looking to the New Testament, we want to see how the faithfulness of God works out in the gospel of the new creation race. On one hand we're shocked to find that in our King James Version, although the word "faithfulness" is used many times in the Old Testament, it does not appear at all in the New. On the other hand, the word "faith" appears more than two hundred times in the New Testament, where it appears only twice in the Old. In both cases, it is a translation of the word *emunah*. Whether it is translated "God's faithfulness" in the Old Testament or "Christ's faith," *pistis*, in the New Testament, it is still a distinctive virtue of God being exercised. We see now the reason faithfulness is not the term used in the New Testament: There is a Person now in the believer who will perform that faithfulness. Faithfulness is the most distinct character trait of God, and concerns God's love and truth.

The Key to the Scriptures

To see the Scriptures properly as God intended, the believer must come to an understanding that the Christ-life is the actual key to unlocking divine truth.

It may be important to look further into the use of these words that we have been dealing with. The terms *pistis* and *pistos* are Greek words that deal with faith and faithfulness. *Pistis* is the noun and *pistos* the adjective. There seems to be no doubt among Bible scholars that the meaning of *pistos* is faithful, but there are many who doubt that the word *pistis* means faith or faithfulness. In the King James Version, *pistos* is used sixty-seven times. It is translated as follows: "faithful," fifty-three times; "sure," once;

"faithfully," once; "true," twice; "believing," three times; "believeth," three times; "what believeth," three times; and "believer," one time. *Pistos* is translated as faithful rather than just as a believer believing because it only makes sense when translated that way. When Jesus began to give the parables, He very strongly emphasized faithfulness in each parable because it was a key to seeing God in man—that man within himself had never been faithful, and all of the parables of Jesus bear this out. Faithfulness was a greater virtue with Christ because He saw that the only faithfulness that could ever be pleasing to God was God's own kind of faithfulness in the believer, and so He lays the foundations for such an idea. It is not what we believe as Christians that becomes imperative, for too many today are bogged down in developing their beliefs, their doctrines, their theology. To do that is to fall into the trap of Satan—never allowing Him who is in you to be faithful. It is not so much what we believe or what our doctrines are that is most important. The most important thing is coming to know Him who is our life.

His Faith and God's Faithfulness

Certainly, it cannot be left to any new creation race believer to exercise faithfulness within himself. This would be so contrary to the finished work that God accomplished through the death of the Lamb. By the work of the cross and Another's paying the price, God was able to place Christ in every believer so the believer now lived by the faith or faithfulness of the Son of God. The New Testament clearly brings this out in the word "faith". We should not make any difference between Christ's faith and God's faithfulness because Christ is distinctly God the Son operating equally with Father God in the Old Testament. In Paul's Epistles where we find the truths of the new creation race gospel, Paul plainly uses the language that is imperative for understanding the Scriptures, as in Galatians 2:20. He says, *"The life which I now live in the flesh I live by the faith* [or faithfulness] *of the Son of God."* This is true to the intent of God and to the believer God is bringing forth in these last days. It is not our faith; it is His faith. It certainly is not our faithfulness that counts; it's His faithfulness.

Throughout the Scriptures, we have certain admonitions such as *"Have faith in God."* A better translation would have been "Have the faith of God." Again, this is true to the intent of God. The Greek word that is translated "faith" in this instance is *pistis.* We see that when a believer is encouraged to have the faith of God, it means a mind renewal is in effect. He already has the faith of God in him, for Christ is in him, the fullness of God. But to express that and to live that requires a mind being given to Christ—one that sees and understands this. Thus the Scriptures renew the mind so the believer begins to express himself by saying, "I have no faith of my own; the faith I now exercise is the faith of the Son of God."

Need for Renewed Mind

Only when we acquire this renewed mind will God be able to honor His dear Son who is within us; only then will we be true "expressers" as sons of God. God works through us in perfect harmony, and we see His Son as our life and our all. This seeing of the Son brings the believer into union with Christ so the believer can shout, "I no longer live; Christ lives in me." Thus, the faithfulness of God—God's character—begins to be expressed by the believer. With this faith of the Son of God in the believer comes forth an expression of the *power* of God. By an understanding that Christ within is the faithful One, the believer is able to express the love of God in places he never dreamed possible. The believer is not urged to try to get this faithfulness or try to get this faith; he already has this faith—he already has this faithful One within him. The believer need only understand that this has taken place, and by the renewal of his mind and the work of the Holy Spirit in that mind, he will begin to exercise his true life in Christ.

In Romans 1:16-17, the apostle reveals the great cornerstone truth of the Reformation church—that the just shall live by faith. This quotation probably is taken from Habakkuk 2:4. Very often natural men are prompted to quote this verse as: The just will live because of their faithfulness. This is, perhaps, the reason so many have failed to enter into the Christ-life and multitudes never come to their completeness in Christ. As long as we see the Scriptures presenting a truth that it is our faithfulness and something that we must come to, we will be deceived. Many have long misinterpreted Galatians 2:20, the line which we have quoted often here— *"the life which I now live in the flesh I live* [because of the faithfulness] *of the Son of God"*—to mean that because the believer himself is faithful, he pleases the Son of God. Paul always advocates that Christ's faithfulness rather than works is the means of our Christian living.

The Effects of Believing

Nowhere in Paul's Epistles does he say that our works will have anything to do with our salvation. We are always justified and forgiven by our simple belief in Jesus Christ. His faith then begins to work through us as a continual living of the Christian life. As long as any believer is intent upon being within himself anything other than what Christ is to him, he not only is unacceptable to the Father, but he also is defeated in his Christian experience.

In Romans 3:21-24 we read, *"But now the righteousness of God without the law is manifested, being witnessed by the law and the prophets; even the righteousness of God which is by faith of Jesus Christ unto all and upon all them that believe: for there is no difference: for all have sinned, and come short of the glory of God; being justified freely by His grace through the redemption that is in Christ Jesus."* Now there could not be any words more plainly stated than these, and it is by such words that the new creation race believer is able to come to the true interpretation and translation of the Scriptures. In fact, it is our fervent belief that as a believer comes to see Christ as all, he will reject anything and everything that does not harmonize and correspond with this idea.

Now, I wish to comment upon those verses from Romans. They say that the righteousness of God, aside from, different from, and without the law, is manifested. How important this is! In the Old

Testament, the righteousness of God was based on man's doing what God said. Certainly, in the New Testament men do what God says, but no longer do they need to do what God says to be saved, for they are saved by Another. They now do what God says because that other One in them, Christ, is faithful, for the righteousness of God comes aside from the law. That is because righteousness is a Person. *"Christ...is made unto us...righteousness"* (I Corinthians 1:30). When we see that this righteousness of God comes aside from the law, we are able to enter into the Christ-life and by that come to the rest He has prepared for us. Verse 22 of Romans 3 goes on to say that this righteousness of God, which is Christ our righteousness, is manifested to the believer by the faith of Jesus Christ. This is compounded evidence that Christ is all. He is the believer's righteousness, and that righteousness is expressed and works out of the believer by the faith of the Son of God, or the faithfulness of the Son of God.

Work of Judaizers

Paul was determined that all believers in his day see and know this. There were many believers who sat in his congregations who were still bound by the law. Some of these were Judaizers. Some of them were those who had spilled over into the Gentile cities and churches from Jerusalem. But many of them, if not all, were either under Peter's teaching that they must have an outward circumcision to please God or they were strong holdovers from Mosaic law, disannulling Calvary and the work of grace. Thus, Paul was very pointed in his message when he said that the faith of Jesus Christ is unto all and upon all them that believe, for there is no difference. Even if you are a Jew, even if you have been a believer in Mosaic law, even if you are an Old Testament law believer, there can be no difference in your need. It is the faith of Jesus Christ working out of you that makes the difference. His reason for believing so was, regardless of what your background is, religious or worldly, all have sinned and come short of the glory of God. Then he climaxes this great truth in Romans 3:24 by saying, '[We are] *justified freely by His grace.*" What is His grace? It is His work at Calvary. The pleasing of Jesus Christ to the Father by bearing sin in His body has given to God the right to redeem. All redemption is in Jesus Christ. How beautiful is the work of identification—that the believer sees himself poured into Christ at Gethsemane. When Christ dies on Calvary, it is Christ dying as the believer. When Christ is buried in the Arimathean's tomb, it is Christ buried as the believer. When He is resurrected on Easter Sunday morning, it is Christ risen as the believer; and of course, as He ascended to be at the right hand of the Father, it is Christ ascended as the believer. All the way through, it is Christ in the believer and the believer in Christ. There is no separation in God's plan, where the believer becomes anything within himself, but He does have a glorious plan where everything Christ is, the believer becomes.

Going on to the Father's House

You must be careful to rightly divide the Word of truth. His faithfulness to God and His faithfulness within us is the only qualification we need to enter the Father's house, for we all simply have believed on the Lord Jesus Christ to be our life. That's not the believing that justifies or sanctifies us. We are justified by His faith and His faithfulness, and we are sanctified only by His life in us and His obedience to the truth. The responsibility to see this *is ours.* The responsibility to make it work *is His.* Grace is what we have to help us in our time of need to see Him as our all, and even this grace *is His.* To further see the intricate part of God's great plan through Paul's revelation of God's intent is the divine correction needed to translate and interpret the Word of God.

To translate and interpret the Bible, we need to deal with Philippians 3:8-9, which says, *"...that I may win Christ, and be found in Him, not having mine own righteousness, which is of the law, but that which is through the faith of Christ, the righteousness which is of God by faith."* Once again we have the clear criterion and key to the Scriptures. Paul is expressing gratitude for Christ's imputed righteousness, by which he is justified. Often when men read this, instead of exalting Christ's faithfulness, they exalt man's faith as a means of gaining a reconciliation with God. Paul's language does not, to any degree, stress that the believer does anything to make this work. He says very pointedly, "I do not have my own righteousness, because if I had my own righteousness and exercised it, that would still be the law." He sees the law swallowed up by Christ, who is now our life. He goes on to say that he has a righteousness which comes only through the faith or faithfulness *(pistis)* of the Son of God. He dynamically states that the righteousness which he has is of God by Christ's faithfulness. Literally, man now exercises the very character of God, and he can do that because Christ in him is the One who expresses this righteousness.

No Transfers

Very often, man-made religion teaches that it is our obedience, our works, our doing, that brings this about. Man would have us believe that it is impossible for Christ to transfer His righteousness, and so many Scriptures are translated to that effect. Of course, this is true; it is impossible for Christ to transfer His righteousness, and the Scripture never teaches that Christ does transfer His righteousness. It literally teaches that Christ is our righteousness. There is no transfer from one life to another, but rather the only life the believer has is the Christ-life.

There is never a transfer of virtues in any believer. When Satan operated through the sinner in death-life, he did not transfer his evil works to the sinner and thereby cause the sinner to commit evil. The sinner *was* evil. He was birthed by father Satan, and by that was a child of wrath and a child of disobedience. It was the birthing that produced the evil works from the sinner. Now that we are born again, we are direct operators of the nature within us. It is not a transfer; it is an automatic outworking of who we are. As Paul says, *"The life which I now live in the flesh I live by the faith* [or faithfulness] *of the Son of God"* (Galatians 2:20). Or, "Because Christ is in me, I have no righteousness of my own and the only righteousness I have is His righteousness that comes through His operation of faithfulness."

Man Has No Nature of His Own

It is important that the believer see that Christ's virtues are never transferred to him. So often in some spiritual circles the believer gets the idea that the Holy Spirit is working on the believer to bring forth fruit of the Holy Spirit. This would infer a transfer and such is impossible. The only life the believer has is the Christ-life. He has no life of his own emanating from his own nature. His only nature is the God nature, which was placed in him at the birthing. Thus, the only manifestation he could possibly have is that which comes by this nature. Looking further into Paul's explanation of the Christ-life, he plainly says, "I want to be found in Him. I don't want to be separated from Him, waiting for Christ to do something for me." How important this is for us to see! To be found in Christ is more than just the head saying, "I'm in Christ." Head knowledge will always defeat the work of the Holy Spirit, for the Holy Spirit who comes as a dove will not strive with our human notions of head knowledge. He will wait until the crisis comes, when we say, "We cannot live it within ourselves, or do it within ourselves; we need the revelation of the Christ-life." When that happens, the believer is able to move out of his own personal righteousness into the righteousness of Christ and enter into His rest.

The normal Christian believer will not make these ideas of Paul work immediately. The great problem is that the normal believer is so bogged down in the quagmire of man-made doctrines that it is almost impossible for him to yield to the Christ within him. Furthermore, if the true gospel is not preached to the believer, he will soon revert to being a covenant and commandment-keeping believer. To do so fits a satanic lie that is upon the whole human race, that if we do our own thing we'll be as gods. All our perfection comes from our love affair with the Christ who is already in us. It is not our faith that brings this about, but His faithfulness working in us. It is not our becoming perfect by our own works, but by our entering into the perfection He already is, by our union with Him.

Christ in Us, as Us

Such teaching as this is completely different from the principles of the Old Testament because the Old Testament is based on man's offering his own sacrifice and trusting in his works to please God. The new creation race gospel is a direct opposite to this. It presents to the believer his need for trusting in Another to do it all. Another will die, Another will shed His blood, Another will bear the sins, and Another will be the life and live in the believer. This other One will allow the believer to exercise all of the virtues and ministries that are in Christ Jesus. It is always the faithfulness of Christ in us working out of us as us that is most pleasing to the Father, and gives Him His greatest pleasure.

We come now to a most important fact based upon the tremendous truth that Christ has been placed in the creature as God's only means of salvation. The believer must come to see that any translation or interpretation of the Scriptures not consistent with Christ being God's all and not consistent with the Christ-life— Christ in us as our hope of glory—is faulty, for the Bible is its own interpreter. It's as Isaiah says to the law and the testimony in Chapter 8, verse 20, *"If they speak not according to this word, it is because there is no light in them."* As is true with all the *I am*s He gave us (in John's Gospel particularly), the believer has to come the very same way. Everything Christ is, he is. As John says later in his first Epistle, *"As* [Christ] *is, so are we in this world."* There is another truth to this. Christ not only said, *"I am the light of the world,"* but He turned around and said, *"Ye are the light of the world"* (see John 8:12 and Matthew 5:14). Certainly, they were not lights at the time and could only become lights because *the light* was put in them; that was Christ in them.

Christ Is Truth

Too often we are justified by our own works in establishing what we believe and declaring that to be truth. The only truth there is is the Person of truth, Christ, and the only way truth is ever found and later expressed by any believer is when he begins to see Christ as his life. Regardless of how we translate certain words, the faithfulness of God manifested by Jesus Christ who is our life is imperative to our Christian growth.

What is very difficult for most people in law-religion to accept is the fact that when any sinner simply believes on the Lord Jesus Christ, this remarkable birthing takes place. This is simply the Father placing His own incorruptible seed in that believer, even as a husband places the seed in a wife, and by that simple action of love, a child is born. The birthing of that child is Christ in us, our hope of glory. When this has taken place, the believer enters into a whole new realm of life, even as a pregnant mother must correct her own living and her ways because of the child in her. So does the believer, by his love for the Christ in him, make the correction necessary for the whole of his being to be as that Christ in him. By simply believing in the Lord Jesus Christ, we enter into the new creation race ideas that are contrary to anything and everything we have experienced or have been a part of in our past lives. Whether our past lives were religious, denominational, or very spiritual, we now see a whole new life by a new "Living one" in us.

It is marvelous to see that as we simply believed on the Lord Jesus Christ and were saved, so we now see that by grace we are kept saved. Grace is His work for us and our continuing to live the Christian life is by Christ in us. The verse of Scripture, John 15:10, that implies we can abide in His love only as we keep His commandments is now enlarged, for we found out that we could not abide in His love and keep His commandments within ourselves. But He Himself in us keeps His own Word, keeps His own commandments, and does it by the exercise of His love through us. If *pistos* means faithful, and there could be no doubt that it does, then *apistos* would mean unfaithful. The New Testament translators have generally translated *apistos* as unbelieving or faithless.

Look at Israel
Because of unfaithfulness, disobedience and unbelief, the children of Israel did not enter the promised land. It is interesting to

note that such unbelief did not hinder the love of God from giving them miracles every day, but the receiving of miracles is not the exercising of truth. Because they were unbelieving and faithless, multitudes of them died in the wilderness. You must see this working in this hour as a light to lead us out of darkness.

Many people today, like those in the wilderness, have ample miracles, signs and wonders working but are in disobedience and rebellion. What is the root of this rebellion? It is a believer who feels that what *he* is doing is right, that *his* way is right, that *his* faith is right, all of this ignoring the Christ within him. This is the example of *apistos,* meaning unfaithfulness. If the adjective, *pistos,* means faithful, then it is reasonable to assume that the noun, *pistis,* means faithfulness. Very often the translators, even in the King James Version, have carefully avoided the use of this word. It is as if man has not yet seen that Christ is his life and his all, and in the translation of the Scriptures has veered away from what is God's truth to man's understanding. As we have said, the term *faithfulness* is not to be found in the King James Version of the New Testament. The closest translation of it is found in Titus 2:10. Here Paul advises Titus to exhort servants to be obedient, *"not purloining, but shewing all good fidelity."* The word *pistin* is translated fidelity. It is very obvious, however, that it is not man's fidelity, but to be consistent with the intent of God and Paul's revelation of that intent, it is the fidelity of Christ in us that's at work. It must be seen at all times that it is never our faith that justifies us but God's faithfulness, Christ in us.

Another term, *pisteuo,* is translated to mean, "I believe." This bears out the simple truth that as we believe on the Lord Jesus Christ, we set into operation the birthing and the living of Christ in us. How important it is that each and every believer have that moment where they have believed on the Lord Jesus Christ and have experienced a radical regeneration—a moment where God, by Calvary and the cross, makes a traumatic exchange of natures. Old nature, Satan, is put out with its death-life, and the new nature, Christ, is put in.

This miracle is greatly emphasized by Paul on the road to Damascus in Acts 9, for when he saw the Lord as his Savior, he immediately cried out, *"Lord, what wilt Thou have me to do?"* (v. 6). Connected with our believing in the Lord Jesus Christ is this immediate responsibility of saying, "I come to You not only to get, but to serve You," at which moment God places His Son in us, who is the faithful Servant. This term, *pisteuo,* is further elaborated upon by the Apostle Paul's writing to Timothy in Second Timothy 1:12, where he says, *"For the which cause I also suffer these things: nevertheless I am not ashamed: for I know whom I have believed, and am persuaded that He is able to keep that which I have committed unto Him against that day."*

How could there be a more definitive truth in the whole Bible than this verse? Here the divine correction necessary for us to see the new creation race gospel is plainly stated by Paul. He says, *"I know whom I have [pisteuo] believed."* This *whom* that he speaks of is the Christ in him. Then, notice by his believing in this Christ, he has entered into the process of Christianity. That process is emphasized by his words that he was *persuaded* that Christ was able to keep him.

God's Eternal Intent

I want to stop right there, because that's the whole of what God's intent was. "I have believed and have entered into a persuasion by the believing *(pisteuo)* that the Christ in me is able to keep me in righteousness, obedience and love, and as I commit myself unto Him, this all works." What a glorious message in one verse alone! The commitment that Paul made to the Christ in him was a mind thing. As his mind was renewed and he saw more and more of who he was in Christ, this persuasion became all the greater. As you grow in Christ and come to see and to know Him as your all and in all, you too will come to the ultimate persuasion, the persuasion of a "kept" believer. At this point of the believer's having this sort of faith working in him, there is no evil day that the believer will fear. There is no time ahead that is too devastating for this believer. He will triumph over the world, the flesh and the devil. The hard times will be overcome. The difficult moments will be overcome. He now rules over death, for he does not fear death anymore. If his earthly tabernacle is destroyed, he has a new building in Christ Jesus. He doesn't fear Satan, for the Christ in him has already defeated Satan, and Satan, as a defeated foe, is ruled over by this knowing believer. It is only when the divine truth of God's intent and Paul's revelation of that intent grips the believer that the Scriptures come alive. Search the Scriptures, for in so searching them you will know that you have eternal life dwelling in you. What do the Scriptures say? They tell us plainly what is God's intent—that is, the putting of Another in the creature. We finally find the key to all of the Scriptures, based on Paul's revelation of Christ in us. As this revelation takes hold and begins to work in, through, and out of the believer, a whole new world comes about. This is the world of the new creation race, a new race of people designated for the Father's house, but now living in the rest that God planned for them before the foundation of the world (Hebrews 4:3).

Chapter 6

Our Glorious Teacher, the Holy Spirit

There was a pause in the proceedings of an evangelical banquet I was attending, and the Baptist preacher sitting next to me turned and said, "I wonder if you'd answer a question for me. You Spirit-baptized people are always talking about the Holy Spirit—what He does, His gifts, His power, etc. What I want to know is, when you receive the so-called baptism, what happens to the Christ already within you?"

I was a bit taken back by his question. After some contemplation, I gave him our stock answer, which I realized—at least to him—was no answer at all. Looking back on that conversation many times, I have become cognizant of the fact that we tend to make the Holy Spirit more than the Father intended and to make Christ less. The idea behind the Baptist preacher's question is a truth that all believers must come to in time: *Christ alone is Savior for the sinner, and He alone is life for the believer.* At no point does the Holy Spirit take the place of or do the work of Christ (Acts 4:12). The Holy Spirit is a Person—the third Person of the Godhead. He has His own personality, His own ministry, and fits perfectly into the plan of God. He is not the Lamb. He is not the Giver of the blood. He is not the Son. In all simplicity, He is God, the Teacher—specifically, the Teacher and Revealer of Christ—

to the sinner by conviction and to the believer as a revealer of the Christ within him.

What has been built up as a theory among fundamentalist and Spirit-filled believers is the idea that once saved, the Holy Spirit represents Christ—even to the taking of His place in the believer. To believe this is to ignore the very heart of the Father's plan. "In Christ" is the most often-stated truth in the Bible. It never says that we are in the Holy Spirit. The "one baptism" Paul speaks of in Ephesians 4:5 is the work of the Holy Spirit placing the believer in Christ. The truth is simple: The Holy Spirit works *outside* the believer in bringing about the *inward* work of Christ. We have not only misplaced the Person of the Holy Spirit, but as believers misusing the works of the Holy Spirit, we have also misplaced Christ as the life of the believer! The Word is pure and simple: we are saved by the Christ who died for us, but that which makes us Christian is Christ *in us.* His death reconciles us to the Father, but it is His life *in us* that keeps us saved and makes us "Christ persons" (Christians) (Romans 5:10).

Christ Only—Our Life

When we make the Holy Spirit our life as well as our salvation, we hinder His greater work of revealing to us that *Christ* is our life and our salvation. This is a reversion to our former state of self-independence—denying the very life we now live is Christ. We have come up with the idea that our old man is now filled with the Holy Spirit. Thus what he could not do before, he can do now. But, as Paul said in Galatians 2:20, we no longer live; only Christ lives in us. The One who lives in us as our "reconciled life" is Christ, and He lives in us by the teaching ministry of the Holy Spirit. The Holy Spirit does not *give* life; He teaches us who *is* our life. The works we do are not the works of the Holy Spirit through us, but rather the works of Christ *as us.* The virtues—the fruits of the Spirit—are Christ's personality working through us. The gifts of the Spirit are Christ's ministries working through us, as us, by the diversification of the Holy Spirit (I Corinthians 12:4). It is plain that making the Holy Spirit some form of Christ not only is a misunderstanding of the Godhead; it also limits the believer in two crucial areas of living.

First, it makes the shed blood of Christ and its ultimate purpose in the believer—the grace of imputation—something less than the weight of the Scripture indicates it to be. Not only is the blood a saving and cleansing power for the sinner, but it is also the life of the believer. Leviticus 17:11 tells us that the life is in the blood, and John said that this blood (life) is in the Son, Jesus (I John 5:11). When the Holy Spirit reveals Christ in us as our life, we are able to see the full and perfect work of imputation, which is Christ doing all as Savior and "Liver" of our new life.

Until we see Christ as our all and in all, we misuse the Holy Spirit by making ourselves something other than Christ-persons. The greater problem here is in the handling of the sin problem. Until we see that the Christ within us does not sin (I John 3:5-9), we will misuse the Holy Spirit to make us sinless. This is not His work, for *only the Christ in us is sinless.* However, the Holy Spirit does help, teaching us that the Christ within swallows up the sins of the flesh that the believer does have (I John 1:7-10). In other words, the real me—Jesus, the incorruptible seed—does not sin; but there is sin in my body (Romans 7:17-20), the container in which Christ lives, which will be corruptible until the resurrection morning (I Corinthians 15:53).

As long as the believer does not see Christ as the sinless One, imputing His sinless nature to us, he will misuse the Holy Spirit to help him live a better life, rather than to reveal Christ as our only life. The Father's plan is to place another nature in us—not to correct the old nature! It was never His intention to bring us to a place of pleasing Him. Lucifer proved that a creature already living in God's house could not please Him. God's plan, boldly conceived and executed before the foundation of the world was laid (Ephesians 1:4), was not to deal with the creature at all, other than in its free moral acceptance of Him. His superb plan was that by the creature's acceptance of Him, He could place another nature (Christ) within; and that Christ-nature would ever be sinless before Him, thus making perfect His plan.

Second, because of the misuse of the Holy Spirit, the believer is hindered from coming into the ultimate provision the Father has made for the earth journey—the *rest* that He provided from the foundation of the world.

If the believer fails to come into rest, his only alternative is work. He works diligently to fit religious ideas and doctrine into his personality and experience. This creates an enormous dilemma, for work never leads to rest. There is no greater self-effort than that of the believer involved in certain faith ministries, or the commonly called "Word of Faith" movement. I know, for I almost destroyed myself trying to believe. The regimen of saying promises, confessing the positive, quoting the covenants, denying the negative, and resisting the devil was greater self-effort than I had ever known. I thank the Father that this cycle is being broken in many lives and that believers are seeing the Christ in them as their rest. Of course, if Satan can keep the believer busy working for what Christ already is in him, then Satan has destroyed his rest. It was never the Father's intention to put chosen sons on this earth to labor and fight for what He was justified to freely give by the slaying of the Lamb.

The Trick of Satan

The real rest the Father planned for us before the foundation of the world (Hebrews 4:1-3) was dependent upon our seeing we could do nothing to please Him. It hinged upon our seeing that Another had taken our place in sin, in crucifixion, in burial, in resurrection, and in ascension. The awful trick that Satan (who is the first preacher, preaching to Adam and Eve in the garden) played on us was to slightly *twist* the Scriptures (as he did with Eve, saying "Hath God said...?") by adding, to the finished work of Christ, our own works. So instead of accepting the finished work of Christ (identification), we are tricked into believing the Holy Spirit must still perfect that finished work in us so we will be more acceptable to the Father. By accepting this, believers have not entered into His rest.

One of theology's strongest points is: *If you don't start off right, you don't end right.* This is the reason so many believers have never entered into rest and freedom from sin. When they were saved (born again), they were more confounded by law than by grace. It was as if more of Moses was preached than Christ. Sometimes preachers forget that *"grace and truth came by Jesus Christ"* (John 1:17). The true gospel contains neither claims, nor commands, nor threats, but is the glad tidings of salvation to sinful men through Christ. This glorious message was to be preached to the vile, stout-hearted, and far-from-righteous sinner.

Modern preachers often err in preaching such a conglomerate gospel—one that embraces a little from the Old Testament and a lot from their own understanding! Although there is eternal truth in every "jot and tittle" of the Scriptures, any passage that, even in the slightest way, indicates that God demands anything of the sinner other than his simple belief that Jesus will save him will start that sinner off wrongly in his understanding of the gospel. One reason there are so many Old Testament works preached in modern theology is that they fit the outer knowledge so well that "We can and must do something to make salvation work." In Paul's New Testament message, the gospel is not our doing anything or becoming anything; it is Christ being our everything and our seeing Him alone as our life.

Perhaps we have lost sight of the true gospel. The gospel is a message from Heaven that God loves sinners. The gospel is that God saw that man could not be what He wanted him to be within himself, so He killed His Lamb (Revelation 13:8) that He might have the right to put into the creature another life—one that pleased Him—the Christ-life. The gospel is the good news that peace was made for the poor sinner through the shed blood of Jesus Christ. The gospel rings a bell of liberty to captives, of pardon to condemned criminals, of peace to rebels, of life to the dead, and of salvation to those who lie on the borders of hell and condemnation. Much gospel preaching today just exchanges the bondage of sin for the bondage of religion. Too many preach today to get the sinner into their own beliefs, rather than to get them into Christ. Therefore, it is not just the gospel itself that heals the sinner, but Christ revealed within. Finally, the Apostle Paul declared in Galatians 1:11-12 that the certified gospel was the revelation of Jesus Christ. Salvation is not the receiving of beliefs by the sinner, but the receiving of another Person, whom God has ordained to be the operating life in the sinner. The gospel is the receiving of Christ—not just what He has done, but who God intends that He be in us. It is not only the acceptance of the gospel, but the acceptance of the Person of the gospel—Christ. The gospel is, as one writer put it with respect to Christ, what the pole was to the serpent (Numbers 21:8).

In Christian circles, being "saved" has meant "giving your heart to Christ." This is most unwisely urged upon sinners as if this were the gospel, causing them to begin their walk with God in the wrong way. It is not what we give to Him. The essence of the gospel is stated in Hebrews 10:19-22a: *"Having therefore, brethren, boldness to enter into the holiest by the blood of Jesus, by a new and living way, which He hath consecrated for us, through the veil, that is to say, His flesh; and having an high priest over the house of God; let us draw near with a true heart in full assurance of faith."*

Giving your heart to Christ is law rather than gospel. It is most proper that it be done, for God Himself demands it; but merely urging that it be done falls far short of the gospel. When we start with the idea that we must do something, or even that we can do something, we are plagued with our own doings throughout our Christian experience. This keeps many from the *rest* God has for them. This is the key work of religion, for religion cannot exist without our doing. The trick of Satan is obvious: if we begin by believing we can do something to be saved, then Satan's seed of religion and self-effort is still planted, and all our days he keeps us doing rather than entering into our rest of just being.

Accept the free gift of salvation from wrath and sin by receiving the Person of the Lord Jesus Christ, and your heart will be His in a moment—being given to Him—not as a matter of *law,* but of *love.* If you have the love of His heart poured into yours, you will feel yourself under the constraining influence of a spontaneous spiritual impulse to give Him your heart in return, and all that you are and have! It is right to give Him your heart, but unless you first receive the open proof of having His, you will never give Him yours.

The Blood—Not Conviction—Is the Foundation of Our Rest

The blood of Jesus is His life. When we say we are covered by His blood, we are saying it is totally what He did at Calvary that saves us. But there is more to the blood than this. It is not only an outward sign that we are saved by Him, but that same blood, as His life, is also *our* life. Therefore, the blood is not only our justification for sin, it is also the bond that ties us to the family in the process of adoption. When Paul says in Galatians 2:20 that the life he now lives is Christ, he is saying that the blood is more than just a covering; it is the actual life of Christ in him. *"For other foundation can no man lay than that is laid, which is Jesus Christ"* (I Corinthians 3:11). Christ is the foundation-stone of salvation laid by the Father; we are to rest on His finished work alone—not on our accomplishments or our feelings. It is of the utmost importance to be clear about the fact that it is the work of Christ *within* us (His blood)—not the work of the Holy Spirit *outside* us—that forms the sole ground of our deliverance from guilt and wrath. We must beware of resting our peace with God on feeling, conviction, tears, repentance, prayers, duties or resolutions. We must begin with receiving Christ, and not make it the termination of some fanciful feeling or conviction. Christ must be *everything* in our salvation, or He is *nothing.*

Beware of falling into the trap of thinking you will be more welcome to God if you are brought through some terrible process of law-work. You are as welcome now to Christ as you ever will be. Far too many believers are awaiting some deeper conviction of sin. Why should anyone prefer conviction to Christ? If you had the greatest conviction of any sinner who ever lived, you would not have one iota more of Christ in you! Conviction of sin is precious, but it brings no safety, no peace, no rest, no salvation, no security. It does, however, bring war and storm and trouble! It is well to be awakened from sleep when danger is hanging over you, but to awaken from sleep is not to escape the danger. In like manner, the work of the Holy Spirit in conviction is merely to convince you that your soul is in danger. It is no more. It is not deliverance. The Holy Spirit cannot bring deliverance. He simply tells of a Savior. He cannot save. It is here that the error of many begins. The Holy Spirit convicts, promotes and inspires us to do something. His work and our doing, however, are not what saves us. Only Jesus saves!

Some have a false sense of security, saying, "Ah, I have been convicted of sin; I have become terribly afraid; all is well with me; I am safe!" Is it well with the seaman who awakens and finds his vessel going to pieces on the rocks amid the fury of the storm? Is it well with the sleeper who awakes at midnight, amid the flames of his dwelling? Does he say, "Ah, it is well with me; I have seen the flames!"

Sad to say, this is the way many believers started their walk with God. They misunderstood the work of the Holy Spirit, believing it was Christ's, and fell short of God's intended purpose—that only Christ be all and in all. To see your need is not to see Christ. To see that you need help is not to see Christ as your life. Often the anxiety to have deep convictions and to be content with them is a subtle trick of Satan's religion to get you to turn away from seeing that Christ is God's everything and that He must be your everything! You must be aware of this to avoid falling into the trap.

Christ Must Be Everything, or He Is Nothing

"Behold the Lamb of God, which taketh away the sin of the world" (John 1:29). Behold the finished work. It is a finished work. We often fail to see that Christ is the alpha and omega of

God's plan. He is the beginning and the end and all in between. He not only died at Calvary, but in God's plan, He was slain from the beginning (Revelation 13:8). This is what caused the writer of Hebrews 4:3 to say that all of God's works were finished before the beginning. What a stupendous thought! It means that it was not our conviction, our trouble, or even the initial work of the Holy Spirit in our lives that started it all. It was finished in God's mind before the creature was ever created, much less before he became a sinner! Christ was the whole of God's thoughts from the beginning, and in His plan He finished it all with Christ. It is never said in the Word that our duties, our prayers, our fastings, our convictions of sin, our repentance, our honest life, our giving, our faith, our love, or our grace bore our sins. It was Jesus Himself who *"bare our sins in His own body on the tree"* (I Peter 2:24); and it is Jesus whose life in us is our salvation now (Romans 5:10). We rest in nothing other than Him!

Christ has done the mighty work;
Nothing left for us to do;
But to enter on His toil,
Enter on His triumph, too!

His, the labor; ours, the rest;
His, the death, and ours, the life;
Ours, the fruits of victory;
His, the agony and strife.

—A.B. Simpson

We do not intend to take away anything from the Person of the Holy Spirit. The Holy Spirit, who is presented as a dove, must always be protected, honored and obeyed. He is tender, patient, longsuffering and capable. But His place in the plan of God is to work out the details of the plan of God—not to be the Savior or life-giver.

The quickening grace and presence of the Holy Spirit is most essential to seeing Jesus as your life. You should recognize His presence as you contemplate the crucified Redeemer; but it is unscriptural to seek the works of the Spirit before you see that the life given to the sinner and the life within the believer is Christ. It is also unscriptural to mix sanctification and justification—partly depending upon one or the other, for Jesus alone is the object on which your eyes must rest for peace. *"It is Christ that died"* (Romans 8:34), and the Spirit's work is to direct you to Him. The continuing work of the Spirit is to reveal that Christ is in you until the only life you live is Christ! Nowhere is it written in Scripture that the Holy Spirit cleanses from sin. Nowhere is it written in Scripture that the Holy Spirit is the life of the believer. Nowhere is it written that the Holy Spirit is Christ.

We must join the writer of Hebrews 2:9 in saying, "But we see Jesus" in all things. Modern-day believers are often more interested in seeing His works than in seeing Him. It is here that we feel the impact of Paul's great statement that he was determined to know (see) nothing other than Christ, *and Him crucified* (I Corinthians 2:2). By looking upon Him who was pierced at Calvary's cross, seeing God's Lamb in action, we become convinced by the Holy Spirit that Christ is indeed God's everything. We must continually *see* Jesus—not our repentings, resolutions, reformations, prayers, reading, hearing or anything of self that would form any basis for our acceptance, pardon or salvation. It is here that Satan's religion will tell us that the Holy Spirit will do all things that make us "more saved." It is never the Holy Spirit working on us to gain salvation within ourselves. It is never the Holy Spirit trying to take the place of Christ as our life. It is our flesh that cries out for us to do something to be more acceptable to the Father. If we do not *see* Jesus as our all and in all, we will misuse the Holy Spirit to do within us what God has already made Christ to us (I Corinthians 2:9-10).

Satan's Religion Is an Antithesis to Christ

When we seek the Holy Spirit to help *us* live the Christian life, we make the vessel more important than the content. The Spirit does not help us live the life; rather He reveals another *in* us who *is* the life. There is no such thing as a believer who, in himself, is living the Christian life. The life is in the Son, and it is the Son in every believer who stands before God as the Redeemed. Because so many have thought that God's plan was that they, themselves, be changed or corrected, they have never come to see Jesus as their life. Consequently, they are never sure that they are saved, or that they have faith, or that God is pleased with them. At times they *feel* justified, and at times they *feel* guilty; at times they are *"alive unto God"* and at times they are dead.

A person can be in only one of two states. As a sinner, you are in Satan. As a believer, you are in Christ. You cannot be in both. It is not that you have a little of the Lord at times and a little of the devil at other times. There is no such thing as Jesus coming in parts, pieces, bits or blessings. The Spirit does not deal with the sinner to bring him some salvation. He brings him to the Lamb, and salvation is total and complete, based on the finished work at Calvary. Likewise, at the moment of belief, the Holy Spirit places Christ in the awakened sinner. It is not a thing, not an idea, nor merely a blessing, but the total Christ and His total Person with all His personality (fruit) and all His ministries (gifts), making that believer ready—perfectly prepared—to live the life of Christ!

Many believers feel that if they do not see some changes in themselves for the better, they have not received God's best. It is not necessary for the believer to see Christ in himself. Christ is there, seen or unseen. This is the great mystery of godliness, and such a mystery can be revealed only by the Holy Spirit (Romans 16:25). God did not say to the Israelites, *"When you see the blood, I will pass over you."* No, He said, *"When I see the blood, I will pass over you"* (Exodus 12:13). Neither is it left up to us to see the mystery of Christ in us. It is God's doing for every born-again believer, whether they know it or not—and whether they know it even now! Many, not knowing that Christ is in them, try to make the Holy Spirit do something to them so they can be more acceptable to the Father. We don't have to wait for the Holy Spirit to do something to us. It is God's doing for every born-again believer.

The Holy Spirit Bears Witness

What the Holy Spirit really did in our salvation, aside from conviction, was to take the shed blood of Jesus Christ into the presence of God and sprinkle it there. God saw that perfect atonement had been made for every sinner and that He was now justified to do His great intention—that of putting Christ in every believing creature. The Holy Spirit bears witness to this truth. By the death of the Lamb, the Father sees His right to place us in Christ; and by that same death on Calvary, we see the finished work in us.

We are prone, because of our past Satan nature, to look at something taking place in ourselves as our ground of peace and rest. We are apt to regard the work the Spirit did for us as the work done in us, which is a mistake. We know that the operations of the Spirit have their place in Christianity, but His work is never set forth as the ground on which our rest depends. That is only in Christ. God did not send the Word, preaching peace by the Holy Ghost, but *"by Jesus Christ"* (Acts 10:36; Ephesians 2:14,17; Colossians 1:20).

The Holy Spirit ministers to us to reveal that Christ is our life. He makes us to enjoy and love our new life in Christ. He makes us to feed upon Christ, the Bread that comes down from God out of Heaven. When we eat of Him, we eat His flesh and blood, and thereby are approved righteous to the Father, and by the same eating, grow up into Him in all things. The Holy Spirit takes the things of Christ and shows them unto us. He is the power of communion, the seal, the witness, the earnest, the unction. In short, His operations are essential. Without Him we cannot see, hear, know, feel, experience or enjoy any part or function of the life of Christ that is in us. When any believer has received a revelation of Christ as his life, this is the first great truth that liberates him. The work of the Holy Spirit, purely and simply, is to reveal the Christ who is our life—not to take His place.

The Holy Spirit is not our title, though He reveals our title and enables us to enjoy it. Our title is the same as our life—Jesus. Jesus is the name of our Father's family, and we do all things in His name, Jesus. The Holy Spirit carries on His work in the soul (mind) of the believer. His prime work is bringing us to a *knowing*—knowing in whom we have believed, knowing who we are in Christ, knowing that in all things we are more than conquerors. His teaching ministry brings us to the place of being *"knowers"* (John 14:20). By this knowing, He teaches us conformity to the Christ within, that He might present every man perfect in Christ. He *"maketh intercession for us with groanings which cannot be uttered"* (Romans 8:26b). He is the Author of every right desire, every holy aspiration, every pure and heavenly affection, every Divine experience. He is working to cause us to see that we are already complete in Christ (Colossians 2:10). He is not that completeness. Christ alone is. Just as in the case of Abraham's servant, His work is to teach Rebekah (the believer) all about her new husband, Isaac (Christ).

The Holy Spirit never teaches a soul to lean on Him. His office is to speak of Jesus. He does not speak of Himself; neither does He lend Himself to anything that might distract from Jesus. He does not have a church, a special people, a special ministry through man, or a special anything of Himself. It is Christ's Church. The Body is Christ. All the gifts and ministries are Christ's, even though the Holy Spirit may diversify them. He can only present Christ's life and work as the basis for our rest.

The Holy Spirit Is Not Our Redeemer

A number of professing Christians have the unfounded notion ingrained in their minds that Christ came as Savior in the fullness of time and, upon being rejected and received up into glory, sent the Holy Spirit to be the Savior of sinners in His stead and that now, whether men are to be saved or lost depends entirely on the work of the Holy Spirit in them, not on Christ—God's gift to all sinners. The Holy Spirit never usurps the place of our Savior or our life. When speaking of the Holy Spirit, Jesus said, *"He shall glorify Me"* (see John 16:13,14). If glorifying Christ is the grand objective and peculiar work of the Holy Spirit, should it not also be the grand objective and constant work of those who believe on Him—especially those who are gifted to minister to the Body of Christ? The whole intention of the Holy Spirit's inspired works, as I have seen them in the Bible, is to teach us Christ and to glorify Christ.

Sinners who believe in Christ are justified from all things: *"Being justified freely by His grace through the redemption that is in Christ Jesus: whom God hath set forth to be a propitiation through faith in His blood...."* (Romans 3:24-25a). At no time in our walk with God is there ever an incipient personal righteousness wrought in us by the Holy Spirit. Few men who have seen Jesus as their all and in all would ever subscribe to such a doctrine; yet it is the latent creed of a great majority of professing Christians. It is, in fact, the universal creed of many who have not seen Christ as their life. It is like a hangover from the old man syndrome. The Satan nature always said to do something when terror came, and this same spirit in many believers still says we can do something and be something within ourselves, even though Christ in us is complete and needs nothing from us. This spirit of error says, "You ought to read your Bible more"; "You need to become holier"; "You need to reform your conduct"; "God will have mercy upon you!" But the Holy Spirit says, *"Behold, God is my salvation!"* (Isaiah 12:2).

The Holy Spirit Is a Teacher

All knowers must go back to the beginning and get started properly if they are to see the Holy Spirit in His right perspective. In the beginning, when the Father elected to place Christ in the believer's life, He knew that doing so would be such a mystery that no one would be able to comprehend it with the natural mind, and that only He, Himself, could ever make the mystery known.

It is at this point that I see the great compulsive drive within the Father to make Himself known and understood. This is a tremendous personality trait in God, wanting all creatures to know all things—especially God Himself. Thus, the two greatest works of the Holy Spirit were to inspire holy men of old to give us the Bible and to bring to believers the revelation of Jesus Christ as the life of the believer. God knew from the beginning that only He, Himself, as the Person of the Holy Spirit, could ever reveal to mankind the liberating secret of the ages, which is the mystery of Christ in us.

The Father waited some four thousand years from the time He *"[chose] us in Him"* (Ephesians 1:4) until He brought about the first prototype in Mary of Nazareth, and finally the first revelation of Christ as the believer's life in Paul (Galatians 1:16). In both of these instances, we see that the Holy Spirit is the key worker, explaining to Mary the awesome thing God had done to her and, later, explaining to Paul that he was separated from his mother's womb for the very purpose of receiving Christ as his only life!

Although the Holy Spirit may have varied tasks and may do many other works, His major role in the Godhead is to reveal the most unbelievable thing the Father has ever done—the placing of His dear Son in the believer. The primary work of the Holy Spirit is that of teacher. This feeling is solidified as I hear Jesus speak of the coming of the Holy Spirit in John, Chapters 14, 15 and 16. First, Jesus says that He must go away—back to the Father— otherwise, the Holy Spirit will not come (John 16:7). Aside from there being only one Person of the Godhead operating on earth at one time—the Father, in the Old Testament days; Jesus, during His earthly life; and now the Holy Spirit in this day of grace—the fact remains that human beings could not possibly have understood the things of the Spirit unless the Christ in the flesh left. Jesus said, *"If I go not away, the Comforter will not come unto you."* The Holy Spirit was going to make known to the minds of men the great revelation of Christ in them. This is probably the background for Paul's great statement that we are to know no man after the flesh—not even Jesus (II Corinthians 5:16). Thus, Christ in the flesh had to leave in order to set into operation the work of the Spirit—that of revealing Christ in us.

We should note what Jesus said in John 14:20: *"At that day* [the day of Pentecost] *ye shall know* [necessitating a teacher] *that I am in My Father* [Christ and the Father were two, yet one in union], *and ye in Me, and I in you. "* Here the Holy Spirit was announced by Jesus as being the Teacher-Revealer who was to bring the knowledge to the believer that as He and the Father are One, so shall He and the believer be one. This great act of union was to be handled by the Holy Spirit, who was to come on the Day of Pentecost with the mission of teaching men that Christ is their life. Christ never deviates from His teaching on the Person of the Holy Spirit being primarily a teacher.

Many believers have missed what Jesus said would take place; this came from religion. Jesus never said the Holy Spirit would save or deliver sinners; only religion says that. Jesus never said the Holy Spirit would be the life or the Spirit of the believer; only religion says that. Religion has robbed God of His greatest feat— that of placing Another in us as our life. Religion attributes many works to the Holy Spirit, causing confusion and ignoring the Spirit's prime mission—that of teaching the believer that Christ is in him. The great power that the believer was to receive on the Day of Pentecost was to come from the Teacher, who was to tell all believers that Christ is in them. That is why the word *after* was emphasized by Christ in Acts 1:8. After that He was come...after He was able to take a mortal mind and renew it...after He would bring all the loose ends of Scripture together...after He, the Holy Spirit, began His teaching mission...then the believer would have Christ's power. Certainly it was not God's plan to give raw power to a believer who was no longer to live (Galatians 2:20)! The power is in the believer knowing who he is in Christ, and then, beginning to live as Christ. To do this, Jesus stressed the importance of the Teacher.

Seven Times Jesus Refers to Teacher

In the three chapters of John where Jesus introduces the Holy Spirit, He never refers to Him in any form other than teacher. Let us look at the record:

1. John 14:16-17—The key word in the 16th verse is *Comforter. Comforter* means "paraclete"—one who comes alongside and instructs. The renewed mind is the greatest emphasis the Apostle puts on the believer's growth. The idea of the Spirit being a Comforter—an Instructor along the way—is consistent. Verse 17 speaks of the Spirit of truth. Christ, of course, is the only truth (John 14:6), and the Holy Spirit is with us to manifest Christ, the truth, to us—a strategic form of teaching.

2. John 14:26—*"He shall teach you all things."* This is a prime statement concerning the Teacher. Notice that the phrase *all things* is the most commonly used phrase in the New Testament, alluding to the fact that God is a part of all things in the universe. Only the Spirit can teach that.

3. John 15:26—*"He shall testify of Me."* A teacher is one who speaks firsthand of what he has seen or heard. This is a form of knowing and points to the Teacher.

4. John 16:7-8—*"He will reprove the world of sin."* The Holy Spirit's main function to sinners is that of making them knowledgeable of their state before God; He does this by reproving (explaining) to them their need of God. The Holy Spirit is a Teacher—even to the sinner!

5. John 16:13—*"He will guide you into all truth."* All guidance is a form of teaching. Just as no man can come to the Father aside from Christ, so no man can find the truth aside from the Holy Spirit.

6. John 16:13—*"He will shew you things to come."* A "shower" is a teacher. Here, the Holy Spirit is presented as a Teacher who, in knowing all things, will share those things with the believer—not just the prophetic things of the endtime, but the things that are coming into the believer's way in daily living. It is an integral part of the believer's knowing.

7. John 16:14—*"He shall receive of Mine, and shall shew it unto you."* This is another form of the Holy Spirit's work of showing. This is His prime work and His greatest mission. God already has placed Christ in the believer at salvation, and the believer does not know it. Only the Holy Spirit can reveal it to him. To do that, the Holy Spirit takes the things of Jesus and reveals them. What a glorious Teacher we have!

For centuries, the grace of God allowed men to claim an inward work of sanctification and an outward reformation that could be understood, comprehended and approved of by the natural man— even the religious man. But that day has passed. The Body of Christ must now see that believers are justified by faith alone in the finished work of Jesus Christ. Because religion has not seen that God has placed Christ in the believer as the believer's only life, it has also taken too great a liberty in misplacing the ministry of the Holy Spirit. The essence of this move of the Spirit centers in His being able to do the work God ordained from the beginning—that of revealing Christ as the believer's only life.

This may appear foolishness to some, but *"the foolishness of God is wiser than men"* (I Corinthians 1:25). Now, instead of preaching holiness—our own holiness—as a ground of peace with God, we *"preach Christ crucified"* (I Corinthians 1:23); for *"other foundation can no man lay"* for either justification or sanctification *"than that is laid, which is Jesus Christ"* (I Corinthians 3:11). Whatever others may do in preaching the gospel, *"I [am] determined not to know any thing among you, save Jesus Christ, and Him crucified"* (I Corinthians 2:2). Amen!

Chapter 7

Is the
Christ-Life the
Only Christian Life?

I would like you to take your Bibles in hand and do some Scripture searching with me. First, from Galatians 4, verses 4 and 5: *"But when the fulness of the time was come, God sent forth His Son, made of a woman, made under the law, to redeem them that were under the law, that we might receive the adoption of sons."*

In the fullness of time, God sent forth His Son. Is the Christ-life the only Christian life? If you have had a revelation of Jesus Christ or if you have ever tasted of heavenly things, you do not doubt it. But the majority of Christians do not know about the Christ-life. They know Christ had a life and that He lived and died, but they do not know that His is the life they are to live as Christians. The mystery that was hidden from men down through the centuries is still hidden from many Christians. It does not make us, to whom Christ has been revealed, special or more important than anybody else, but it does put us in a place where we must advocate a message that is generally unknown.

Is There Another Life?
Is there another Christian life, other than the Christ-life? Is it possible that Christianity is a combination of the Adamic nature and the Christ nature? Is it possible that Christianity is

a combination of the carnal, the earthly and the spiritual? Is it possible that God intended for us to talk about this deeper, richer life, but never really experience it? Is it possible that He intended the experiences we have had to overshadow the fact that we are to live the Christ-life? Is it possible that God really intended that there be degrees of believers, that there be no common bond, that there be no single stature? Was that His plan? Is Christianity intended to be a hodgepodge of believers who are simply saved with little else to identify them as believers—if, in fact, they are? If Christianity is not believers living the life of Christ (as He lived it once, He will live it again in them), then what is it? What is Christianity? Is God ever definite on this subject?

We have literally believed in Christianity that Christ is only the epitome of our personality projection, that He is a creation of our own personality. He literally does not have a distinct nature of His own, but rather is a product of what we are. We think we manifest Christ by our own makeup, that there is no single standard, for if there were, then there would be only one church and one people of God. So we have logically concluded that Jesus is simply the projection or manifestation of our own personality.

The Bible Says It All

The historical record of the Scriptures is clear regarding the true life of the Christian. It is my conclusion, from the study of God's Word, that one of God's most painstaking acts is making sure there is only one Savior, one Lord, one Christ. The scriptural and historical record is clear on this subject. When God sent forth His Son in the fullness of time, made of a woman, made under the law, He made sure that Christ was not just another good man like Enoch. God made sure that Jesus was not a great prophet like Isaiah or an important man like Solomon. In fact, God made such pointed statements as, *"A greater* [man] *than Solomon is here,"* so He is not Solomon; *"A greater* [man] *than Jonas is here,"* so He is not Jonas (Matthew 12:41-42). Some men thought that He was Elijah or Moses raised from the dead, but Jesus rejected this theory by asking Peter, *"But whom say ye that I am?"* And Peter said, *"Thou art the Christ"* (Mark 8:29). Jesus was not Abraham raised from the dead; He was not Moses raised from the dead; nor was He Elijah come back. Jesus of Nazareth is a distinctive product of God's eternal wisdom. Carefully, God planned it this way.

The Bible is a letter which was written to us from God, designating who Jesus is. We should have no problem in locating the Christ-life, for out of all the other lords, all the other professed christs and saviors, all the other miracle workers, all the soothsayers, fortune-tellers, spiritualists, demon-possessed, those heaven-sent, or angels, there is no doubt. Out of all them, the Bible narrows down to the one life we ought to live, down to one single individual and leaves absolutely no doubt. In basics, in rudiments, in programs, in ideas, in faith, in walk, in speech, in hearing, in saying, in telling, in going, in living, in dying, in doing—in all things, we are narrowed down to one single example.

I believe the Bible is just that clear and distinct in pointing out that Jesus Christ, the Son of God, is our life. In Genesis 3, God began bringing forth a Son in the fullness of time by narrowing the choice of our life down to one-half of the human race. *"And I will put enmity between thee and the woman, and between thy seed and her seed; it shall bruise thy head, and thou shalt bruise his heel"* (Genesis 3:15). God narrowed the Savior down to womanhood, thus eliminating one-half of the human race at the very beginning. *"God sent forth His Son, made of a woman"* (Galatians 4:4).

There can be no doubt about it. Many of the great truths of the Christ-life evolve from this fact. Why is it that Paul said that in weakness we shall bear our greatest strength? Our Savior is produced in God's plan from the weaker half of the human race. He is to be born of a woman, and the principles begin to evolve out of God's prophetic utterances of how He will designate one life to be our life.

Eve Believed

In my study, I came across something in the fourth chapter of Genesis that does not have a lot to do with my subject, but while I am this close to it, I want to point it out to you. The first verse says, *"And Adam knew Eve his wife; and she conceived, and bare Cain, and said, I have gotten a man from the Lord."* I did some research on this verse, and it came to me that most scholars agreed that Eve believed she had brought forth the man-child who was to be the Savior of the world. That is why she makes this statement in the first verse, *"I have gotten a man from the Lord."* She only brought forth Cain, but she was strong in believing this prophetic utterance.

But now, back to this subject, let us go a step further. Turn to the ninth chapter of Genesis, where we see that God eliminates two-thirds of the nations of this world in bringing forth our life. Verses 26 and 27: *"And he said, Blessed be the Lord God of Shem; and Canaan shall be his servant. God shall enlarge Japheth, and he shall dwell in the tents of Shem; and Canaan shall be his servant."* Shem, Ham and Japheth were the sons of Noah. Two of them were rejected—Japheth and Ham. One son rises up as the promised seed. Thus God has narrowed down to one-third of the nations of the world, for all nations of the world flow out of the sons of Noah. God has eliminated Ham and Japheth and said that they shall not have the promised seed. So this Christ-life will not come out of the nations aside from the descendants of Shem. If you want further information on this, in the eleventh chapter of Genesis, we have all the descendants of Shem listed. The generations of Noah and Shem deal with the production of the Lord Jesus Christ as our life.

Soon after this, another choice is made. Of the seed of Shem, there comes forth a man in the Ur of the Chaldees named Abraham. Let us read about it in Galatians 3:8. *"And the scripture, foreseeing that God would justify the heathen through faith, preached before the gospel unto Abraham, saying, In thee shall all nations be blessed."* God has eliminated, now, not only two-thirds of the world's nations, but 99 percent of the nations. Verse 16 of that same chapter says, *"Now to Abraham and his seed were the promises made. He saith not, And to seeds, as of many; but as of one, And to thy seed, which is Christ."* God has limited the world to one nation and has said that nation shall bear the seed. What seed? Christ. This is God, painstakingly and meticulously bringing forth the one single life that all men must have.

Isaac Believed

Let us go further. In Genesis 26 we see God's next step in bringing forth our life. Abraham had several sons, among them Ishmael and Isaac. These two sons figure predominantly in the plan of God, and God had to make a choice between these two sons. In Genesis 26:2-4, God speaks to Isaac. *"And the Lord appeared unto him, and said, Go not down into Egypt; dwell in the land which I shall tell thee of: sojourn in this land, and I will be with thee, and will bless thee; for unto thee, and unto thy seed, I will give all these countries, and I will perform the oath which I swear unto Abraham thy father; and I will make thy seed to multiply as the stars of heaven, and will give unto thy seed all these countries; and in thy seed shall all the nations of the earth be blessed."* God has now, in one single family, limited His plan to one single son—Isaac.

There is truth given to us on this passage in the ninth chapter of Romans. *"Neither, because they are the seed of Abraham, are they all children: but, In Isaac shall thy seed be called"* (Romans 9:7). In the New Testament, the message is very strong in presenting the Christ-life in order that they not believe that just any Israelite will bring forth a Savior—that the heathenistic truth that "every man is his own god" should not flourish. God says, in the New Testament, that He wants all Jews to know that the plan of God is now down to one single son of Abraham—Isaac and his seed.

page 129

A Sceptre Shall Arise

To continue, when we look at Isaac's life, we see that he has two sons, Esau and Jacob; and it is necessary for God to further narrow His plan of bringing forth a son. Let us turn to the Book of Numbers and see God moving, once again, in a supernatural way to bring forth our life. *"I shall see him, but not now: I shall behold him, but not nigh: there shall come a Star out of Jacob, and a Sceptre shall rise out of Israel, and shall smite the corners of Moab, and destroy all the children of Sheth....Out of Jacob shall come he that shall have dominion, and shall destroy him that remaineth of the city"* (Numbers 24:17,19). God has narrowed His choice down to one single grandson—Jacob.

I would like you to see that every time God makes a prophetic move, He does the unusual. It is not a natural, rationalized decision that God makes. Did you ever wonder why God chose Jacob over Esau? Did you ever wonder why God chooses the least rather than the greatest, the smallest rather than the strongest? It is because He wants to show us that He is definitely pinpointing one life. He is not using the wisdom of man; He is not rationalizing as natural man would; He does not want us to end up with a life we interpret into our own. He wants us to see that the coming forth of the Christ-life is supernatural, and that God must manipulate it. It cannot be the ordinary; it must be the unusual. If God is to have sons on this earth, it will be of His own choosing; it will be of His own will. He will birth them Himself. He often chooses the profane, the ungodly, the unyielded, the sinful and the lying, and changes and shapes them by living through them. He does this to show that it is not everyday normal living that He is interested in, but a people who are what they are by the grace of God and not by the circumstances of time.

To go a step further, turn to Genesis 49 and see another choice the Father had to make. Although God allows Jacob to love one of his twelve sons more than any other, He does not allow him to have his way when it comes to bringing forth the promised seed. What a beautiful story evolves from God's choosing and eliminating powers. In Genesis 49:8-10, we see God's choice of Jacob's sons. *"Judah, thou art he whom thy brethren shall praise: thy hand shall be in the neck of thine enemies; thy father's children shall bow down before thee. Judah is a lion's whelp: from the prey, my son, thou art gone up: he stooped down, he couched as a lion, and as an old lion; who shall rouse him up? The sceptre shall not depart from Judah, nor a lawgiver from between his feet, until Shiloh come; and unto him shall the gathering of the people be."* Although man chose Joseph, God chose Judah, who did not have the great thrills that Joseph had of rising to be prime minister. You see, Joseph is merely an illustration of the life; he is not the life. So God does not choose the way man chooses. Here again, He does not use the things that man understands, the principles man sees with his natural mind. He chose Judah.

Judah, the Lion

In Psalm 78:67-70, we see one of the strongest statements God makes concerning our life (Christ). *"Moreover He refused the tabernacle of Joseph, and chose not the tribe of Ephraim: but chose the tribe of Judah, the mount Zion which He loved. And He built His sanctuary like high palaces, like the earth which He hath established for ever. He chose David also His servant, and took him from the sheepfolds."* Do you see it? He chose not Ephraim; He chose not Joseph; He chose Judah, the lion, and eliminated all others.

We see, again, God's next program of elimination in narrowing down the one life that we should live in Isaiah 11:1,2: *"And there shall come forth a rod out of the stem of Jesse, and a Branch shall grow out of his roots: and the spirit of the Lord shall rest upon Him, the spirit of wisdom and understanding, the spirit of counsel and might, the spirit of knowledge and of the fear of the Lord."* God has narrowed down, again, out of Judah's family this time, one family called Jesse.

Time moves on, but the fullness of time has not yet come. Many lives have been chosen by God, but the fullness is not yet come.

Until we come to fullness through the revelation of Jesus Christ, there are many parts of the Christ-life we fall into. See how many phases God leads His people through. He chooses Jacob over Esau; He chooses Abraham out of all the families of Shem. Likewise, God continually keeps narrowing down your walk. You may have started out as a Methodist, changed to a Baptist, then decided to be a Lutheran, and maybe got married and decided to go to the Episcopal church. You wandered from religion to religion, and then one day got saved. All of this is God's manipulation in your life, narrowing it down to the one single life He wants you to live.

The Fullness of Time

This is why you should never despise God's dealings in your past life. We have not come to the fullness of time; we have not come to the fullness of sonship; we have not yet become the image of the Son of God. So God has reserved the right, in dealing with His people through the generations, to continually narrow them down to a focal point—*the fullness of time.*

Out of all families of Judah, God has narrowed it down to one family—the family of Jesse. An important point here is that of all God ever chose, none was so humble, so meager, as was Jesse and his line. Abraham was the richest man in the Ur of the Chaldees; Shem was one of the greatest nations on earth; but when it is narrowed down to Jesse, we are dealing with a common, everyday believer, one through whom God would do His greatest work. Little Mary of Nazareth is not just kin to Abraham, or Jacob, or Isaac, or Shem. She has her greatest identity in God's prophecy with that meager family God chose out of Judah—the family of Jesse. They were not great; they were not rich; they were not famous. They were just common people, but that is where Mary has her identity, for the Scripture says that she came from the house of David, the seed of Jesse. Only God could have planned it like that, for He is bringing forth *my life*. This is the history of my life; this is the background of my life that I now live in Christ Jesus.

Looking back into the family of Jesse, we turn to Psalm 132:11-13: *"The Lord hath sworn in truth unto David; He will not turn from it; Of the fruit of thy body will I set upon thy throne. If thy children will keep My covenant and My testimony that I shall teach them, their children shall also sit upon thy throne for evermore. For the Lord hath chosen Zion; He hath desired it for His habitation."* Where is Zion? We have seen already, for the third time, that the Scripture calls the man God chose as His promised seed to be Zion. What an interesting thought. Jesse had eight sons, and another divine choice must be made. Who will God choose out of these eight sons? We saw that Jacob had twelve sons, and that the most chosen to Jacob was Joseph; but God rejected him and took Judah. Now we have Jesse with eight sons. Since God did not choose the youngest of Jacob, surely He will not choose the youngest of Jesse; but you see, that is man's reasoning. God is in the process of bringing forth *my life.* The life that I now live (Christ) will not be manipulated by human hands; you will never put His life in a box and tie it up with a neat ribbon and call it worship or doctrine. You will never put Him into rituals and ceremonies. He will not fit into man's plan.

Where Is Zion?

His life is always different from man's. You can come to a service ready to sing your song, but He may want you to shout. You can come ready to preach, but He may want you to deliver the sick. You can come ready to pray, and He will want you to sing. You will not put His life in a box. You will never write the life of Christ on a program and say, "At 10:00, we will do this; at 10:15, we will do that; etc." Jesus is not the product of man. Contrary to what man would have done, God did not want the youngest of Jacob; yet He did want the youngest of Jesse. So He took the little lad from the backside of the desert where he was herding sheep and chose him to be the promised seed who would bring forth *my life.*

Do you see what He is doing? The life I now live in Christ Jesus is God's product—not man's. People have said to me, "You should not preach to the sinner that Christ is a mystery. Just preach the simple gospel and tell them how to get saved." My friends, that is not the Word of God. In a sense, the gospel is so simple that if anybody will accept it by faith, they can be saved; but in another sense, you do not fully understand it. I cannot understand the choices God makes, but I am not supposed to. I am to trust in Him because the life I now live is not of man. I am not to be the product of Abraham, Isaac, Jacob, Judah, or Jesse; the life I now live is the life of the Son of God.

Narrowed to My Life

We must narrow this down again. David had many sons, so God, through the process of elimination, must choose again the son who most pleases Him. In First Chronicles 28:5-7 we read, *"And of all my sons, (for the Lord hath given me many sons,) He hath chosen Solomon my son to sit upon the throne of the kingdom of the Lord over Israel. And He said unto me, Solomon thy son, he shall build My house and My courts: for I have chosen him to be My son, and I will be his father. Moreover I will establish his kingdom for ever, if he be constant to do My commandments and My judgments, as at this day."*

Once we reach Solomon, the next great promise of distinguishing the Son of God as our life is the promise in Isaiah 7:13-14: *"And he said, Hear ye now, O house of David; Is it a small thing for you to weary men, but will ye weary my God also? Therefore the Lord Himself shall give you a sign; Behold, a virgin shall conceive, and bear a son, and shall call His name Immanuel."* Once again, out of all the household of David, God has limited the kind of life that we are to live to one single virgin. But there may be thousands of virgins in the household of David, so it must be one single virgin who has been given to God, who has the ability to believe and to have a babe without knowing a man.

He Is Different

This is the narrowest highway that prophecy has ever walked on. God has narrowed down *my life* to the most impossible and

page 134

unbelievable situation. His choice now goes beyond all finite comprehension. Why does God do this? He wants to make sure that I am not an imposter. He wants to make sure that Adam never rises up and says, "I am God; I am the life that you ought to live." He has it narrowed down so that we have no doubt as to what life we shall live. It is a virgin who knows not a man; she must have the ability to bring forth a child, having never been touched by a man.

Do you not see something here? Two things are important: my life must be born of a virgin, and that virgin must descend from the root of David, who is of Jesse's household. Only the miraculous power of God could work this out. My Lord is so arranging the life we should live that He will not allow an imposter.

No Imposters

Notice that He has made the Christ-life such a miracle that no man on earth could impose such a life. No church could bring forth such life. No one can say that he knows all about that life unless he fits into the rudiments of God and has had a revelation of this same Jesus, born of a virgin, made of a woman, made under the law. Unless you have that Christ, you do not have the true Christ. God has so lined it up and has so placed it, historically and prophetically, before us that there is absolutely no doubt about who Jesus is. We cannot say, "It does not matter what church you go to; it does not make any difference what you believe in, so long as you are really born again. My friends, that is not so. It all makes a difference. My God, with a fine-toothed comb, went through one civilization after another to bring forth *my life* according to His will. He reiterates to us the kind of God He is and the reason He makes choices the way He does. It is all part of the background of the Savior who is *my life*.

There was another important stipulation, which is found in Micah 5:2: *"But thou, Bethlehem Ephratah, though thou be little among the thousands of Judah, yet out of thee shall He come forth unto Me that is to be ruler in Israel; whose goings forth have been from of old, from everlasting."* It is not only a virgin who shall bring forth *my life,* but she shall do it in a describable town called Bethlehem Ephratah, the least of all the cities in Judah. The place of His birth is stipulated. His address is plainly written. Notice that out of all the continents, God chose one, Asia. Out of all the states in Asia Minor, God chose one, Canaan. Out of all the areas about Canaan, God chose one province—Palestine. Out of all the areas of Palestine and all the cities of Judah, God narrowed it down to one—Bethlehem Ephratah. Only God could have done that.

One Life, One Church

I want you to go with me on a little adventure and see how keenly God wanted us to have *one life*. Not only is it Bethlehem, and not only did Mary bring forth Christ in Bethlehem, but the circumstances surrounding His birth are just as miraculous as God's choosing David from the backside of the desert to be the promised seed. Mary was living in the wrong place; so in order for her to bear the promised seed, she must get to Bethlehem Ephratah. She must be moved there to have that baby if God's plan was to be perfect. Several hundred years before, God said He would be born in Bethlehem—born of a virgin. It had to happen like that or there would not be one true gospel. The hodgepodge of religion we have in America, with a church on every corner with a different interpretation, is devoid of this truth. But if Jesus is born in Bethlehem, then, mark it down; there is one gospel, there is *one life,* there is one Church, and that is Jesus. There cannot be a church on every corner with a different interpretation any more than there could have been many christs. God's plan points to one Christ, one way, one interpretation.

So Mary has to get to Bethlehem. Notice how God manipulates this. During the reign of Caesar Augustus, God did a lot of political manipulating. You may think God is not interested in politics, but He is. He has His eye on all nations. He is keenly aware of every political maneuver among the nations. God has His hand on all of it. He has always been a political manipulator so that He could work out His plans. He did it with Pharaoh; He has done it all the way through history. So God began His political manipulations to get Mary to Bethlehem.

During the reign of Caesar Augustus, there were three great tax collections. The one we are most interested in is the second tax collection of Caesar, which was announced four years before the birth of Jesus Christ. When that tax collection was announced, the Jews in Palestine raised up in arms and said they did not want to pay any more money to Caesar. So the Roman government, being fairly democratic despite the dictatorship, allowed the Jews to elect for themselves a commission that was to argue the tax problem at the Senate in Rome. It took a period of time to get them elected. It took another period of time to orient them to the need and a long time for them to travel to Rome, after which they had to await their turn in court. They finally presented their petition, only to have Caesar completely reject it. In the process of all this, four years had passed. The Jews were happy to have this period of relaxation from taxes, but that was not why it happened. It was God manipulating. When the commission failed, they were turned back, and Caesar began his collection.

The Tribal Identity

It took a long time for them to get down to Bethlehem, Judea. They went, province by province, city by city. The tax collectors had a lot of trouble with the sabotaging Jews, and everywhere they went, there was static. Nobody was in a hurry to pay taxes, but it was God who allowed that tax collection to be held up for four years. God was waiting for little Mary, who was only nine or ten years of age when Caesar announced the tax collection, to become old enough to bear a child and to get over to Bethlehem so that Jesus could be born according to Micah's prophecy. He was born right on time, by the right woman, and in the right place. There could be no duplicator. There could be no imposter.

In the fullness of time, God brought forth His Son. Not only was the infant Jesus born at the right time, but when He was born, the Son of God had to come forth with Him. When He comes forth,

He must not be a man of men, but the Son of God. That is the great difference.

There are at least two general predictions about time given in the Scriptures that will help us to know God's timing in bringing forth *our life.* The first is in Genesis 49:10: *"The sceptre shall not depart from Judah, nor a lawgiver from between his feet, until Shiloh come; and unto him shall the gathering of the people be."* This states that before the tribe of Judah loses its identity, Jesus must be born. The record shows that prior to the birth of Jesus Christ, all of the other tribes, except Judah, dissolved and lost their identity.

The word sceptre means tribal identity, and the Scripture reads that the tribal identity shall not depart from Judah until Shiloh comes, meaning that all the other tribes of Israel may dissolve, but one of them must still be in existence for this baby to be born in Bethlehem. Otherwise, he would be an imposter. We do not sing about Ephraim, Joseph, Dan, or Naphtali; we sing about the Lion of the tribe of Judah, because when He came, anyone could see that He was the Lion that was spoken about in Genesis. He came out of Judah. Praise God! We know that the tribe of Judah was still alive because it had a king. He was Herod, king of Judah, king of the Jews. Also, the tribe of Judah still had its governor and the Sanhedrin.

Search the Scriptures

In time, Jesus stood before Herod. He met with members of the Sanhedrin. It is very interesting to note that the tribe of Judah was dissolved when Jesus was twelve years old, after which they kept only a *form* of government. God did not recognize them once Jesus brought forth a message. There was old King Herod, but what was he? An imposter. There was a government of the Sanhedrin, but it was a bunch of evil men because God had dissolved the tribe as far as His blessing being upon them.

There was a second prediction made in Malachi 3:1: *"Behold, I will send My messenger, and he shall prepare the way before*

Me: and the Lord, whom ye seek, shall suddenly come to His temple, even the messenger of the covenant, whom ye delight in: behold, He shall come, saith the Lord of hosts. " What is the second prediction? He would come to His temple. Does He not do so? We see Him ministering in and about Herod's temple; we see Him about the pool of Bethesda; so He does come to His temple. That had to be fulfilled while that temple was standing. In A.D. 70, the temple was destroyed—God, alone, manipulating in the time element. My friends, the evidence is clear and astounding. God has not left the life of the Lord Jesus Christ to you and me to figure out according to our own ideas. I must call upon you, as Christians, to search the Scriptures as never before. Perhaps one of the greatest faults we have in this day is depending upon our religious experiences to carry us through.

The life I now live is not an interpretation of the Christ-life. I ran into a man who said to me, "I am not a Christian; I am not religious at all." He said, "You know, I believe in certain truths in the Bible," and he picked out things like the golden rule and said "I try to live by this." My thought was that this man was not so far off. Multitudes of born-again believers are the same way. They have picked out of God's Word certain facts that complement their personalities and their makeups. People come to me and say, "I don't think God wants everybody to give his life to Him." But the question is, Are we sons of God? Have we been born into the family of God? If so, our history is very clear-cut. It is very distinctive. It comes right down to the point that God has one Son.

Jesus Is the Word

It is declared by John in the third chapter of his Gospel that God so loved the world that He gave His only begotten Son. It was a choice that was made through the centuries. It was not an idea that exploded at the last minute, with God deciding to use the product of the virgin, Mary. It was the Son that God had throughout centuries, generations and civilizations brought down to one single act. The Holy Spirit would breathe upon a virgin, who would go to Bethlehem and bring forth a manchild whose name would be called Jesus; but more than that, He should be called Emmanuel—God with us, God in us. There was to be no doubt about it; there is one Savior, one life.

God has not written a book so that in the end we could come up and say, "I am going to live like Abraham." God has not written a book so that we can take the good out of Moses' life and live it. He is not our life. Moses was just a tool in God's hand. My life is Jesus. I am not to be like Moses; I am not to be like Paul, Peter, James or John. God narrowed it down so no flesh and blood could be *my life.* When I want to know how to live the Christian life, I look at *my life,* who is Jesus. He is the Word. It is clearly printed. It is documented. It is truth. God did not throw it out and say, "Now, you do what you please with Jesus." He gave us one Christ, one Lord, one hope, and by virtue of His life in us, has made it possible to live His life. Of course, in the beginning you may not live all of it. His grace makes up the lacking, and that is the beauty of the Christ-life. Mary, herself, was not perfect, but she brought forth the Son.

She herself needed the grace of God to make it through. I want to tell you that you can travel all over this world, but if you find one single contradiction, one single reason why we should not live the life of Jesus Christ today, then the gospel is the biggest farce that was ever written. However, God did not fail one single time in bringing us a Son supernaturally; neither will He fail in bringing us forth as sons. He will bring forth the Son in us. He is leading and directing in our lives in the very same way. The issue is before you. God called many, but He chose very few. What is the difference? It is Jesus—His life.

Chapter 8

The Benefits of Understanding Spiritual Pre-Existence

When we think about pre-existence as born-again believers, we are faced with what we have termed in the Christ-life as one of the three classifications of Scripture passages upon which the whole plan of God is based. This classification of Scripture is found in Ephesians 1:4. It says that the believer was chosen in Christ before the foundation of the world. "Before the foundation of the world" is an idea explaining the pre-existence of every born-again believer. It shows that the believer in Christ was planned before anything was created. Therefore, all things created are secondary and have nothing to do with the believer planned in Christ before the creation of the world.

Jesus Lived in the Knowledge of His Pre-Existence

When this idea gets hold of any believer's consciousness, he immediately begins to receive tremendous benefits from this understanding. The facts are simple: there is nothing in the world that supersedes God's placing the believer in Christ. As the believer comes to see this, he moves into a realm of living that is above and beyond the natural mortal world, and, of course, it is an understanding that goes beyond all carnal-minded comprehension. We have only to look into the Christ-life itself to see how He lived in this realm of understanding by His knowledge of pre-existence. Christ's recognition of who He was and where He came from shone throughout His entire life as bright as the sun. Many of Christ's statements clearly show that He did not regard His own existence as having begun with human birth, nor His real status as flesh and blood. He said once to His disciples, *"What and if ye shall see the Son of man ascend up where He was before?"* Then He added, *"It is the spirit that quickeneth; the flesh profiteth nothing"* (John 6:62,63). Christ's unparalleled knowledge of His true spiritual being, forever God-derived and sustained, brought Him an unsurpassed dominion over all of the discord and limitations that were attached to the material, mortal and temporal existence.

The Created Man Has Dominion

As it was with Jesus of Nazareth, so it is with the believer today. Jesus, having stepped out of the realm of eternal glory where nothing created could hinder or oppress that eternal quality, began to operate in His daily life by healing the sick, casting out devils, and raising the dead. There was nothing in the temporal realm that ruled over Him. Adam was given, in Genesis 1:26, dominion over everything in his realm of environment. It was God's intention that Adam, the first man created, was to live and move and have his being in a world over which he had authority. Yet Jesus came to be the life of every born-again believer and His pre-existence ruled over even what God had given to the first created man. Christ was before all things were created and, as Colossians 1 says, not only was He before, but all things were created by Him and for Him (v. 16). The first chapter of John's Gospel says that there was not anything in existence of which He was not a part (v. 3).

This same Jesus lives in the believer, and when the believer comes to the understanding that the very life he now has is a life pre-existent to this mortal and material world, he is able to move into a spirit realm hitherto unknown. Our hearts should leap for joy at this prospect of learning that Jesus knew about man's spiritual pre-existence. This meek Nazarene, who was so steadfast and adamant about His pre-existence, was by that very knowledge able to nurture an inseparability with God that made Him mighty. His knowledge of His pre-existence and of His very nature, which was God in Him, gave Him the spiritual insight of truth and love that literally destroyed all the forces of the flesh and the carnal mind. His very understanding that He was God's man—even before Adam—caused Him to be a true reflection of God and the very voice of God, doing the works of God. Jesus declared, *"Before Abraham was, I am"* (John 8:58). Now that same Jesus lives in every believer. As Christ bore the great consciousness of who and what He was by God in Him, so we can come to that same understanding of Christ in us.

The Lord Is Our Dwelling Place

The supposition that God is somehow blended into all matter and created things is a pantheistic doctrine presenting a false sense of existence that cannot stand in the light of God's Word. Although God is the Creator of all things, it is only man who shows forth the Spirit of God, and it is the work of the Holy Spirit to reveal this marvelous life of God that has been released. Whenever a believer accepts the idea that it is his natural birth which supersedes all things, he has entered into an error that will rob him of the prerogatives of being a Christian. If we adhere to the glorious truth given in Psalm 90:1, which says, *"Lord, Thou hast been our dwelling place in all generations,"* we can enter into a relationship that goes beyond all finite comprehension and brings us to true sonship in Christ, providing all the benefits and prerogatives of that sonship.

The Christ-life message rolls back the clouds of error and brings forth the Christ of truth; it literally lifts the curtain on man, showing him that as a born-again believer, he is indeed a true son of God and literally coexistent with his Creator before the foundation of the world was laid. When we begin to understand man's spiritual pre-existence with God, we enter into benefits we never knew before; but at times this new, vibrant knowledge causes considerable mental and emotional upheaval. Why? Seeing our oneness with Christ literally pulls the rug out from under our natural lives' claims to dominance and reality. This is an absolute necessity, for at some time during the growth of the believer a devastating moment must come, when the natural birth—or the knowledge that the natural birth gives us our real life—is made to be error. As Peter says in his Epistle, we are born again not of the corruptible seed, but of the incorruptible seed (I Peter 1:23). This plainly gives us the understanding that the corruptible seed is our natural birth and is now superseded by, literally overwhelmed by, and perhaps even laid aside by, our spiritual birth.

Our true life comes from God. It is only as we are in harmony with the God-idea of our true existence that we are able to move into the fruits and benefits of our existence in Christ. However, we need not be surprised that the carnal mind resists being set aside. We can rest assured that the Christ-life truth will prevail over any temporary sense knowledge. It means that our born-again experience, birthed by another father, Father God, must at some juncture of the believer's life take pre-eminence over the birthing by the natural father. Until the believer sees that truth, he will never be able to enjoy eternal life now in his temporal body.

As a good example of how we can benefit from the under-standing of our spiritual pre-existence, take the issue of human relationships. Even when the child has been out of the nest for years, few beliefs of the mortal mind have as tenacious and as discord-producing a hold on people as the notion that one individual creates another and therefore in a sense possesses him. This limiting human attachment often holds the parent in bondage even longer than it does the child, but it eventually has to yield to a more enlightened appreciation of God as the only Father of the believer. So the sooner one takes this mental step, the greater his joy and freedom. Sometimes parents and children both wish they could rewrite their human histories and live out those events and circumstances of early life that have lingered to mar their present happiness and well-being.

Working Free of Guilt

Fortunately for all, the spiritual truths that the Christ-life reveals of our inseparability from the Christ within can heal these past hurts and bitter feelings. The spiritually accurate view of creation blesses both parent and child. Combined with spiritual growth and regeneration, it supports one's efforts to walk free of the guilt and condemnation some parents are tempted to feel at having done a less than perfect job of rearing their children. The truth of the Christ-life coming through revelation knowledge can wash away the emotional conflict and bitter memories some children harbor toward their parents. Both parties, in their true spiritual being, are simply sons of God and are actually governed by God's unerring wisdom and unfailing love.

Sometimes people who undergo psychiatric therapy and trace their emotional difficulties to past human events or hereditary factors admit to a great feeling of freedom when they are told it is okay to resent those whom they consider the cause of their difficulties. Oh, how the carnal mind deceives us! What looks like liberation turns out to be a worse bondage, since hating another actually magnifies our self-independence, brings us back under Satan's pulls, and compounds our suffering. As one prays for the Father to heal emotional wounds and debilitating memories, it is imperative to view one's existence as it literally is. Our existence is always, in the spiritual sense, a continuously harmonious union with the Christ who is in us. To veer away from this union is only to unnecessarily burden ourselves with hurt and torment. It is here that the continued enlightenment of the Christ-life can empower one to begin to feel love—the very love of the Father—exercised by the Son within.

Demonstrating Christ-Life Forgiveness

It means that all the parties involved in a supposed unfortunate relationship are made aware of the true nature of God as it is exemplified by the individual believer. Disharmony and disunion with the Christ within is certainly never a part of God's ideas. This spiritual fact must be proven in the individual's experience through his own redemption and demonstration of Christ-life forgiveness. The believer who comes to see Christ as his all will finally understand Paul's teaching that things appearing to be of the antichrist are opposites of God and are intended to bring us to the true knowledge of God. The purpose of these illusionary events in any believer's life is to bring about godly chastening and to rebuke human consciousness, which is contrary to Christ-consciousness. They turn the believer away from a material, false sense of life and happiness to true spiritual joy and a true estimate of who he is in Christ. Increased spiritual knowledge brings an increase in spiritual love. To see Jesus in another human brings about more of Jesus to the entire world. It means that, as Jesus saw the world, so does the believer see the world and Christ will rule with authority over everything in that believer's environment.

With that same Jesus in the believer today, he too can rule over all in his realm. This means that where the Christ-life is in operation, there is abundant life. When Christ-life love begins to operate, it brings about wonderful changes in all that the believer contacts. As the believer puts off the old man, meaning the old knowledge of doing things, to his delight, and more often to his surprise, he finds himself feeling something of the tender compassion and forgiving love that motivated Jesus. As a result, glorious miracles begin to take place wherever he goes.

First, he feels the restorative, healing Christ within him, not only enveloping him, but enveloping everyone whom he thinks about and contacts. As a result, he disburses the glorious light from Christ to other mortal beings who heretofore have been obscuring the spiritual truth of Christ. Second, he realizes the truth that the real man, God's eternally loving and lovable Christ, never did anything that was contrary to the healing of human relationships. In this reformed, compassionate, Christ-enlightened state of thought, all blame and bitterness melt before the glorious warmth of the infinite, ever-present, all-encircling love of Christ.

Eternal Life Now!

There is another very important aspect of the pre-existent Christ that must be mentioned. It is simply that in Christ, the believer now has eternal life dwelling in him. This eternal life is not only eternal future, but also eternal past. This means that, when one is born again and receives the nature of God, it will cure all human pride in his natural birthing and natural family lineage and background. Either view of one's ancestry is erroneous according to the facts of the Christ-life since they would limit the good that God intends for each of His offspring to enjoy. Feelings of superiority or inferiority concerning one's mortal ancestry give way before the recognition that one has been eternally in God.

In growing to adulthood, we usually lean less and less on our human parents for direction and support. Just the opposite happens as we demonstrate our union with Christ. We find ourselves adopting an even more childlike dependence on our heavenly Father. Praying to God in this way keeps our thoughts obedient, humble, and more awake to the reality of our life in Him. By this, we have more of the dominion and joy that are God's intention for all of His sons.

One important thing we need to be alert to in handling the carnal mind is its insistence that it has always been true in the past. When believers begin to receive mind healing, especially concerning relationships, they must not allow a mental image of the many things they have not been delivered from to prey upon them. To do so confuses their thought and disturbs their sense of peace. One must turn to God and begin to invoke His spiritual laws—that since the new birthing, *"old things are passed away; behold, all things are become new"* (II Corinthians 5:17).

As the believer begins to see union with Christ, God's divine love enables him to perceive that man's true being cannot be destroyed by the things that are temporal, or by the circumstances and situations against him. As we begin to see Christ as our all and in all, we have the comforting and eternal fact that the Christ-life can never be interrupted by anything that concerns the corruptible seed or the old life.

By His Stripes We Are Healed

A true being can never be separated from God the Father. We can grow in Christ until true consciousness—the mind of Christ—is no longer impressed with the beliefs of the past or the frailty of the present or the impending impairments that come with time. All of these obvious temporal and illusionary aspects are overcome and defeated at the cross of Christ, for by His stripes we are healed. Furthermore, all of our circumstances and situations in life are planned by God and are ordained to be stepping stones in our lives to the greater understanding that He who is within us has already overcome all things—even death, hell and the grave. Then, because He is in us and operates as us, we too are victors. Understanding that man in his thinking is a reflection of the Christ in him, we can claim immunity from any discord or defect there may be in life's daily operations.

Nothing disturbs the perfect functioning of the Christ who is within us. Since mankind is a reflection of this Christ, as even the universe is a reflection of this Christ, all things will function according to God's idea if we let them (Colossians 1:16-17).

Satan Is a Liar

Satan will often come about with the lie that there is physical disharmony in our bodies and souls, as well as in the universe, and that nothing will work out right. To believe such is to become separated from the Christ within, and in this separation there is bred doubt, fear and unbelief. The believer can and must identify himself daily with being the direct offspring of God, eternally existent in the mind of God, for the believer was chosen in Christ before the foundation of the world (Ephesians 1:4). Thus, all of the conditions and circumstances of life, including even Satan's lies, are progressive factors bringing to light the blessedness of

page 148

our new birth in Christ, and presenting us ever available to God's healing in body and soul. It is God's plan that all of His sons enjoy the infinite, inexhaustible, omniscient love of God.

Chapter 9

New Testament Ethics and the Christ-Life

There is no place where religion shows its ugly head any more than in forcing believers to adhere to some law—a law that says if you do not do this or that, you will not be pleasing to the Father; a law that hinges on the believer's work in his flesh. Actually, all *law-keeping* can be done only in the flesh. Satan, the progenitor of religion, works continually at keeping believers laboring on something that is already a finished work. To round out his religious dogma, he uses God's servants to preach and perpetuate doctrines and ideas, most unknowingly, that will keep the believer working where no work is needed.

Satan Works to Hinder God's Plan

Satan's reason for this is twofold. First, he doesn't want the believer to come to the knowledge of who he is in Christ Jesus. It is simple—keep the believer trying to earn blessings by everything he does and there will never be any time or place to find out who he is in Christ. Second, Satan wars against world-evangelization. Those chosen from the foundation of the world to be in Christ are the focal point of Satan's battle. These chosen ones are those who have displaced Satan in the Father's house and are those upon whom Satan has taken out his enmity against God. How sad that with all the religious effort put forth these days, the statistics of reaching the world with the gospel have not changed in the last 50 years. This not only sends multitudes to hell without ever hearing the gospel, but also delays the coming of the Bridegroom for His Bride, the Church. We will not go home to the Father's house until all those chosen have had a chance to hear the gospel. It is wonderful to know that our real life—the life we now live in the flesh—is the Christ-life, but with Paul we groan to get out of this fleshly body and go on to the Father's house. This cannot and will not happen until the world has heard the gospel. Although more money is being spent on spreading the gospel than ever before, it is obvious that money, talent, ability and personality are the work of the doers. The true gospel that pleases the Father can come only from those who are *be-ers.* The work of the doers can easily be motivated by Satan, while the work of the be-ers is Christ at work. All doing, in time, is motivated by certain laws—laws that often start in the Spirit but end in the flesh. I say this because all the important works of the Father were finished before the foundation of the world (Hebrews 4:3).

Many Are Preaching the Truth

Now, it is necessary to say that the kind of gospel one hears is imperative to this understanding. If the only gospel preached is that of doing, then there will never be an understanding of the finished work of the Father. That shows the far-reaching extent of Satan's influence in religion. Today's believers operate for God out of the premise that they must do something to please God. Having no knowledge of the Christ-life, or having the knowledge and not the outworking, they never allow Christ to be the doer. How necessary it is at this point for the believer to receive a revelation of Christ as his only life (Galatians 1:16)! This revelation alone will project the believer from his own self-effort to the Christ in him. This thought highlights the essence of this current move of the Spirit, which we know as the Christ-life. It is in this move of the Spirit that many are coming to see Christ as their all and in all. Without the Father raising up voices to speak boldly as the Christ who is in them, there can be no growth in the current Church. But thanks be to the Father, many are being raised up to preach the message of the revealed Christ (Ephesians 1:17). The tide working against this move of the Spirit is great, but the people whom the Father is raising up to preach Christ are bold, noble and enlightened, and cannot be stopped. They will, in time, bring a whole new concept—new to the current Church but certainly not new to the New Testament Church; new to those whose whole gospel has been that of self-effort. Those who preach Christ in His fullness will for a time be ferociously fought; they will be as strangers in a weary religious land. They will be pioneers making the first trail across the wilderness, fighting all the rigors of a perilous journey, but they will succeed. They are the living Christ in their various human forms and knowing this is their ultimate weapon against Satan. The sad thing about the battle that these pioneers must wage is it appears to be a battle against the doing of good and against godly brethren who are doing that good.

First, it always appears to be doing good if souls are saved, the sick are healed, or the world is blessed. In the natural, these things appear to be the work of Jesus of Nazareth, but it must be remembered that Jesus Himself raised the criterion of works when He said in Matthew 7:22-23 that any works that were not the will of the Father were not done by His servants, but rather by the servants of Satan. Dear believer, do not feel bad if you begin to see the difference between the law, which says a thing must be done because it is good, and your knowing that if it is not Christ doing it, it is not of the Father. Satan will attempt to put you under condemnation, but your in-Christ knowledge will persevere.

Second, when you speak out against the law of self-effort, you will also appear to be speaking against some brother who propagated that work. He will probably be very sincere and very anointed in what he is doing. He will probably be doing more works on the surface than you may ever do, but what does it matter if it does not please the Father? If it is he doing it and not Christ as him, it won't matter. You will be severely attacked for speaking out against such works, but with the living Christ within you who fought against all religion—Moses' religion, Abraham's religion, and Israel's religion—your voice will be blessed by the Father and many shall come to the knowledge of the Lord.

The Seven Areas of Satan's Traps

In the modern church, there are at least seven areas where the law is most predominant in leading the believer away from his fullness in Christ.

1. Doctrine. Satan works to keep the believer from seeing Christ as his life. Most doctrine in the church today is man-made. This does not mean it does not have some good in it—most doctrine does. But any truth not started and finished by Christ is harmful to our seeing Christ as all. Christ is the Alpha and the Omega. John was able to finally say that his entire doctrine is Christ. Now, the way Satan tricks believers over doctrine is by the Scriptures themselves. Almost all progenitors of some religion or doctrine start with the Scriptures as a basis for proving their point. They are plucked out of context and therefore nullify the Word of God, the Person of Christ. It is as Jesus told the Jews in John 5—that they had no life in them for they did not see Jesus in the Scriptures. They were searching the Scriptures, they had doctrine, but they had no life.

Through my years of searching to know God, I have seen, again and again, hungry souls find some Scripture passage or some doctrine that became a security blanket to them and essentially blocked their search for the real Christ. I have seen those friends willing to die for their Christless doctrines. The traps that Satan sets for these are in the areas of eschatology, perfection, church polity, commitment and service. Sad to say, there are those claiming to be Christ's who will disfellowship you, harass you, and even kill you for disagreeing with them on any one of these subjects. This is the law of religion at its best. It is Satan trying to keep hungry hearts from coming into the Christ-life.

All Truth Flows Out of Christ

It is to be noted, however, that all who come to see the Christ-life will believe in and establish truths flowing out of Christ. By no effort of their own will they enforce their actions—not by the Scriptures, not by workable works, not by any successes. Their only life is Christ, and their only actions are His. We must never forget that there is not any law that says we must do anything to become a Christ-person other than simply believe on the Lord Jesus Christ. Likewise, there is no further obligation to being kept saved than having Him in us. If God sees Christ in us as our only hope of glory, then it is a trick of Satan to urge us to see that something else will perfect us. There is nothing that we believe or that we practice or that we do which can add anything to Him in us. Whatever we do in these areas of living can only hinder Him from being our all.

The true test for a believer concerning the issues of doctrine is all summed up in our seeing Jesus (Hebrews 2:9). The Father is not so interested in what you believe; His greater interest is in whom you believe. If you do not see Christ in something you believe, throw it away. If Jesus is not the substance of all your knowledge, it has no life in it. I am becoming bolder and bolder in suggesting that any believer wanting to *come to full stature* in Christ ought to be willing to start at point zero, doctrinally, that the proper foundation be laid to contain the Christ, who offers nothing but Himself as life.

We must cease in the ordeal of trying to fit Jesus into our current knowledge. Christ is not an add-on, doctrinally. I cringe every time I hear theological terms such as christological, as if that were another doctrine we needed to learn and add onto current knowledge. Far from it; Christ is not an add-on. He is *all and in all*. He is the reason there is a world in the first place, and more so, the reason the Father has chosen us to live in His house. Modern religion has notoriously misused Jesus by attempting to add Him onto present doctrine. This add-on dilemma has produced a modern Church specializing in getting from God more than anything else. Of course, the Christ in the believer is not a getter but a Giver and the ensuing conflict the believer goes through by the misuse of the Christ within only leads to more needs, and thus more getting.

Cubby-Hole Religion

It is here that Satan attempts to deceive the very elect. He tricks believers, especially ministers, into trying to fit all the new things they hear into present doctrine. I call this idea of present doctrine *cubby-hole religion.* These cubby holes are established doctrines that have been accepted through years of search and study, and when anything new comes along, these believers attempt to fit the new truths into the existing cubby holes. If they fit properly, according to past teaching, they are accepted. If they do not fit, they are rejected and often the presenter of the truth is branded as being unscriptural. By this process, Satan hinders believers from becoming complete in Christ. That is why we stress that those who handle this Word of Life be thoroughly trained by the Spirit. Aside from all else, it must be plainly stated that when any doctrine becomes a law that makes one more acceptable to the Father or produces more self-effort or gives more confidence in one's self, it is Satan who is enforcing the law that has already been fulfilled in Christ and in many instances has been done away with by Christ.

2. Self-Perfection. For centuries—in fact, ever since the days of the New Testament writers—men have sought a way to be holy and thereby evade a holy God's wrath. There have been holiness and sanctification movements since the Church began.

There have been at least two outcomes from man's attempts to be holy. Both of these attempts have been motivated by religion, and thereby Satan has had his hand in them. The first outcome of man's thrust toward holiness was that it eventually ceased to be an inward work of grace and became an outward demonstration of the flesh. It finally became necessary that men prove their own righteousness by adhering to some outward code. Certainly, the Christ who came to possess men as they were at conversion, taking them just as they were, untrained, untaught, untried, and with corruptible bodies, would not place a demand upon them to be anything within themselves. His prime purpose in coming was to take control of them by Himself, becoming their holiness and righteousness. It was never to be in their doing that they would be holy, but by His Person in them.

There were many well-meaning servants of God, teachers and theologians, who were to be swept up in this tide of self-effort, and in their defense I say that the time for knowing Christ as our all and in all was yet to come. Their desire to please God was honorable, but it always led to self-effort.

Satan's Self-Effort Law

The second outcome of man's thrust toward holiness was the most devastating of all—that Satan, by religious acts, saw to it that the self-effort to be holy became a law. If one did not agree with the principle of holiness presented, he could not be saved and would go to hell, and thus would be disfellowshipped. All of this, of course, ignored the fact that salvation is a Person—a Person who is in the believer. It also nullified the great work of the Father at Calvary. By Calvary, the Father fixed it so that Christ the Lamb would be the life, the righteousness, the holiness, and the hope of the believer. It is here that Satan set out to blind the believer to what the Father had done. The believer, blinded, ignorant of Calvary, and tricked by Satan, started working to become what he already was.

However, the saddest part of this snare is how men can become so confused and frustrated that they will disfellowship anyone who does not see their doctrine. That is exactly what Satan wanted. He has them seeing Scripture, but not Christ. He has them proving their points, but not from the Word. He has them dying for what they sincerely believe, but never coming to know the Christ who is in them. All the years I have been preaching the gospel, I have witnessed a most sorrowful situation. When there was a believer who did not match the outward appearance of the rest of the believers in that body, he was worked on by all of the religious tools Satan could muster. All who did not conform were criticized, ostracized, humiliated, sermon-clubbed, and finally, if they did not straighten out, were put out. How simply Christ handled this problem with Peter, the reed, and with Judas, the devil. It should be noted, however, that religion cannot so simply handle such problems because self-perfection has been turned into a law. Where there is law, there is no Christ-life. The two are incompatible.

A Baptism Which Produces Knowers

Self-perfection is further seen as a work of law in believers receiving the baptism of the Holy Spirit. When believers are taught that they need the Holy Spirit to live the Christian life, when they are taught that they need the baptism to have power, or when they are taught that the Holy Spirit makes them anything within themselves, they enter into self-effort and finally, into law. It is Christ who is the believer's only life. If Christ is the life, then it is His power, His gifts and His works. Satan, by religion, would like nothing better than to get the emphasis off the Christ within and back on the believer's need to do something. How sad that a believer, already crucified with Christ at the cross, is tricked into thinking that now he has come to the Christ-life, he is something within himself. As it was with Jesus, who said that His words, His works, and His life were all from and of the Father, so also must the believer see that the life he now lives is Christ, and it is Christ's words, Christ's works, and Christ's life that he manifests.

There are so many today who need to hear the words of Christ in John 14:20 concerning the Holy Spitit's coming on the Day of Pentecost. Here He said that the believer would *know* that as He is one with the Father, so would we *know* that He is in us and we in Him. There never has been a believer who, within himself, could do anything. It has always been Christ's life in the believer, and it always will be. We are admonished to be filled with the Holy Spirit, for this is a work of God, bringing the soulish part to knowing the Christ within. It is glorious how the Father planned all of this, but it is important to see that making a law by fellowshipping or disfellowshipping others is a trick of Satan. Let all those who hunger to know God allow the Holy Spirit to fill their minds, for when He comes, He sees nothing but Christ, speaks of nothing but Christ, and reveals nothing but Christ.

3. Faith. Without faith, it is impossible to please God (Hebrews 11:6). What an idea! This puts faith in a position that nothing else holds. But faith needs a "Word" definition. The Word says, *"So then faith cometh by hearing and hearing by the word of God"* (Romans 10:17). This statement immediately puts faith in the area of the mind and knowledge. What we hear from the Word is what brings faith. But perhaps someone will not know about faith as it really is, from what is said in this verse. Let me paraphrase it: *"So then, true knowledge comes from hearing Him who is a Person, the Person of the Word."* Notice that it said faith comes by hearing. Hearing means that someone must speak. It is not just reading the Scriptures that brings faith, for that would be only seeing. It says "hearing" because there is a depth attached to knowing real faith. That depth is stated in the "hearing by the word." The Word is a Person whom we must hear. When we see something, we are prone to evaluate what we see, but when we hear Him, there is no evaluation necessary. This is how real faith comes—not by just reading the Scriptures, but by hearing Him who is the Word speak to us.

Now, without this kind of faith, the faith in which He is speaking to us and in us as the Word, we can never come to the ultimate living, where we live by the *"faith of the Son of God"* (Galatians 2:20). It is at this point, when man tries to see on his own what he needs to do to have faith, that Satan interjects some religious act which, in time, becomes a law. The greatest self-effort I have ever witnessed is by those who try to get faith. They go from meeting to meeting; they buy every book on faith; they contact every preacher whom they hear has faith; they give money to those who require it to share their faith; they will go into any new doctrine or even a far-out cult if they think it will bring faith.

It is an endless and unceasing labor to get faith so they can get what they want. Now, if you cross those who are promoting such things, you will be strongly rebuked. These methods have become laws of men, and these laws are strongly protected by outward results. Sometimes the claimed outward results, such as health and prosperity, are true and sometimes they are just promotion. In it all, Satan, by religion, is working to get believers to see Christ do something for them, rather than have Him be somebody in them.

The Old Testament Kind of Faith

Also, when the faith hinges on what the believer does, then greater faith is nullified. That greater faith is the "faith of the Son of God" who is in the believer and is the life of the believer. Finally, the believer comes to see that it is His faith that is working from within and is working by "hearing" the Word Person. Praise God for the Word in us. So much of the confusion over real faith comes from the Old Testament and the law of Moses. These had no Christ within. These had no faith of the Son of God. These had no Savior who had paid the price for all the Father had to give His sons. These were expected to please God by their own self-effort. These prospered and were healed by their own adherence to some given law.

If you see this clearly—how the Old Testament saints lived and were blessed by their doing—you will see how Satan keeps believers of the new creation race from living the life that is in the Son. He does it by causing them to ignore the miracle of the in-Christ position. He does it by getting them to ignore the finished work of Calvary and instead to work to earn their inheritance.

Another warning should be made about deception. Great error exists today in preachers who make no distinction between the teaching of the law and the Day of Pentecost. There is no teaching in the Old Testament for the new creation believer except as he sees Jesus in the verses. Furthermore, there was a radical change which took place on the Day of Pentecost, for that was the day the Father began to form the new creation body. With the forming of that body, there was a whole new gospel to be preached, for prior to that time, there was no Christ in the believer. But with Christ as the believer's only life, a new gospel was needed.

As this gospel spreads, we see the results that Paul said would take place. He said that the believer would lack for nothing and that the believer could *"do all things through Christ"* (Philippians 4:13,19). How wonderful these days to hear the testimony of those who have learned this Christ as their life. They are blessed and the blessings come spontaneously. They are healed of killing diseases without the self-effort of human faith. Imagine the joy of knowing consciously, every day, that you are a Christ-person, and that He, as you, has put every enemy, every disease, every evil spirit, and every power that could possibly work against you under His foot. Imagine knowing that the finished work of Calvary is daily working in you as Him, for the life you *now* live is Christ. Imagine knowing that the same Christ who defeated Satan at the cross is the only *you* there is to the Father, and that you are coming into that same mind, the mind of Christ, as your way of living and knowing. There is no law needed to enforce this new creation life. It operates from the finished work of Calvary, and most of all, directly from Him who is in us. When the believer understands this truth, he will be free for the first time from human laws that have kept him from being the Christ who is his only life.

4. Prayer and Fasting. When I was just six years of age, my mother, who was a Baptist, received an experience called the baptism of the Holy Spirit. Just as she had served God as a Baptist, she, with the same fervor, served the Lord as a Spirit-filled believer. With eagerness she pursued all that was being advocated. Among the many new thrilling things she participated in was the experience of prayer and fasting. It seemed in those days that one was never mentioned without the other. In fact, I grew up believing that prayer and fasting were one and the same. It seemed that every time there was a prayer meeting, there was fasting also. I remember numerous testimonies of those who had received miraculous healings and answers to prayer, just because they had prayed and fasted. Now most of the belief in prayer and fasting was based on the verse that says, *"Howbeit this kind goeth not out but by prayer and fasting"* (Matthew 17:21). Based on this verse, almost all hard-to-get things from God came only by prayer and fasting.

There is a place for *prayer and fasting.* Yet in so many instances this ministry has become a law in that if you do not do it a certain way or with a certain style or under someone's command, then you will not be blessed. Men are always attempting to organize prayer. It cannot be done, for new creation people are no longer outsiders trying to get God's attention and favor, as did the Old Testament saints. They are full-fledged sons of God by the Son in them, and they speak and pray to God on another level—the level of a son who has the full inheritance and who comes behind in no spiritual gift. No one can control or command their relationship with the Father. No program or promotion can produce any more fervor or anointing than they have as the Son in whom the Father is well pleased. There is a relationship between the Father and the Son that cannot be entered into by anyone else's promotion or controlled by anything else. It is personal, it is vivid, and it is overwhelming.

Old Testament and Four Gospels Under the Law

Before going any further, we should look at the scriptural input on the subject. So much of what we know about prayer and fasting comes from the Old Testament and is based on the law that something must be done by one's self if he is to get God's attention. Also, the ministry of Jesus in the four Gospels was based on the same theory, as He carefully carried out the fulfilling of the law, especially before the Jews rejected Him as their Messiah. Although there is much help for the new creation believer in the renewing of his mind from the Gospels, he must ultimately look to the Epistles to get the Christ-as-the-believer message, where the full gospel is given for those who have become knowers and "livers" of Christ. The law that says the believer must do something or be somebody within himself is overwhelmed by the believer's knowledge that he is a Christ-person and that his relationship with the Father is radically different from that of any other Old Testament personality. He sees, hears, understands and knows differently. No other believer prior to the Day of Pentecost had that standing before God.

Paul gives us this distinctive gospel for the new creation life. In First Corinthians 7:5 he discusses the man-woman relationship, and speaks of fasting in the light that Satan would love to break up the husband-wife relationship by stopping the two from being one with each other and from respecting one another. To control this, he suggests that they give themselves to prayer and fasting. In Second Corinthians 6:5 he speaks of himself being *"in fastings."* Nowhere does Paul speak of prayer and fasting *bettering the position of the believer.* Satan's trap is to get the believer to believe that anything he does will cause him to have a better standing with the Father, which puts him back under the law. The law annuls the Christ-life. It breaks up the union of the believer with Christ and precipitates the believer into an adulterous affair.

Fasting in the Absence of the Bridegroom

There is one occasion when Christ says an important thing about fasting. He had been asked why His disciples had not fasted as had John's disciples, and He said that as long as the Bridegroom was present with them, they were not to fast, but they were to fast in His absence. In our waiting as the Church—the Bride—to be finally joined to the Bridegroom, we fast. This kind of fasting is likened to where Paul said that we groan while awaiting deliverance from this body. Certainly the bringing of our bodies under subjection to the "treasure," Christ within us, is a noble form of fasting, but we must not be deceived into believing that bodily subjection by fasting will enhance the Christ within. He is total and complete, and nothing we can do

page 163

will add to Him. The bringing of the body under subjection is to give Him the liberty of spontaneously living as us.

Praying is not something the new creation believer does, it is something he is. His very life is a prayer; everything he does is a prayer. He is never separated from the Christ-life, and Christ is never separated from the Father. There is constant communion. Wherever he goes, he goes as Christ—Christ on the job, at school, in the home, driving the car, etc. The total consciousness of the knowing believer causes everything he does to be a prayer action. The knowledge of God doing and working in him constitutes perfect communion and is spontaneous living. It cannot be put on, or legislated, or organized. It is not forced by the believer. It cannot be forced by others. Its center is the Father, as is demonstrated by Christ in both of His prayers. Its Father-center is oneness with the Son who is in us.

Pray-ers Are Lovers

This point is not to demoralize praying, but rather to show that true prayer is an act of the Son to the Father. Those who are lovers are pray-ers. Love is the key to finding a time for prayer when the burden is more than natural. Jesus left the multitudes to pray. He was in the desert alone in prayer. He often went apart to pray. This was the Father-love working in Him. It will work in you also, not by the pressure of others or of things, but by love. It cannot be timed; it cannot be charted by others; it cannot be taught by others. It is so completely a love act between the Father and the Son that it is really no other person's business. When others get involved, it tends to become a thing of the law and loses its sweetness, its truth, and its merit. When a new creation believer prays, he enters the deepest communion and the most thrilling experience he can have. Even if he prays in public, it will be as if others were entering into a private conversation between intimate friends or lovers. Law separates the kinds of praying we tend to do, as if God has changed. This is the kind of praying the publicans did in Jesus' day.

I make a point of this because I feel the world has fixed, in its mind, the believer as a hypocrite. Much of this mind-set comes from the way we pray in public. We seem to put on a little show and the deep intense feelings that a believer has with the Father get lost.

Our greatest witness to an unsaved world may be lost in hiding the deep relationship with the Father. How could our love be more clearly demonstrated than in our talking to the Father? We have not manifested this as we should because the law, rather than His Spirit, has taken control. Although there is a place for you to be alone with Him, there should never be an inkling of separation from Him by anything that you say or do. The whole world awaits the witness of those who truly know God. As such, we must no longer hide the true union we have with God.

5. Witnessing Spirit. The other day, while traveling to an institute on an airliner, I witnessed a passenger across the aisle from me begin to make a common witness to an unbeliever. He sat in the middle seat of a row of three and was rather vocal, thereby catching my attention. He asked the person on his right if he were saved, and that person mumbled something, so he turned to the fellow on his left and asked if he were saved. The answer was negative. The man pulled out a booklet I immediately recognized as the *Four Spiritual Laws* booklet and began to go through it. The man he was talking to tried to avoid him. He turned to his magazine, but this did not stop the other man. He ignored him, but this still did not stop the man. As it continued, I sensed the utter discomfort of the witnessee. I was uncomfortable, too.

An Embarrassing Situation

Nothing would stop the person doing the witnessing short of an embarrassing situation, and I started praying. I asked the Father to overrule the situation and bring about good. I am not sure that this happened, but after going through the four laws, he prayed a prayer and it was over, with the witnessing believer settling back feeling he had won another soul. Now I don't mean to be critical of anyone helping others to accept Christ. A world is going to hell, and there are few who are stopping it. But my embarrassment and that of others on this occasion was based on the fact that some law was dictating to this man, a law that said, "You will not be a *good* Christian if you do not witness to others." There is no place in Christianty where the law that a believer must do something to be somebody is more evident than in witnessing. It all starts when a believer is converted. At that time, most will tell them, "Now you must pray and read your Bible and *witness* every day to be a growing Christian."

There is nothing wrong with the doing of any of these things. They will, in fact, be done. The error is in attaching these things of doing to being a good Christian. A Christ-person will do all of these things, but not *to be* who he is. He does these things *because* of who he is.

This is one of the most popular traps of Satan. He wants us to force souls to come to God. When they are forced, then a pattern is established and they will continue to force others and themselves to serve God. By this, he has set aside the Christ within them who is the Light of the world.

Many Have a Christless Religion

Because of the spurious methods the modern Church uses today to fill up the buildings by any and every means possible, I am certain that there are multitudes of church members who are not born again. But that is not the whole problem, The other part of the problem is that they think they are born again and by this thinking have become oblivious to any true gospel that might save them. Modern religion will lead them on into other experiences, such as faith-living, the baptism of the Holy Spirit, and even the preaching of the gospel. Still, with all this they have not come to see Christ as their only life.

Jesus was very plain as to how true witnesses come about. His most prominent word on this was from Acts 1:8, where He said,

"But ye shall receive power, after that the Holy Ghost is come upon you: and ye shall be witnesses...." For long, too long, this verse has misled many. It does not say that if you get the Holy Ghost you will have power to witness. If that were the case, the multitudes who have received the Holy Ghost would have evangelized the world.

On the contrary, most of the world still has not received the gospel. By this misinterpretation of the verse, a law has developed that says you can do nothing of yourself, so the Holy Spirit will give you power to be a witness. Of course, what is lacking in this interpretation is the new creation gospel. Self, as a self, is never empowered. It is the Christ within who becomes the self. The verse says that after the Holy Ghost is come upon you, you shall receive power. Why would Jesus have the Holy Ghost coming upon the believer? The answer is simple. Until the Holy Ghost comes to inform the believer of who he is in Christ, he can never exercise the true power. The believer has no power and is never given power. Jesus said in Matthew 28:18 that all power in Heaven and earth was given unto Him. That means that there is no power to be given to the believer. It is all in Christ, and Christ is in the believer as the believer's only life. That is why the Holy Ghost must come to every believer. Only by the Holy Spirit will they know that Christ is their life and that out of His life comes power.

The Holy Spirit Is the Teacher

When the Holy Ghost comes, a teaching process begins. He will teach the believer that Christ is in him and that he can do all things by Him. The *power* is in the *knowing* of this. To believe, as many do today, that *they* have power and that the Lord has given *them* a ministry is a retreat back into the law which says that man can operate without the Christ-life if he is holy or good enough. The cross in the heart of Paul makes every believer aware that he must be crucified to flesh, that he died *with* Christ, and that he (the believer) no longer lives. The trick of Satan is to take this dead man and give him power by denying that it is Christ in him who is life and power. Somehow modern theology has become so twisted that the coming of the Holy Ghost upon a believer does away with the Christ who is the life in the believer. Now the believer thinks that within himself he has power. This is one major reason the world does not have the gospel.

Jesus said in John 12 that if He would be lifted up, *He* would *draw* all men unto Him (v. 32). He did not say that *we* would draw them. He did not say that our programs would draw them, or that churches and preachers would draw them! It is clearly stated. He would do the drawing. He would do the witnessing. How could this happen? Only by Him being in the believer and operating as the believer. The world is seeing churches and men but not Jesus. The world is hearing songs, sermons and teachings, but not Christ. The only way we can lift Him up is as He flows out of us as living waters. It is only as they see Him that they will know Him. Acts 1:8 says that we will be witnesses *unto Him,* to the ends of the earth. *Unto Him* is the key, not unto ourselves, or our church, or our program. It all has to do with Him—only Him. When every born-again believer begins to see Him as his all and in all, the world will know it as greatly as the world knew that Jesus of Nazareth was passing by. When every believer lays hold of the "revelation of the mystery" that Paul spoke of (Romans 16:25) and has it operating in his life with knowledge, then will the world have the gospel and then will the Father have true witnesses.

6. Commitment. This has to be one of the most important religious subjects with which I could deal. In fact, there is no part of religion that can operate without it, yet there is no place where the law of doing is any more prevalent. When any new convert falls in love with God, his first act is to make a commitment. In my walk, there have been many times I had to make a deep commitment to be able to continue, as if I were not being sincere or loyal to God if I did not do something. The sad thing is, they only lasted a short time before I failed, gave up, and then in time, out of guilt, made another one to make up for the other. Now, don't mistake what I am saying. I am not against a commitment. Far from it. I am against the need of a believer having to make it. I failed in my commitments because there are no committing abilities in me. I cannot be committed within myself. That is why I failed in the past. Now I see that the committed One is Christ.

Religion Wars Against Rest

Commitment is the one great area of rest that all new creation believers come to. Religion does not like this. Its main power is in keeping men committed to the program. Thus, there are innumerable programs constantly promoted to try to get God's sons to do the Father's work. How sad! It means that there is not enough of God's love and power working in the believer to cause him to function as a son of God. Here is where the law takes over. One of our students showed me a letter the other day from a TV preacher who apparently was having difficulty paying his bills. The letter said that if the student would honor his request, the student would be blessed, but that if he did not, judgment would come upon the student. There were several illustrations given of those who had disobeyed this plea and how they had suffered. Now, that is the law at its best. *Guilt is the grease that runs the wheels of religion.* In this hour of extreme faith promotion, there is more evidence of guilt than there is of faith. This is Satan in his antichrist spirit at his best. People who commit themselves to God or any program out of guilt will fail. Yet, this seems to be the only way modern religion knows to operate.

The Adulterous Wife

We can come to the knowledge of the Son of God and be committed believers as we never dreamed possible. Just the thought alone is thrilling! Him in me. His life, not mine. His power, not mine. His commitment, not mine. The Christ who is in me is the committed One. He has never failed. He is sinless, and that is the life I now live. He is faithful, and that is the only faithfulness I have. He is the Giver and the Lover, and that is the only true manifestation I have. When you get that fixed in your thinking, then commitment is a daily and unending thing. But when men say that you must do this or do that, then He is nullified. Like a wayward wife who does her own thing, separate from her

page 169

husband, so does the believer-wife separate herself from the Christ-husband. The wife must want only to do the will of the Husband; she is never a true lover if she operates any form of separatism from Him. This is where those who use the law enter. They see a wife operating on her own and urge her to do their thing, which may be contrary to the Husband, and by so doing, they have separated her from the very One who is her source and life. These even will tempt her to an adulterous affair with something that says, "If you do this, you will be blessed, or feel better, or be relieved of your guilt." Soon she is, in the guise of commitment, waging her own battles, living her own independent life and woefully neglecting her Christ-husband.

There is a need for the truly committed. But this need is automatically met by the response to the greater need of believers. That is the coming to the revelation knowledge that Christ is your only life.

When I began teaching the Christ-life message, I had an obsession that no one should be asked to do anything for the Lord in order that the message of Christ in them would not be even a little bit diluted. At times I have wondered when there would ever be anyone committed enough to help spread the gospel. But praise the Lord, now there are many who are totally committed to the Christ-life gospel. But here is the miracle. *No one has been asked.* All have, in time, come to me and personally said that the Christ in them wanted to do this or that. It has been beautiful to see Him alive unto the Father. Now all of our leadership and co-workers are committed by Him to Him, and worldwide evangelization of the Christ-life message is in view.

We Must Know Nothing but Jesus
I believe that the modern Church could do much better operating like that. To have that, however, a radical change must take place. That change is in the preaching of the message. Until the message of the Christ-life is preached, there will be few who are committed. Until the Church boldly says what Paul said—*"For I [am] determined not to know any thing among you, save Jesus*

Christ, and Him crucified" (I Corinthians 2:2)—there will be few committed. Perhaps most of all, until the leaders of the Church can demonstrate a Christ-like commitment, few others will respond. We need shepherds who will lay down their lives for the sheep if they are to have committed sheep. We need those who can love the brethren. We must see that among the committed are not only the highly trained and talented, but also the feeble and less honorable (I Corinthians 12). This is the way Paul treated the subject, and unless many of these ideas are working, man-made law will take over. It is a perilous day when many souls are weighed in the balance and a greater and more glorious gospel is needed to save the world. That message is the Christ-life. It is an open message—open to all—and we plan, as Him, to cover the earth with its essence, so all will have an opportunity to know. The committed everywhere will hear, and the Christ within them will respond to His own Word, and the world will know the difference.

7. Money. When Martin Luther posted his 95 Theses on the church door, amazingly, many of the things that he protested against dealt with money. Religion of his day had become so money-minded and secular that a believer could do nothing without money being involved. Every blessing of the Scriptures came to the point that money was required if the believer was to receive it. Every event in a believer's life, such as childbirth, marriage and death, were all centered upon money in one way or another. In fact, there was a planned monetary aspect by the church for everything that could possibly happen in a believer's life. These gifts, given to the church or the clergy, were called "indulgences." Indulgences were supposed to bring the giver added blessings. They were to provide him protection. They were to bless his family and business. In fact, believers paying for or buying blessings and protection from the church had become so common in Luther's day that, finally, salvation was attached to the giving. The believer could make indulgence for eternal life if he paid in enough money. It was at this point that Luther balked.

More and more, the message of grace was diluted by indulgences. So he not only took the bold step of differing with the church, but also openly defied it by saying, "The just shall live by faith," and be saved by that same faith and nothing else. At the very risk of his life, he caused a revolution that began the glorious church we are now a part of, the Reformation church. What he really accomplished, after more than 473 years have gone by, was to settle the fact that the Church could not save. A sinner was saved only by believing on the Lord Jesus Christ. The other problem of indulgences is still with us.

Carnal Blessings by Carnal Giving?

I would not mislead anyone into thinking that religion today would outrightly say that salvation depended on money. The fact that it is done is a most guarded and covered action in the Church today. No one would say that money had anything to do with a believer getting saved. Yet we live in a day in which virtually no TV preacher can preach a sermon without the issue of money being major.

The thought is always planted by someone that, "If you love God and want His blessings, you will help with this program, or you will help build this building. Or if you want to have your business blessed, or you want to prosper, or you want to be healed, then join our money crusade." It is always done in careful use of Scripture, by such scriptural connotations as plant a seed, reap a harvest. Or the more you give, the more you'll be blessed. Or in the more desperate case, if you don't give, God won't bless you and something worse will come upon you. All in all, things have changed very little since Luther's day in this area of stewardship. We can call it whatever we will, but it is the same problem that Luther had in his time and there is no better term for it than indulgences.

The problem with indulgences is they revert the believer to trusting in the law. It is a law that says what we do makes the blessing greater or brings it quicker or causes God to respond more. It is a law that blinds us to seeing Christ in us by drawing us into a separated state of doing something on our own. The believer-wife today is roaring through life separated from her Jesus-husband as if He didn't exist. She seeks her own place and her own blessings. This is the essence of the law—to separate us from Him who is our Provider, our Love, our Life, our All.

Money and Faith

It is a strange fact that most of those who are involved in these money schemes of our day also most loudly advocate the message of faith. It is even stranger that those who go after the money for the Lord are able to trust God alone for every miracle but that of their own finances. They alone can pray the prayer of faith and take the credit for someone's healing, but they need the help of everyone present for God to supply the needs of the preacher. This, of course, is a subtle trap of Satan. Having been at this stage of service for many years, I know the deceitfulness of Satan. I know what it means to trust for and get miracles in everything but finances. I see, today, many who are so trapped. They *trust God* for miracles and *trust the people* for finances.

Now, I know that this statement may fall flat on the ears of many who read this. But this great move of God we call the Christ-life has in its center the real faith of the Son of God working. The Church of Jesus Christ can no longer tolerate the carnal attitude that God cannot supply money for His program. We must go back to the Scriptures that say that God can supply all our needs according to His riches (Philippians 4:19). This means that for God to do it, He can do it all. When any believer has a need, he need only tell the Father what it is. If the Father wants to meet it, He will make a way. When we, by our schemes and programs, intervene and separate others from the Christ in them, we have done a disservice that no blessing received from their giving can make up for. We have placed them in a separated place of doing their own thing because someone else said to do it. On the other hand, the Father is well able to show His committed what they should do, and they will do it without reluctance.

It is to be admitted that any group of believers coming to this place will need to be severely trained in the things of God. They will need to know Christ as their only life. That will take a deep commitment on the part of the leadership to faithfully bring them to that understanding. What will be absolutely necessary is the preaching of the total truth, Christ in you. Only when the modern church can bring its believers to the gospel centered in the revelation of the mystery will all of the financial needs of a local body be met. Only then will there be plenty and more to spare in the coffers of the Lord's House.

It Is Not How Much to Give

You may ask, "How is a believer to treat his personal finances?" To begin with, all things must belong to the Christ who is the life of the believer. This knowledge will require a revolution. Up until now, most believers having nothing but the gospel of separatism have operated their finances as if they were their own, with no regard to the Christ-life. We are quick to say that all is Christ, excluding our finances. There is little wonder that the Scriptures say that the love of money is the root of all evil. Yet the matter is quickly resolved when the Christ within the believer begins to handle the matter. It is *all* His. The issue is not how much belongs to the Lord, for it is *all* His. Paul, teaching from the viewpoint of Christ as the believer's life, never mentions percentages that belong to the Lord. To him, it was *all* His. The question to the Christ-person is not how much to give, but how much to keep. The God in us is a *giver*.

This means that at least two things are necessary in order to be free from the law connected with money. First, the believer who sees Christ as his all will not have to be auctioneered into giving. The Lord's gift will come spontaneously from the true Giver. A loving believer will always see ahead to the need and be prepared to meet it, whether it is the need of the church, the program, the preacher, or another brother. As Paul said, we were to lay up gifts so that there would be no collections when he came (I Corinthians 16:2). Second, the message of Christ must control the *wants* of believers and the ministry. God's provision to His Body will always be comparable to His needs in the Body. When we strive to make others adhere to our personal needs and wants, we are under a law and have nullified the Christ-life. He who said that He would supply all our needs is also the One who gives the vision for His ministry. The two are always parallel. In the end, all the works done in the flesh will be burned. Only by seeing Jesus as our all can we ever enter into the rest that He has prepared.

We Can Do Nothing to Please God

The law that says we can do something within ourselves to please God is the focal point of the Spirit's attack these days. God will have a people who know nothing but Christ and Him crucified. This people will come from all over the earth and will dynamically proclaim the majesty of the Christ within. They will make known the revelation of the mystery, and that knowledge will liberate multitudes now in bondage to religion. They will be a people who will serve the Father as true sons, who will have joy unspeakable in that service. It is not a closed society, nor a select group. Its glorious message is from Paul to everyone who hungers after God. Its enemy is Satan, who works mostly by religion. But the Father, who controls Satan, uses even his devices for gathering together those whom He has chosen to be His. So often it is the works of Satan that turn the needy to God. That is what is happening in the universe, and all who long for freedom can enter into its glory this very day!

Chapter 10

The Radical Basis of Christian Fellowship

That which we have seen and heard declare we unto you, that ye also may have fellowship with us: and truly our fellowship is with the Father, and with His Son Jesus Christ (I John 1:3).

I was visiting a church, and the service was good. I was blessed. But near the end of the meeting, the preacher brought up the matter of the fellowship pledge cards. As I listened, I was alarmed to learn that fellowship in that body of believers was contingent upon adherence to the conditions on the pledge cards. Since that time, I have seen many bodies of believers who base fellowship with one another on such pledging.

Some days ago, I heard of a church that was splitting. Several members were at issue with others in that body and some were going off to establish another church. The issue was doctrine—specifically, who was to be in leadership.

Recently a young man came to my office in deep depression. His pastor had warned him that if he did not curtail his witnessing and soul-winning and conform to the church's program, he would have to put him out of the body.

Radical Departure From the Early Church

To some, these incidents may seem normal and rational, for that is apparently the way the system works today. In fact, in some churches there is literally a police-type action in the receiving and controlling of believers. The end result of this attitude is a radical departure from the spirit of the New Testament Church. Spirit-filled circles are deeply marred by division. Almost all have their own rules and regulations that determine whom they will accept and whom they will reject in fellowship. Most groups have written and oral codes that act as a basis of judgment of others.

This could be the greatest besetting sin in religion. It has caused the deepest division—in some cases, outright rejection—on the grounds of failure to conform doctrinally. Unless the creed, the confession, and the constitution of a particular system is fully endorsed, fellowship is denied.

When we speak of fellowship, we are speaking of our acceptance of other Christians. This brings up at least two important questions: What does it mean to "accept" other Christians? On what basis should we accept other Christians? Paul seems to resolve these questions in just one way—by the justification of faith, alone. I too feel that justification by faith alone would solve all the disunity in religion.

Jesus Christ, alone, can create and make fellowship among men by means of His death and continuing life in the believer. What He has done provides the basis, and what He is doing in us continues His justifying the Father and binding us together. God accepts as perfect what Jesus did and accepts Jesus in us as our basis of justification with the Father. God, therefore, declares men perfect and acceptable because He accepts Jesus Christ as perfect and acceptable—and Jesus is their only life to the Father.

If God accepts a believer in Christ, what right have we to reject him? If God declares all men righteous by virtue of Christ's being in them, are they then unacceptable to us?

This is probably one of the issues Paul had in mind when he wrote Second Corinthians 5:16: *"Wherefore henceforth know we no man after the flesh: yea, though we have known Christ after the flesh, yet now henceforth know we Him no more."* Obviously, believers judge other believers by fleshly standards. They are all we can use to judge as our senses are the only vehicles we control. Yet Paul says we are to know no man after the flesh. It is here we are lifted into another dimension of understanding—Spirit knowledge—the only knowledge by which we should see our brother.

With regard to fellowship, the only question we should ask is, *"Does God accept this person?"* If He does, no man or institution has the right to regard that person as unacceptable.

Works Must Not Be the Basis of Fellowship

Paul clearly taught that all men who sought to be acceptable before God or man could not stand on their own works (Romans 3:20; Galatians 2:16; Ephesians 2:8-9). There will be a day when all men stand before God and He will examine their works and render a verdict. Their only hope will be in the Christ who is in them (Romans 2:6; I Corinthians 3:11). Acceptance is a free gift now. Christ in the believer has provided all that is necessary and has been made unto us wisdom, righteousness, sanctification and redemption (I Corinthians 1:30). This is a legal truth, and we can depend upon it because Jesus is the basis. Men ignore this truth when they judge other men, leaving their only basis for judgment in the flesh, by which we are to know no man. In fact, the only way works can possibly be judged is by the flesh. Sad to say, this is the basis many have for fellowship.

The modern church is so far from basic Bible truth that these Pauline truths seem far out. Yet that is where the great move of the Spirit is today. The Father is restoring the *spirit* of the Word, as well as the letter, through the revelation of Jesus as the only life the believer has. That life of Christ in the believer is the only life the Father sees and accepts, and the heart of the current revival is that men must see what the Father sees to have fellowship.

Until all men see Christ in each other as the only basis for fellowship, we will never have true fellowship with the Father and the Son or with each other. These days, there is a great effort in

page 179

religious circles to "make us all one" or "to bind us together." This is human effort, at best, and is most unrewarding because we have started in the wrong place.

We cannot be one with each other until we are one with the Father and the Son. We cannot be one with the Father and the Son until we are one with ourselves. Until the believer is one with the Christ in him, totally reconciled, dead to his own self-independence and married to the Christ within, all effort to please the Father or one another is useless. That we might be *one* is not to make different groups *one*, but as Jesus was *one* with the Father, so must we be *one* with Him.

The Merits of Christ

If any believer is rejected by another believer—especially one who is already accepted by God—then the Christ in him has been rejected. The merits of Christ are fully accepted by the Father, based on His sacrifice and sinless life. These are Christ's merits. His merits are for everyone who trusts in Him. If we treat such a person as unacceptable, we are saying that the merits of Christ are unacceptable. Our true faith in Jesus Christ can be measured by our acceptance of those who are trusting those merits of Christ. If we deny the Jesus who is in others, we are denying His very merits that are in us. This means that failure to fellowship with anyone who is trusting the Christ in them as their only salvation is a serious defect in our faith. If we cannot forgive those whom God has forgiven, then we stand unforgiven ourselves. Forgiveness must reach the point that regardless of one's flesh, by which we are to know no man, we see Jesus in them as the Father does and the fellowship then is with both the Father and the Son.

Acceptance means that we should never ask people to do anything in order to be accepted by us. Acceptance must never be by works. True acceptance can be only by trust in the Savior's dying and doing in us. We cannot ask for any deed to be done or not to be done. We must ask only, "Are you trusting the finished works of Christ for salvation, and do you believe that His merits are in you?" If God requires no works, we should require no works.

"Church Hoppers"

When I first came to Dallas to pastor, I soon saw that there were "church hoppers" coming to our services. These were people who truly loved God but had never settled into a local body. I saw these as hungry, seeking people. As I began to preach Christ, many of them were set by the Holy Spirit into our body. Some of the workers around me said that we should put these people on probation—make them prove themselves first. I asked how this should be done. Most of the answers were based on works, which I knew was not of the Father. Finally, after waiting on the Lord for some period of time, the Holy Spirit, through Paul, spoke that I and our body of believers should accept all who confessed that Jesus was their life—their only life. If God had put Christ in them by grace, there could be no greater standard. If they were in Christ, they certainly had a right to be in His local body at our place. What a relief this brought to all concerned. Now, in fellowship, we had Christ in His rightful Lordship.

Even though works include such spiritual measures as water baptism or confirmation or studying catechism, acceptance and fellowship must come by Christ in us, alone. Then all of these things may follow as love tokens.

In this current move of the Spirit—the revelation of Christ as all and in all—we are again seeing the essence of a biblical fellowship. Believers fellowship and are led to a fellowship on the basis of the knowledge or "mind" of that fellowship. Believers who are led to the wilderness or desert experiences to know Christ as their life will be led to fellowship with those of like mind and spirit. We have no right to reject anyone from fellowship, but can and want to accept, in love, all hearts into whom the Father has birthed His Son.

The Here and Now of In-Christ Theology

As it has been so many times in the past moves of the Spirit in the Reformation church, people are slow to accept the new and feel that the old must be constantly solidified. That is how works take over faith. It was so with Luther, Calvin, Wesley and others who were great instruments in fulfilling a major part of the moves of the Spirit in re-establishing the New Testament Church by the Reformation. We see the same thing today. Once again the Father is re-establishing a major truth to the Reformation church—*the truth of Christ in us*. Just as there was great misunderstanding of the Reformation fathers, there is equal misunderstanding today. Because many in the past could not see what God was doing, they did a very human thing. To protect what God had already done, they established criteria—man-made criteria—for acceptance and fellowship. In doing so, they were trapped by Satan and missed the greater move of the Spirit. This is happening today. The in-Christ truth is not new at all. It was taught first by Paul and fully experienced by the New Testament Church. Yet, for all its truth, many could miss God's best. The end will be as it has been in history. Men will solidify their present doctrines and make their truth the only way to have fellowship with other believers, thus shutting out the fullness of Christ. When a believer is saved, or born again, God instantly does a wonderful thing. He places Christ's nature in the believer and takes out Satan's nature. This is instantaneous. It is here-and-now reality.

Only One Way of Salvation

God has but one way of salvation, and that is Christ in us. Christ does not give salvation; He *is* salvation. If a believer does not know that Christ in him is his life, that does not stop the Father from making it so. For the last 474 years (since Luther) most of the Reformation church has been ignorant of this fact. Although they used words and had it as a fact in their heads, it still was not a Spirit-taught truth, as Paul said it must be. That is where the current great move of the Spirit is. God has now chosen to reveal the Son in every believer as the believer's life. It could not be accomplished until the Father was ready—as it was with Luther, Calvin and Wesley. Always, God moves in the *"fullness of the time."* That time is now for the Christ-life message, and this has been the major move of God—worldwide—for at least the past twenty years. My point is that every believer has Christ in him and every believer can and ought to be living Christ. It is a here-and-now reality. This message of Christ in us is not new, but its advocates will be branded, as were the Father's teachers before. An age-old ruse will evolve that in order to be accepted, one must adhere to the system of old to have fellowship. Although this may hurt some for the present, God moves on and brings all things unto Himself in time. We praise God for the pioneers who see and enter into the fullness of Christ at the risk of disfellowship.

We must not fall into Satan's trap of measuring other believers by our own works. As God accepts us in Christ, let us accept all others in Christ. The acceptance must be here and now. It is at this point that our faith, which is literally His faith in us, must work. If God puts His Son in the believer, then He is able to keep the believer by that same Son. It is here we so often lose faith. What we do is revert to a human faith, ignoring the real faith of Christ. I cannot trust myself to believe in another's walk—as to whether it is sound, scriptural or sinless. It is here that I need His faith in order to see Him in another. And when I see Jesus in him, I can rest. It is not my affair to accept or reject. It is Jesus I see. A marvelous thing happens to the other at this point. If others know that you see only Jesus in them, they will automatically purge and cleanse themselves of their independence and self-interest, thus binding themselves to that same Jesus who is all. If this sort of action should hinder or even destroy any fellowship or institution, then it should die and be re-established in Christ.

God Accepts the Ungodly Who Believe

If God declares a man acceptable here and now, does that mean He declares ungodly men acceptable? The answer is an unequivocal "Yes!" God does declare ungodly men acceptable (Mark 2:17; Romans 4:5). Those who have absolutely nothing to commend themselves are commended by God. He accepts men and women on the grounds of His own acceptance of the sacrifice of Jesus Christ. We often forget that the sacrifice of Jesus was not for man, primarily. It was the Father's sacrifice to justify Himself in redeeming mankind and putting Christ in the believer. The fact that Jesus died to save sinners is of secondary importance in the Father's purpose.

Even with this in view, however, God does not destroy all standards of morality by accepting impious men who lack integrity. No, God must—and will—honor all His law by meeting its requirements Himself.

God is able to accept the ungodly who believe because of the slain Lamb. Although this is a statement made by most religious leadership, it is not an openly practiced truth. We must ask ourselves the question, "Do we really accept the ungodly into our fellowship, even as the Father has?" So often it appears that the past background of holiness teaching, which placed so much emphasis on what man does rather than what God does, tends to motivate the fellowship—especially the fellowship with the newly-saved.

To see believers take hold of the sacred things of Christ, desecrating them by worldliness and outwardly sinful habits with no inward change, is going too far in the opposite direction. Most sincere believers are uncomfortable when believers who claim Christ as their life bear no likeness or image of His character.

The one thing that is strategic in the Christ-life message is when one sees Jesus as his all-in-all, this consciousness brings him daily under subjection and into perfect union with Christ. This is not only inward, but outward. Although I cannot better myself at all, Jesus in me can and does, so that the impossible things I could not *overcome* myself are daily overcome. Even though it is Jesus in me, His inward presence is causing me to grow up into Him. We may begin our walk in Christ with the simple understanding that Christ in me brings a change in my outward man—in living, in health, and in service. What things were impossible before in my consecration now are swallowed up by His abiding, and I and all others around me can tell it.

We Must Understand Imputation

The merits of Jesus are imputed to the believer. If we find ourselves unhappy with those with whom God is happy because of Christ, what does that say about our regard for Christ? Justification is of the ungodly. As important as our ideas of sanctification or holiness or Spirit-given catechisms or by-laws are, none of these is the basis for fellowship with others. If this were the case, new converts would never be able to enter the fellowship of believers.

There are many in the Body of Christ who never enjoy real fellowship with one another because they continue to set their own rules, ignoring His justification. That is why it is futile to attempt to make all groups one in fellowship. When we see Jesus in each other, we will have that fellowship, and the Body of Christ will be one. Fellowship must become a here-and-now reality, as we know no man after the flesh (II Corinthians 5:16).

Acceptance in Christ Alone

There is no greater truth expounded by Paul than the truth that all acceptance is by the gift of grace, which is found in Christ alone.

The same is true of the expression "only by faith." This means that a man is acceptable to his fellow man through believing in what God has done in Christ. There are no requirements. One need simply trust in Christ. It is grace *alone,* not "grace *and....*" It is Christ *alone,* not "Christ *and....*" It is faith *alone,* not "faith *and....*" If anything is joined to grace, Christ and faith, then it is not the justification of God, but the justification of man. Often people say, "I like the message, but...." The Word must stand on its own. It cannot be compromised by anyone's rules or personal ideas. Truth is truth, regardless. It is not ideas that set us free; it is truth. The acceptability of another in Christ must be on the grounds of Christ alone, and not on the grounds of faith in Christ plus certain denominational allegiance. Such allegiance never plays a part in our acceptance. There is no *defacto* righteousness on earth. I am not saying we should have no denominational allegiance, but only that it does not secure acceptance with God or with our fellow man for us. What we want to avoid is the growing denominational righteousness or party righteousness that is coming from so many believers. This spirit bears the same image as the one from which we were delivered when we began to see Jesus as all in all.

A Christ-person (Christian) who is Spirit-filled is no better than any other believer—Methodist, Baptist, Pentecostal, or whatever. Being Spirit-filled is not justification. Only Christ, and He by the Father at Calvary, justifies. In Christ, there is no weak or less honorable believer (I Corinthians 12:22-23). We might alter the wording of Paul and say that there is no one denominationally righteous, not even one (Romans 3:10).

In the final sense, I am not advocating fellowship with no scriptural justification. What I am saying, and saying as loudly as I can, is that *faith in the crucified and risen Savior entitles a person to fellowship with God and with His people!* When we see that basis of fellowship common among believers, we shall have taken a giant step toward the Father's house and will accomplish world evangelization in the process.

The Tyranny of Religion

How is it that the Church of today has forsaken the biblical basis of justification by faith as the only basis of fellowship? A quick look at the beginning would give us some insight. Before the foundation of the world was laid, God put Lucifer (son of the morning) on this planet, our world-to-be (Isaiah 14:12). It is obvious that with all the worlds the Father had, He surely could have put him somewhere else.

The fact that He didn't shows that the Father had a future purpose for Lucifer. He was to be God's agent, working out some of the intricacies of the plan to get new sons. The very heart of the

Father's plan for Lucifer was the institution of religion. Lucifer, while in the Father's house, had full opportunity to know and live the very life style of the Father. Instead he took the knowledge the Father was giving him and turned it into his own purpose and manifested rebellion. He had available to him the Father's ways and character, but chose to manifest his own way. This was the beginning of religion.

The Father saw this and decided that this "use of his own way" in independence could be the main training factor for His new sons. Thus, Lucifer was placed on the same earth as the chosen sons in order that religion might become the opposite of God's ways to show the new sons the true way. We must remember that the Father often trains by our first doing the opposite and by that contrast coming to the knowledge of Him.

Lucifer (Satan) created religion as an opposite of God's ways from the very beginning. The first man, Adam, clearly shows Satan's influence in religion. Adam not only duplicates Satan's rebellion, but also does the first religious act by hiding from God and covering himself with fig leaves.

Until today, there have not been any two acts of religion more obvious than these two. There is no greater force in religion than the force that makes a sinner, and even a saint, want to hide from God and cover his guilt. Of course, this is impossible; yet religion continues to deceive multitudes into thinking that believing certain doctrines and joining some group will hide them from the wrath of God. Then, in a sense of false security, they cover themselves with doctrines. Satan, the instigator, has polluted all mankind from Adam's time until today, and made religion the tyranny that destroys everything that would bring mankind to peace with God. Whenever religion is made central, a way of salvation, or the determining factor in our relationship with others, it becomes an instrument of demonic tyranny.

Subjection to religion then becomes the worst form of human enslavement. "Getting religion" of this kind is an evil thing. Religion tyrannizes by division. More separations and conflicts are caused by religion than by anything else. Religion divides friends and destroys fellowship.

Christians Are a Strange Group

The verdict of one historian on Christian religion is rather harsh: *"Christians have always been a cantankerous lot, feuding, fighting, and quarrelling over theological questions which most people do not understand, much less care about"* (Robert Wilken, *The Myth of Christian Beginnings*).

When Roger Williams embraced the principle of religious liberty, the New England Puritans forced him to flee for his life. Williams found asylum among the American Indians, and many were converted to Christianity. When his former brethren invited him to return, Williams made the famous reply, "I would rather live with Christian savages than with savage Christians!"

Religion confines Christians to sectarian ghettos where their vision becomes so narrow and their love so cold that they can only worship with birds of the same theological feather. Religious commitment often makes members of one religious group paranoid toward other Christians. Not only can religion make us hostile or paranoid, it can also make us arrogant. It is the Pharisaism of Christ's day, reproduced.

The Tyranny of the Closed System

The classical systems of theology tend to act as closed systems, imprisoning the minds of millions of Christians. We are certainly not exempt from the slavery that systemized theology brings to Spirit-filled circles. In areas of faith covenants, confessions and daily rote, all are presented as necessary to knowing God. After a time, these ideas become the basis for fellowship. Finally, the getting of things—body healing, carnal things, etc.—becomes the criterion of spirituality and those who don't get them are faithless or sinful. In time, those who get the most rise to authority and further enforce the basis of fellowship by their own standards. This is a far cry from the grace preached by Paul. The lacking of grace in holiness and Spirit-filled circles, along with the lack of a

page 188

Bible understanding of justification, has been great. A religious trap set by Satan has long persisted, based not on what God did at Calvary, but on one's ability by his or her own faith to produce those works.

When "received works" become the criterion of fellowship, grace is effectively negated. When there is no Bible grace, rules and creeds take over. The confession of being born again—washed in the blood of Jesus—no longer counts. Although those things are elementary, they are only part of man's requirements. On the other hand, God requires only that we believe on the Lord Jesus Christ to get into His house.

The ultimate of the closed system is seen among "oneness" believers. At the beginning of the Latter Rain Outpouring in the early 1900's, these believers likely received a revelation of Christ as their life; but being before God's time to release such a truth as we are experiencing today, and being without sound fundamental Bible teachers, it became perverted and unscriptural. As a result, they have created a closed system of fellowship which narrows them to being exclusive of all other Bible groups and even the Word.

The tyranny of the closed system was prophetically seen by the early fathers of the Latter Rain Outpouring. They spoke strongly against any and all attempts to organize people who were taught by the Spirit. Finally, for lack of a Christ-centeredness, they gave in to the organizing of groups. Of course, groups cannot organize without rules, but as the fires of the move of the Spirit abate, the rules take over more and more. The idea, however, is priceless. Today, those who see the whole of this current move of God are persuaded that the hope of the Church is for the Holy Spirit alone to control and lead. We are of the persuasion that as Christ alone is the life, we would not only lose the essence of His abiding but the thrust of the very move of God, should we move toward a closed system. This is a day of liberty. We are, for the first time, beginning to see the rest and refreshment the Father planned from the beginning. What a dilemma it would be to return to religion that bases its works on our efforts to receive!

The Tyranny of Tradition

Because Satan is basically religious in his ways, he uses the power of tradition to keep us from the fullness of Christ. In the Charismatic renewal, we witnessed his devious ways, startlingly. Although many were receiving and being filled with the Spirit, as well as talking in tongues and exercising spiritual gifts, many were still wedded to and continuing in churches that openly denounced the work of the Spirit. This shows the power of tradition. It also shows that the free gifts, freely given by the Father to all who ask, do not produce life—Christ-life—in the believer.

Many of these who were rabid traditionalists left their old traditions only to create new ones with Charismatic overtones. Soon, in Spirit-filled circles, such things as covenants, confessions, authorities, standards, rules, worship, praise, success, and many others became the new traditions.

The sad thing about tradition is that it comes through man. It is a sign that man has ceased to hear from the Father and must rely on the good of the past. Thank God, Paul handled this forthrightly. He said that we should forget the things of the past and move on into the future (Philippians 3). Perhaps the greatest bondage in tradition is our substituting it for life—Christ-life. We are tricked into believing that the things of the past are better than a present-tense living by His faith. Tradition then becomes a tool to bind the mind from living in Christ.

In a challenging article entitled "The Treacherousness of Tradition," James D. Smart shows that Protestants can be worse than anyone in matters of slavery to tradition. Smart declares:

> ...but what few Protestants are likely to acknowledge is that they, too, have a distressing problem with tradition. The statement can be made and can be supported with a mass of evidence, that in North American Protestantism, in the actualities of both church and personal life, tradition is a much more powerful shaping force than the Scriptures. What complicates the situation and conceals the

problem is that most of our churches are, by their constitutions, committed to the principle that the Scriptures alone, or the Word of God in Scripture, or the Gospel according to the Scriptures is their only rule of faith and practice. Any questioning of that rule would, at once, be condemned as the most flagrant heresy. However, when we look with open eyes at what actually happens in our churches, and what has been happening through much of their history, we have to recognize that the prevailing influence frequently has not been Scripture but tradition.

Two illustrations would be sufficient—one Presbyterian and one Lutheran. Most Presbyterian churches, for 300 years, have been plagued by the endeavor of some of their members to make the Westminster Confession of Faith, in all its details, an absolute and infallible criterion of faith and practice, which would anchor the church's mind and heart in the mid-seventeenth century and cause it to be unfit to face the emerging issues of our time. The Westminster fathers wisely insisted upon a continuing subordination of the Confession to the Scriptures. Their Confession was church tradition, intended only as a guide to a right understanding of the content of Scripture, and therefore, to be corrected should new light emerge from the Scriptures. Confusion of the Confession with Scripture itself, and a failure to make clear the fact that all confessions, as interpretations of Scripture, are church tradition, produced generations of confusion and conflict among Presbyterians. Parallel with this is the present situation in the Missouri Synod Lutheran Church.

The president of the church and his followers, under the impression they are preserving the pure teaching of the Scriptures, have fastened on their church, as an iron law, a set of interpretations which would make fellowship with them impossible, not only for anyone who accepts the historical-critical approach to Scripture but even for Martin Luther himself! A Lutheran church which would exclude Luther is surely an anomaly. How can such a strange thing happen in America?

It can happen because Protestants think themselves free of the problem of tradition. Or because they think themselves to be applying the Scriptures directly to life, and remain blissfully unaware of the extent to which their minds, their actions, and their whole conduct as churches are shaped by traditions of varied origin rather than by any word that is to be found in Scripture. The Catholics have the problem out in the open where they can deal with it and where the full perilousness of dealing with it is apparent.

We Protestants are less fortunate. For us, the problem is and has been concealed for centuries and our official pronouncements and constitutions create, in our minds, the illusion that we have no such problem. But from its place of concealment, it ever plagues us and confuses the life of our churches. We have no pope who gives visibility to the authority of tradition, but we have for years had a profusion of little popes who have known how to mobilize the tremendous power that is latent in tradition.

The Tyranny of Independent Group Life Styles

Every local church has a tendency to produce its own life style. That is sort of a miniature cultural development. Although diversity is inevitable, and even necessary, and may even be pleasing and led of God, many problems in fellowship develop. Real problems are seen when any group begins to equate their life style with spirituality. Soon pressure is put on members to speak, sing, pray, and even dress alike. Psychologically, this could be the leadership putting controls on the people to make sure of their allegiance to the body. Holiness groups are notorious for all their members dressing alike—especially the women. Maybe not in uniforms, but in such like dress that they are identified immediately as "one of them." Often, in Word of Faith and some Pentecostal groups, there are certain forms of worship which are prerequisite to entering in—much as it is in denominational churches that force every worshiper to their own creeds and confessions.

Now, the major problem that develops from this is that sooner or later all who worship here will begin to exhibit the spiritual mannerisms of this place. In fact, it will be either consciously or unconsciously demanded as part of the fellowship.

Our Grace Christian School experienced this some time ago. Our football team was to play a church school in another part of the city. Our kids were excited and practiced and planned hard for the game. On arriving at the other church's field, as our kids were getting off the bus there was an unexpected jolt. The pastor of the church saw that our girls were dressed in jeans, as was our custom for all athletics, and went to our coach and told him that he could not play with them because of the jeans. He did not believe a Christian should wear jeans and he would not be identified with it. All our confused kids could do was reboard the bus and return home.

The pastor, of course, had a right to his own beliefs, but the issue had gone so far that he was forcing them on others. There was no fellowship aside from his life style.

How, then, are we to enforce our beliefs? Are we to ignore what we believe to be right because others may not like it? Any enforcement of beliefs to the extent of barring other Christians from fellowship is error. I know this will seem radical to many. Yet, for Christians to base fellowship on anything other than Christ is error.

The pressure for conformity to group pressure is enslaving. Although there is no intent here to preach the acceptance of those who flagrantly transgress the truths of Christ (and I want it clearly understood that the Christ-life fellowship I speak of can be expected only from the born-again), we still must not presume that our "cult's taboos" are the standard of Christian fellowship.

The liberty that we have in Christ has freed us from religion. Paul, sensing that the trap of religion would be doggedly set for those who closely follow Christ, strongly urges us to *"stand fast therefore in the liberty wherewith Christ hath made us free"* (Galatians 5:1a). He also spoke of those believers who were *"so soon removed from"* the gospel that he had preached (Galatians 1:6).

Religion, masterminded by Lucifer, is ever ready to *force* the believer away from the Christ-life. Now that Christ is our all and in all, we must not be drawn into any forms of worship as being "the only way to do it," or into any methods of service as being "the only way to do it," or into any group piety as being "the only way to live it." It is never our way of doing a thing that pleases the Father. His only *way* is Christ, and Christ is all that pleases Him.

Since the Father accepts only the Jesus in us and the Jesus we are as the *real* us, how important it is for us to see only Jesus as our life.

The Problem of Churchianity
Very often I hear people say their church and worship is best because they are not bound by denominationalism—thinking that denominationalism is belonging to some staid corporate group that has long since lost its fire. Far from it. Many independent churches fit the mold of denominationalism as well as any. In the dictionary, the simple definition of denominationalism is "one of a kind." This means that a single church, with a single set of rules of conduct, can be denominational. It is not denominationalism that is the error, but churchianity. This is where believers place their things above Christ. This is also why so many have such rigid rules of fellowship—to protect their things—things like buildings, faith, revelation or piety. This is churchianity and should not be confused with any corporate structure.

In closing, I see four things about churchianity:
1. Churchianity relates directly to religion and, in the end, saves no one.

2. We confuse our churchianity with the gospel when we allow it to provide us with identification different from other believers.

3. We confuse our churchianity with the gospel when we think that our way makes a person more acceptable or more pleasing to God.

4. We confuse churchianity with the gospel when we include or exclude anyone from our fellowship on the basis of adherence to our own church tenets.

The time is at hand, and now is, when the Father will have a people who see Jesus as their life—their only life—and confess to know nothing other than Jesus Christ, and Him crucified. In the end, this will be the radical basis for Christian fellowship—the only basis.

Chapter 11

The Faith of
the Son of God

Long ago, I had to learn what *faith* was. My adventure into faith began in 1947 when I first started preaching. At that time there were two great healers in the world who were drawing great crowds—William Brannon and William Freeman. They really did stir me and I felt I wanted to be a "healer." Their theme was "faith and healing," and I could see that having miracles in a ministry was a great asset to soul winning. I knew I had to have faith—healing faith!

It was at this point that the Spirit began to teach me faith. Even though I was saved and filled with the Holy Spirit, I did not know Christ as my life; thus the Spirit could not teach me about the faith of Christ. The only faith I could comprehend was the outer faith brought by the outer knowledge, which manifested itself in outer works. I was building *my ministry* at this time, and I needed all the faith I could get! All the Holy Spirit had to work with was this degree of understanding. Knowing Christ as my life was to come later. Nevertheless, the Spirit used what I yielded; so, from my hunger to have my own healing ministry, the Spirit began to teach me faith.

As I look back, I realize John's three levels of understanding were at work in my life (I John 2:12-14). In the beginning, the Spirit knew that I was at a child level and needed the Father to do for me whatever I wanted—just as we attend to a baby's needs. As a result, many were saved and healed in my meetings. As I learned to do the works of Jesus, the Spirit led me into the son stage. My faith had now grown to where I knew I had power over the devil. This is the general stage the faith churches are in today. I praise God for the many wonderful things that have been and are happening at this stage. For many years, I stayed at the son level. In time, the Father moved me on to the stage of His ultimate faith—the faith that the life I now live, I live by the *"faith of the Son of God"* (Galatians 2:20).

Faith Is God Knowledge

In this process of learning faith, the Spirit first taught me that faith is nothing more than the knowledge of God in action in the believer's life. This simply means taking what God says, putting it in the mind, and acting upon it. Then the Word comes alive in me and I am able to perform His works. When this faith knowledge comes, you turn it to work in the body. So mine was turned toward healing and prospering the body. But after a time I saw this was not the full intention of God, and I was to learn much more.

I saw that to teach the father stage, it was not faith I needed, but a *revelation of Jesus as my life.* This could not happen until I knew what the Father had known from the beginning. What is it He knew from the beginning? He knew that He had planned for another—Christ—to be the life of the believer. This was instituted before the world began (Ephesians 1:4). To reach the father stage I must also know *Christ as my life.* Only then would I be ready to be taught the *real* faith.

It is a great struggle to leave outward faith and come to the *"faith of the Son of God."* The critical step between the son stage and the father stage is indeed perilous. Most believers, when they see the price to be paid, draw back—at least until some crisis pushes them on to Christ's fullness. It is grievous to watch a hungry heart see the fullness, only to draw back into the comfortable security of the outer knowledge. This is, in fact, a drawing back from entering into *His* faith to continue in *our* faith.

Satan will do all he can to keep the believer from entering into that rest promised in Hebrews 4:3. This rest comes only by the faith of the Son of God. Satan's work will be manifested through religion, and many will be tricked into resisting the Father faith because of the apparent loss of their faith. The Son has power over Satan and knows it, and one who has Father faith knows, from the beginning, that the devil is a defeated foe and is only used of the Father.

Yet, the hungry will press on to the fullness, knowing there is no comparison between their faith and the faith of the Son of God. The other day, while I was meditating on these things, the Spirit in me said, "The hour is come to feed the hungry with the bread that comes down from God out of Heaven!" I answered, "I want to do Your will, Lord; just show me the hungry."

The Problem of Feeding the Hungry

Then the Spirit said an awesome thing: "You will find the hungry *everywhere,* because the modern *superchurch* program, even with its signs, wonders and miracles, will not be able to feed its hungry." With this Word of the Lord, I was given understanding. What a thought! Not a new thought at all, for every hungry heart has long known that the basic church program does not answer the cry of those wanting His fullness. Things necessary for a superchurch to foster, promote, pay for, and maintain growth are things that are cumbersome and unnecessary to those seeking the Christ-life.

This is not to imply that by moving into the Father faith principles we cease to see the visible signs of active faith. Far from it! We really begin to see something far more important; it is *His* faith working—not *ours.* We must never forget the plan of God is not for us to become anything in ourselves. We are *in Christ.* He is our all in all; everything *He* is, *we* are! So, we need nothing of ourselves, other than the giving of ourselves (our bodies or vessels) to Him to live through us. We are only containers. He is the life!

Let us consider exactly what the *"faith of the Son of God"* is. First, it would be well to establish a sure direction to take. The whole of God's plan centers in Christ being the only life in the believer, and all Scripture is given to us on that basis. Everything the Father has said and done hinges on Christ-in-man as the only life God recognizes. In our Scripture searching, this is the first thing we are to see. If we do not see Jesus as total everything to God and to us, we will never come to the *"knowledge of the Son of God."* The ultimate of God, in bringing about perfect union between the believer and the Christ in him, must become the final key to the Scriptures.

Although it may seem sometimes that I am *forcing* the idea of Christ in us through the use of many Scripture passages, it is because they have been misinterpreted before. Satan's greatest goal is to separate us from the Christ in us, who is our only life to the Father. Many of the newer translations of the Scriptures are weakened because of the constant vigilance of Satan, keeping us separated from the Christ already in us. So, if it appears that the issue of our union with the Christ who is in us seems to be overstressed, it is because I see Jesus as *total everything* to the Father and to the understanding of His Word. Although many of the translators never saw in-Christ truths—and could not, for it was not God's time (only now is the Reformation church beginning to see His final truth)—we are finally seeing that only the Holy Spirit can teach us Christ. Nevertheless, whatever the translators failed to see, the Father still plainly said (the Greek and Hebrew adequately bring it out), and the Holy Spirit is teaching it to the hungry. Praise God! The hungry do not need to know Greek and Hebrew when they are taught by the Holy Spirit! The only ones who will ever know who they are in Christ are those taught by the Spirit.

Have Faith in God

Now, back to our subject: What is the faith of the Son of God? Mark 11:22 says, *"And Jesus answering saith unto them, Have faith in God."*

This Scripture needs our careful attention. Some translations read, "Have faith in God." A more accurate rendering reads, "Have the faith of God." Only by such rendering would it be consistent with the total plan of God. It is the very heart of the plan of God that He be justified to place another Person in us by the death of Jesus, His Lamb. If He is only going to trust that other One, Jesus in us, as our salvation (Romans 5:10), consistency requires that He trust only Christ's faith as our faith. The Father knew from the beginning that He could not trust man (Adam) or any creature, whether that creature was already in His house (Lucifer) or in His perfect garden. If He was to save man by the life of Another, He would also depend upon the faith of Another.

In the New Testament, an oft-used term is *pistis Iesou Christou*. It is usually rendered as "the faith of Jesus Christ." (Galatians 2:16b). The original plainly brings this out, even though many newer translations render it as " faith in Jesus Christ."

To show how important it is to render all translation from the in-Christ position, we need only look at Romans 3:22: *"Even the righteousness of God which is by faith of Jesus Christ unto all and upon all them that believe: for there is no difference."* Many are quick to say that God sees only Christ as our righteousness, yet they still have not seen that our righteousness (which is Christ) is not on the merit of our faith, but on the merit of His faith. Even as He is our righteousness, He is our faith; better still, our righteousness works strictly by His faith. If we have no life of our own, we have no faith of our own. It is His life and His faith.

Exactly where does *our* faith come in? We know that only those who believe in the Lord Jesus Christ are saved. This believing is a faith that God, by provenient grace, gives to us. If He did not give it, we could never be saved. Yet, this believing faith is not the faith that keeps us. Believing faith comes out of the first real crisis the sinner faces—the crisis of being in great need, yet unable to save oneself—one *needs* the help of Another. It is this other One who saves; but even more, it is this other One who *keeps* us saved. Because it is His life alone that God trusts as our salvation, it is His faith alone that God can trust.

The "First Faith"

A great text is Romans 1:17: *"For therein is the righteousness of God revealed from faith to faith: as it is written, The just shall live by faith."* Here it is plainly written that there are two faiths. Why two faiths? Because the believer moves from his initial understanding of God's saving him to the more mature knowledge of Christ being the saving life in him. The first faith is exercised by a free moral agent, seeing and accepting the salvation of the Lord. After a time and the revelation of the mystery, the believer "sees" Christ's faith as being his only faith.

Throughout the New Testament, *pistis* means "faith *of* Jesus"—not "faith *in* Jesus." But there is more to it than that. *Pistis* alluded to faithfulness—not just faith. Scholars referred to the Hebrew word *emunah,* which in the Old Testament is consistently rendered "the faithfulness of God." Translated into the Greek, the meaning is the same as the word *pistis.* In the New Testament, the phrase then means "the faithfulness of Jesus Christ," or "God's faithfulness revealed in Him." This means the faith of man is literally based on the faithfulness of the Christ in him. The believer who has no life of his own now has no faith of his own; and the life he now lives in Christ, he lives by the faith of the Son of God.

The Father Depends on Christ's Faithfulness

Only the Father could accomplish this. To do so, He depended on the sacrifice of the Lamb, slain from the foundation of the world. Just as He knew He could not depend on a creature pleasing Him, and that He must place another nature in us, so He depends only on Christ in us to be our life, and He depends only on Christ's faithfulness in us to be our faith.

In regard to Paul's usage of *pistis Iesou Christou,* Greek scholars say it is used at least 24 times; every time it is used, it refers to the faith *of* the person—never to faith *in* a person. There are seven places it is used which we would do well to look into:

1. Galatians 2:16—*"Knowing that a man is not justified by the works of the law, but by the faith of Jesus Christ [pistis Iesou Christou] , even we have believed in Jesus Christ, that we might be justified by the faith of Jesus [pistis Iesou Christou] , and not by the works of the law...."* The Father wanted His sacrifice for sin to be the total sacrifice. Man must be totally justified by the finished work of Christ at Calvary and have no trust in the law to save him. There cannot be a mixture of law and Jesus; it must be *pure Christ.* Thus, Paul says that the Christ already in the believer, and *only* He, must be the trustworthy One. If God knows that He cannot depend on man to do what is right, and that He must depend on Another (Christ), He will depend on the faithfulness of Christ to fully justify His saving the believer. The verse may be taken as relating Paul's believing to Christ's firm adherence to the will of God in the work of atonement and redemption:

...a man is not justified by performing the law, but only by means of the faithfulness of Christ. So even we believed on Jesus Christ, that we might be justified in Christ, as a result of His faithfulness to God's will and not as a result of our keeping the law (paraphrased).

Verse 20 of the same chapter amplifies this. To be justified in Christ is to be crucified with Him and to live by (or in) that quality or attitude of constancy by which the Son of God loved me and gave Himself up for me.

2. Galatians 2:20—*"I am crucified with Christ: nevertheless I live; yet not I, but Christ liveth in me: and the life which I now live in the flesh I live by the faith [pistis] of the Son of God , who loved me, and gave Himself for me."* This has become the golden text of the Bible to those who are in union with Christ. I never cease to marvel at the plan of God. To think that He would place Christ—His only Son—in us goes beyond all comprehension.

page 203

Then, to boldly say that Christ in us would operate out of our flesh is unbelievable—so unbelievable that great numbers of born-again believers try to do away with their flesh, or flesh works, never coming to depend on the *pistis* (faith of Christ) in them! This has become the greatest trap set by Satan for believers. If Satan cannot keep a believer from trusting that Christ is his life, he will try to keep him from relying on Christ's faith. For so many years, I—and many others like me—relied on works and self-effort to please God. All this time, I had Another in me to whom God was looking for my salvation. Then, in God's time, I received a revelation that Christ is the life in me, and Satan began his last deceit. He tricked me into believing my flesh was so dirty that Christ could not live in me, and this blinded me to seeing that the life I now live in the flesh is by the faith of the Son of God (*pistis*)! There will always be sin in our flesh (body) (Romans 7:17-20). God never intended to save bodies until the resurrection morning! Until then, the life we live in these bodies (flesh), we live not by *our* faith or *our* works, but by *pistis Iesou Christou*! As my dear friend, Norman Grubb, says, "I didn't ask Him to live in me; He chose me for Himself, and if He doesn't like me, it's His fault!" So the knowing believer depends on Christ in him as his life, and he depends on the *"faith of the Son of God"* that Christ will live as him. It is not just Christ in us, but *pistis*—Christ as us!

3. Galatians 3:22—*"But the scripture hath concluded all under sin, that the promise by faith of Jesus Christ might be given to them that believe."* In this verse, the *pistis Iesou Christou* is the means by which the Abrahamic promise overcame the obstacle posed by the interlude of the law and was made available to all who should believe—meaning that it is not man's faith, but Christ's faithfulness that saves. Supporting that thought is a verse in Romans 15:8: *"Now I say that Jesus Christ was a minister of the circumcision for the truth of God, to confirm the promises made unto the fathers."* This "firmness" of Christ (in this case, His faithful servitude to the will of God) is the *pistis*

Iesou Christou that is the ground of man's confidence and trust as he seeks a standing before God. What has happened to us today is that we accept religion, or church doctrine, as grounds for our standing before God. We have been tricked by Satan, whose greatest tool is religion. It is only Christ's faith in us that is acceptable to the Father. We are not only saved by grace (God's total effort), but we are kept saved by grace *(pistis Christou).*

4. Romans 3:22—*"Even the righteousness of God which is by faith of Jesus Christ unto all and upon all them that believe: for there is no difference."* This verse is an enlargement upon a most important text, First Corinthians 1:30. There Paul says that Christ has been made unto us righteousness. We are righteous—and kept righteous—only by the faithfulness of the indwelling Christ. The only manifested righteousness we have is Christ's! We cannot make or develop a righteousness of our own. He is our righteousness and it is pistis Christou (His faithfulness) that causes it to continue.

5. Romans 3:26—*"To declare, I say, at this time His righteousness: that He might be just, and the justifier of him which believeth in Jesus."* What a glorious thought! We are not justified by our own works, but by the *"Justifier"* who is in us! The one thing God knew about human beings was that they could never prove faithful. This unfaithfulness first began with Lucifer, who was in the Father's house. Probably it was his unfaithfulness that provoked much of the plan of God. God knew that if a son (Isaiah 14:12) already living in His house could not be faithful, then there was no way He could make a free moral agent who would stay faithful! Just as the Father instituted the *"mystery of godliness"* to get sons like Himself, so He instituted into that plan that Jesus in them would be the Faithful One. All God's creatures are unfaithful in themselves. The one purpose of this writing is to show that God cannot depend on man's putting his faith in Christ, for such an act would nullify the righteousness of Christ. God's righteousness has been manifested by the character of Christ's work and not by man's faith in Christ; for how can man's faith be said to have

page 205

demonstrated God's righteousness? Rather, Christ's faithfulness, in death itself, makes possible an atoning sacrifice that redeems lost men. Christ is the Immovable Rock established by the Immutable God, upon which He invites men to take their stand without flinching.

6. Philippians 3:9—*"And be found in Him, not having mine own righteousness, which is of the law, but that which is through the faith of Christ [pistis Christou], the righteousness which is of God by faith [pistis]."* In this verse, Paul is seeking a righteousness— not his own, but that of God—which is through the faithfulness (*pistis*) of Christ. The fact of Christ's faithfulness in Paul has become firmly established because of the many trials and sufferings he has experienced. Paul has already seen that he could not have made it on his own faith. He has come this far by the faithfulness of the Christ whose life he lives. It is obvious that the knowing of the Jesus who is now Paul's faith has come through much suffering. Paul also sees that the future will hinge not on the faith that he has, but on the *pistis*—the faith of Jesus. Multitudes in the faith movements today are being torn apart by Satan. Men tell men to get faith. They say that without faith it is impossible to please God. They say that if you get faith, you can have anything you want—health, prosperity—anything. The fact is, however, that sometimes we get what we want, and sometimes we get what He wants! When I was in the healing ministry (I still pray for the sick, and God heals), I would tell those who did not get what they wanted that it was because they did not have faith or they had sin in their lives. Of course, I did not know Jesus as my only life at the time, much less know that the real faith was His faith in me—not my faith at all! It must boldly be said here that until a believer has received a revelation of Christ as his life (Romans 16:25) he can never see, working through him, the faith of the Son of God.

When Paul saw that Christ's faith in him was his only faith and righteousness, he was willing to suffer the loss of all things that made him what he was. He reasoned, "If the life is Christ, and I live that life by His faith, then I do not need my life, my righteousness, or my faith!'' To come to this level of understanding—the Father level—one must be taught of the Spirit (I Corinthians 2:9-10).

7. Ephesians 3:12—*"In whom we have boldness and access with confidence by the faith [pistis] of Him."* All of this means that *pistis* designated a quality of firmness, or fixedness, or constancy which, as Paul discerns it, exists at three vital points in the scheme of salvation. First, there is the *pistis* of God Himself—His eternal immutable character—displayed in His Word and His action, notable in His righteousness and His salvation. Second, there is the *pistis* of Christ, seen in His unflinching obedience to the will of the Father, His faithfulness to the promise of blessing through the seed of Abraham, and to the loving purposes of salvation—even in suffering and death. We do not have to say this is God's faithfulness in Christ; it is Christ's own faithfulness (*pistis*), peculiar to His own role in the Godhead. Finally, there is the faithfulness (*pistis*) of believers—evoked, no doubt, by the faithfulness (*pistis*) of God and the faithfulness (*pistis*) of Christ—yet a quality in the believer himself and, therefore, properly distinct from God's and Christ's, for ultimately it is Christ *in* us, *as* us. Our faithfulness (*pistis*) is expressed in both our trust in the Word of God (renewal of the mind) and in the work of Christ for us at Calvary and His steadfastness in us.

Chapter 12

Living
as Knowers

During the course of the journey from earth to the Father's house, a traveler is often confronted by various clichés and terminologies. One term used by Christ-life believers is the word *knowers*. I suppose that the word has many different meanings to different people; but to me, it helps to define the essence of who we really are in Christ. In one of our Institutes, I had said that a true believer was a be-er" rather than a "doer." My pronunciation of the word "be-er" confused one student and she stopped me in the middle of a lecture, asking "Why do you keep saying we must be 'beers'?" I realized, then, that my inflection of speech was making the word "be-er" sound differently to her than it was meant to sound.

We have no term in this Christ-life move that is more blessed than knowers. As a young believer, I found great blessings from Paul's statement, *"I know whom I have believed"* (II Timothy 1:12). This statement became a real anchor to me, and my simply knowing Christ as my life was the main part of all my believing. It is not so much *what* I believe or *how* I believe, but *in whom.* Through the years, I found myself using the term *knowing* so much that the word has evolved into *knowers.*

Paul Was the First "Knower"

Though the Father announced before the foundation of the world (Ephesians 1:4) that all believers were to be chosen in Christ, it was still some four thousand years before the Father actually brought it about. This great moment finally came about through the Apostle Paul as he went into the Arabian desert (Galatians 1:17). It was here that he received the revelation that Christ was in him and was his only life. Paul was the first recorded one to know the Christ-life for the believer.

This knowledge that Christ was his life constituted the greatest knowledge the Father had ever released to mankind. Although great amounts of information had come to man during the centuries, none was so liberating as this. It was the secret that God had hidden from the prophets and men of old, but finally released to make man a completed being for the first time.

This places Paul in the most strategic place in all of history. Paul had already received Christ as his Savior on the road to Damascus, but he did not know that Christ was his only life until the Father revealed it to him in Arabia. He did not just receive a new experience. What he got was knowledge—the knowledge that Christ was his only life. This made him a knower—the greatest knower who had ever lived.

This knowledge—the revelation of Christ as his life—flowed throughout all of Paul's writings. From that point on, he would say again and again that the greatest need of the regenerated believer was knowledge—the knowledge of what really happened when the believer was saved. The heart of that knowledge was that God had actually put another life—the Christ-life—in the believer, but more than this, God did not expect the believer to live his own life anymore, but the life he was to live was Christ (Galatians 2:20).

Along with this great knowledge came a revolutionary truth that God would no longer look to the believer for anything. The Father had already experienced the failure of one of His own to become something. This was the creature, Lucifer, who had already lived in the Father's house and was called the *"son of the morning"* (Isaiah 14:12). God knew that if this so-called son of the morning could not please Him, there would be no way any created, free, moral creature could ever please Him.

So it was planned that the Father would take a part of Himself—God, the Son—and place Him in everyone who needed salvation; and by that placing of another life in the believer, He would have the sons He wanted.

The Beginning of Real Knowledge

It was this great truth that made Paul's writing different. God revealed to him the great secret that literally held the world together. He was eventually to say that everything in the universe depended on and functioned only because Christ was total everything (Colossians 1:16-17). This was an unbelievable knowledge that could be known only by the teaching of the Holy Spirit (I Corinthians 2:9-10).

Almost every one of Paul's prayers centers around asking the Father for this knowledge. Paul saw that even though believers were saved, they had no knowledge that Christ was in them. It is mind-boggling to think that the Father would place another life (Christ) in the believer and not make the condition for receiving it the knowledge of what had happened. Yet, that is just what He did.

I believe His reason for doing that was so He might be justified in bringing many sons to His house, and also to bring about His process of adoption. By His past experience with Lucifer, He knew that just a created son in the house was not good enough; He needed a son who had His very nature. However, although the Son's nature was a grace gift, the issue of the son having the knowledge of this was to be left to the exclusive teaching of the Holy Spirit (John 14:16). With Paul, it was only by the teaching of the Holy Spirit that the believer actually came to the knowledge of life. It was the revelation of Christ as Paul's only life that prompted him to say that real knowledge came to the believer only by such a revelation (Ephesians 1:17).

This great revelation that Christ is the life of the believer is the thrust of the move of the Spirit today—not only that Christ is the life of the believer, but that the believer, and Christ in him, have become one (I Corinthians 6:17). This union between the believer and Christ formed the first basis of knowledge necessary to fit the human being into the world as the Father intended from the beginning.

The world is not out of order. Satan does not rule the world. The situations of life are not hopeless. The real problem is our lack of knowledge—Spirit-taught knowledge. More and more, believers are seeing Christ as God's all and in all.

Laying a Sure Foundation

When Paul received his revelation of Christ, he immediately began to teach its liberating knowledge. Galatians 1 tells us that after the revelation, he went to Jerusalem to share his great truth with the brethren there. He was somewhat rejected by these brethren who knew Christ so well in the flesh (II Corinthians 5:16). They could not see Christ being in them. This possibly was the basis for Paul's lack of fellowship with them. Later, we know that Peter and John learned Christ in the same way, for their Epistles speak of it.

Regardless, Paul returned to his missionary work and firmly established believers in the Christ-life. Churches sprang up and believers were seeing Jesus as their all. It was some years after the experience in Galatians 1 that he wrote the letter to the saints in Rome. His Roman Epistle was written to established saints and was consistent with the flow of all his writings—that the spiritual criterion of the believer is Spirit-taught knowledge.

Paul recognizes that just as he has been Spirit-taught of the Christ-life, he must now help all believers see their place and union in Christ. Looking into Paul's method of bringing this knowledge to believers is part of my mission in this writing.

Until believers today come to this knowing of the Father's original plan, they will live under the bondage of various religious ideas. Any and all religious ideas will be set aside when His Spirit reveals Christ in the believer.

As the believer sees Christ as his life, he will become obsessed to be *one* with Him. No longer will he tolerate any division of Christ (I Corinthians 1:13), such as a believer saying that he is a Baptist Christian or that he is a Charismatic Christian. He will come to see that he is never, in any way, separate from Him who is his all and in all. It may be that he attends a Baptist or a Charismatic church, but the knowledge of who the believer is—a Christ-person—will prevail at all times. I believe it is the Father's ultimate intention to bring every hungering heart to this knowledge. Even as Paul became a knower, so shall we.

The Key Is in Romans 6

Paul became aware that, although one may have a revelation of Christ as his life, the mind being degenerate will often revert to its old way, which is total ignorance.

Paul is often saying, *"With the mind* I do this or that" (Romans 7:23,25; 8:5,7). He knew that which all *knowers* must learn—that the mind is constantly making choices, that those choices are the basis of our love toward God and that the love of God flows out of the believer's life as a result of his choices. Thus a knower's true tool of service is his mind.

Let us take a look at a knower's use of his mind: *"Likewise reckon ye also yourselves to be dead indeed unto sin, but alive unto God through Jesus Christ our Lord"* (Romans 6:11). The important word in this verse is the word "reckon." It is a knower's word, and in its highest sense, it points to knowing and making the knowing work. The word comes from the Greek word *logizomai,* which is defined as "one who takes inventory, makes an estimate, or thinks on a certain thing." To reckon, for a knower, means to count on the Christ within for all things, never leaning to one's own understanding. There are several essential principles to becoming a knower.

According to Webster, a principle is "the law of nature, or the method by which a thing operates." The word in the Greek points to Christ as the *Logos,* in that it is the elements of His life and His discourses that make a principle. Our Father works according to His spiritual principles to bring us to His purpose in our lives. He brings us, for instance, to the reality of our *identification* on the basis of knowledge. This knowledge comes by seeing the Word alive in the Scriptures. As we see Jesus living, dying, buried, resurrected, and finally ascended, we become *knowers* of *identification.*

The truths of identification are those facts from the Word that reveal to us that it is really us dying as Him, and finally, that it is us being resurrected as Him. It is not that He did it all for us; He did it all *as* us. As foreknown believers, our Father judicially placed us in His Son on the cross, so that we died unto sin in Him and are now alive unto God in Him.

The Principle of Faith

The simple faith that God meant what He said in the Word brought us salvation. We believed and were saved. That was really our first experience with faith. Then, as we began our walk—our daily living—we grew in faith. We learned that coping with the believing was a fluctuating ordeal; some days it worked, some days it didn't. But the principle of faith was working.

After all has been defined and said about faith, real faith is nothing other than God's knowledge in action in the believer's mind. In time, that knowledge changes from what the believer thinks and believes to the very faith of the Son of God (Galatians 2:20).

Knowers finally come to a life of rest, for the life they now live, they live by the faith of the Son of God. This principle literally means that the issues of life are in the Father's timing, and that all things are working out according to the Father's plan.

The understanding of the time element in the believer's knowing is the real test of his love for God. Knowers accept the time principle as an ordinary process of growth. They know, on the one hand, that they are already eternal beings in Spirit, but on the other hand, that the Father has reserved the earth journey as a means of working out the adoption process.

This takes the entire lifetime of the believer; the knower sees this, fits it into his thinking and never becomes alarmed that things are not as they should be.

The Principle of Pattern

There is a *pattern* throughout our spiritual development. Whether we realize it or not, even though we were ignorant of what happened at our salvation, our knowing began right then. Our coming to knowledge comes as much by the negative things that happen as by the positive. Our ignorance at conversion is of use later on in our experience, as we look back to see how God has led us.

With our hearts full of love and zeal, we became active for the Lord as the new life began to emerge. All went well for a time—possibly for several years. Then a deadly declension set in. We were so busy enjoying our new experience and activities that we inadvertently began to neglect the Source of our new life—both the written and the living Word. The inevitable result was a reversion to the enslaving influence of law, sin, independence and the world. It was then that we began to feel defeated, heartsick and wretched. This failure is necessary. It is the firmest foundation of all knowers.

Finally, after years of failure in both life and service, we were prepared to see something of the wonderful truths of our identification with our Lord in His death and resurrection. We saw that He not only freed us from the guilt and penalty of sin, but also from the power and domination of the principle of sin. A pattern begins to form that will repeat itself every time we get away from Spirit knowledge. It is a pattern of believing, struggling and failing. This seems to be the pattern that is evident when the believer is in the child and son stage (I John 2:12-13).

Now, what about the pattern of our father stage—the stage in which we come to the place of knowing our identification truths? Just as we became knowers of justification truth in our baby stage, so we grow in the father stage by knowing our identification truths.

As we reach the father stage of growth, we intensify the pattern. We want everyone to become knowers too. In our zeal to bring others to this liberating truth, we not only want to share, we also make openings for sharing. We are surprised to discover that few fellow believers are receptive. Many become antagonistic, and some even accuse us of falling into error.

These are times when we limp home, not quite as enthusiastic as we were when we started. Although these seem to be very hurtful times, they are a part of the pattern for growth. So, in time, a knower comes to the place of realizing that he came that far by grace and that others will have to do the same.

Making Our Knowing Work

At this stage, especially when we get hurt by a fellow believer, we tend to get careless about our knowing from the Word. We forget about the liberating truths that have set us free for longer and longer periods of time. We hoped that everything would be spontaneous, but alas, the unregenerated mind needs to be renewed (Romans 12:2). We have begun to depend on experience rather than on the constant flow of His faith through us. We have the mind of Christ available, but such a mind needs to be renewed daily. This daily renewal takes place as we *see* Jesus Christ in all things and concentrate on the Word rather than on experience. Depending on experience brings defeat!

The pattern is now completed. Our failure in the identification phase is the same as in the justification phase. It is at this point that many believers begin to waver in their hope and expectation of freedom from the old life and abundant growth in the new.

Their confidence in the truths of *identification* begins to wane. How many defeated Christians have exclaimed bitterly, "I tried Romans 6, but reckoning didn't work for me!" The ones most discouraged turn back to Romans 7 as a result of this seeming failure. Some even turn to the alluring, flesh-satisfying, experience-centered errors of holiness and self-sanctifying groups. Whatever it may be though, *all* that is outside the realm of Spirit-taught knowledge—that the believer is in union with the Christ within him—will result in compounded failure and bondage. "*...having begun in the Spirit, are ye now made perfect by the flesh?*" (Galatians 3:3)

Patterns spring from *principles.* There is a definite and essential principle underlying this pattern of seeing the truth, reckoning upon it, experiencing the good of it for a period of time and then, failure. As Norman Grubb often says, "You go wrong before you go right." Therefore, take heart, fellow believer, for the Father is ever working according to His principles, patterns and purpose for us.

When the Holy Spirit brings us to a new and higher plateau of truth in the process of our growth, we see it, we reckon upon it, and we appropriate that which we understand. This is the training of a knower. We must be careful, however, to see that every new experience goes through this cycle. We must not be deceived into believing that each time we see the cycle working, it will be the last time we go through it.

The Principle of Need

It is our master Teacher, the Holy Spirit, who is in charge of this training. He makes the decision for you to fail after your eager beginning. He does so because you must leave the stage of just *wanting* more of knowledge to *needing* it. At this point, He will apply the *principle of need.*

The Father, in supplying our wants, does not set within us the true basis for being knowers. This is proven as we witness the extreme promotion of the positive thinking message in religion.

For the believer to get what he wants instead of what the Father knows he needs only delays the adoption process and keeps the believer from becoming a knower. There is wisdom in the Holy Spirit allowing us to fail. This failure moves us from our infantile enthusiasm to the place where we must dig in and settle down to the explicit truth of the Word.

Before we can grow in an aspect of truth, we must be established in the knowledge of it. In every area of our spiritual growth, it is one thing to begin on a new plateau, and it is quite another to *"through faith and patience inherit the promises"* (Hebrews 6:12). Our immaturity was understandable during the milk of the gospel stage, but now it is time to put away childish things and enter the training of the father stage. We have partaken of the meat of *identification. "But strong meat belongeth to them that are of full age, even those who by reason of use have their senses exercised to discern both good and evil"* (Hebrews 5:14).

We often grasp a truth in our need and desperation, but our initial knowledge is insufficient to enable us to persevere. This is particularly true of those in the ministry. Preachers are notorious for taking part of a truth and preaching it without knowing it. We will face this regularly in the current move of God. That is true not only of preachers. Anyone not willing to sit and learn will say words and clichés and rely on past understanding to make others think they are knowers. But time is their enemy and they will not persevere.

The process of adoption is devastating to those who want to cut corners. Remember, the Father has already had one in His house who attempted to deceive Him. He will not have another. In order that the truth may take hold in us and become a living part of us, the Holy Spirit will remove every token experience from us. But wonderfully, He will allow us to retain the knowledge we received during the ordeal, and it will be of benefit later on.

Establishing Knowers

We are to be established in the *truth* that we might grow in grace and the knowledge of the Lord Jesus Christ (II Peter 3:18). A cloud of sadness hangs over religion today as so many in leadership are using human promotions as a basis of ministry. It is seldom that one is seen to hunger after the things that concern only the Father. Human promotions are always directed toward human needs.

This is the child stage of a believer's growth, and it will not stand the test when the Spirit changes the life circumstances to the negative. The Father can and wants to meet our needs. His greater desire is that we become expressers of the Christ He put within us. The believer's using and misusing the Father to meet only his needs is the major breeder of separatism in his life. Separatism is the prime work of Satan. If Satan can get the believer thinking on his own, living on his own, and seeking for the Father only to meet his needs, he has separated that believer from the Christ within.

There is no place where the Holy Spirit ceases to create hunger in the believer. When we cease to be hungry, our knowledge is only head knowledge, dead and devoid of the Spirit of Christ. As Paul said, *"...I follow after, if that I may apprehend that for which also I am apprehended of Christ Jesus"* (Philippians 3:12). All believers already have Christ in them, but they are living their own separated lives. They have Christ in them, but do not express His spirit. They are not yet knowers.

The principle of time underlies all of God's dealings with us. Growth takes time! *"But the God of all grace, who hath called us unto His eternal glory by Christ Jesus, after that ye have suffered a while, make you perfect, stablish, strengthen, settle you"* (I Peter 5:10). Failure in living our knowing is certainly not failure of the truth—the Word—reckoned upon. Never! Without the Scriptures and the Word, we would have absolutely nothing. It is by Jesus, the Word, and only by Him, that we ever learn anything about the Father.

The Holy Spirit, our Teacher, will use the *written* Word to reveal to us the *living* Word. Never for a moment is the written Word to be slighted or bypassed. We are to allow the Holy Spirit to teach us as we study, meditate and reckon ourselves to know the Christ who is in us. *"According as His divine power hath given unto us all things that pertain unto life and godliness, through the knowledge of Him that hath called us to glory and virtue: whereby are given unto us exceeding great and precious promises: that by these ye might be partakers of the divine nature...."* (II Peter 1:3,4).

The written Word, authored and administered by the Holy Spirit, is the vehicle by which the Father and the Son come to be known to us, and we to Them. Still, as to really knowing the truths—such truths as are in Romans 6—nearly all of us stop at the written Word. It is as though we stand there with a death grip on a handful of truth, repeating and confessing with conviction, "I believe this is true, and I know it, I know it, I know it!"

We are not made knowers by simply knowing certain truths. We are not delivered by believing only in the liberation truth! Certainly, we must believe and appropriate these truths, but the actual liberation comes as a result of our intimate personal fellowship with *Jesus, the Liberator.*

The principle is that liberation is in the Liberator. When believers allow head knowledge to take over, they limit the Holy Spirit in His God-sent mission of revealing Christ as the believer's life. To expect freedom of the Christ-life to spring from knowing a few facts is to ignore God's rights, through Christ's sacrifice, to make us sons. He has bought and paid for the believer's salvation, and He has the right to limit our final knowing to the work of the Holy Spirit.

Our freedom from our past Satan-life (we were his children; he was our father [John 8:44]) was completed, positionally, through our *identification* with Christ on Calvary. There, we died with Him, and from there we enter into resurrection life. This is the essence of our in-Christ position. From this position in Christ, we enter our experiential freedom and growth. First we see ourselves in Him. Then we see Him in us. We cannot expect one without the other. They are linked inseparably, and this understanding makes a *knower*.

Three Essential Steps

There are at least three important truths foundational to the knower. First is the truth of *reckoning*. The elusiveness of the mind, retaining and exercising its knowledge on a continuous basis, requires the reckoning. Our reckoning finally becomes a heart-set attitude. In time, we say with Paul, "I have died unto sin; I am alive unto Christ." Now we are ready to let the Spirit *set* the Word in our minds, literally bringing about the mind of Christ. Paul was a great knower. He knew that God's knowledge in the believer's mind was necessary. So, four times in Romans 6, he says that the believer must know certain things.

In verse 3 he says we must know we are as dead to sin as Jesus was dead at Calvary. In verse 6 he says we must know that the old Satan-way we did things is crucified and that we don't need to serve sin any longer. In verse 9 he says we must know that just as Christ is alive forevermore, so are we. In verse 16 he says we must know that in our minds we each make a decision as to whether we will serve our self-independence or the Christ who is in us.

These four things we are to know are the foundation of the liberty we have in Christ. There is a twofold process of growth always working in the believer's life: "...*always delivered unto death...that the life also of Jesus might be made manifest in our mortal flesh*" (II Corinthians 4:11).

Second, a believer cannot become a knower until he becomes aware of his union with Christ. Paul spells out this union in at least seven different ways. He says the believer is a vessel (II Corinthians 4:7), a temple (I Corinthians 3:16), a wife (Romans 7:3), a branch (John 15:2), a servant (II Corinthians 4:5), a body (I Corinthians 6:19), and a house (Hebrews 3:6). Each of these is incomplete within itself. Each must have another joined to it in order to be complete.

It is impossible for a human being to be complete within himself. Humans are only containers—they contain either Satan or Christ. Once we accept Christ as our Savior, He also becomes our life. He is our life because God birthed Him in us. We were dead previously in our sins, but now alive—not just because of what Christ did, but because He is birthed in us. He does not just give life; He is life.

The Principles of Abiding and Resting

No one can read John's writings without getting a feeling that he knew something that is elusive to us today. He is constantly saying "abide" (John 15:4,5). This was his terminology for Paul's in-Christ message, but the wording of John takes it a step further. What the term "abide" really means is best expressed in the Greek. The Greek word is meno, which means to stay put—continue where you have been placed by the Father—in Christ. Abiding is perhaps the most costly blessing that the believer comes to, but it is also one of the most precious. Satan's greatest attack on the believer is to separate him from the Christ within. He wants to break up the union.

Abiding in Christ as our only life is the first of the twofold victories. The second is our *rest*. We are to rest in the living Word. A separated believer never comes to rest. He is constantly doing something to keep his salvation. In time, he gets worn out and cranky and few things of the Spirit satisfy him anymore. He needs rest. He already has that rest, but sees it only as a thing—an elusive thing—and not as a Person, Christ, in him. The only way a believer can live as a knower is to come to the abiding and the resting.

Third, we see the real liberation in this final step. In this knowledge, we are ready to walk out into the world as Christ-persons (Christians), unafraid and ready to serve. In our *union* with Him, He is now ready to walk in us and express Himself as us. He has the liberty of bearing His fruit and power through us. Our union with Him has brought rest and we no longer, in self-effort, try or attempt to perform on our own. We awaken every day as Him. He, as us, goes to the job, to the school, and to the world. We open our mouths and He speaks. We put His hand to the task and His legs to the walk. It is as if we no longer live; He is living through us. Knowing that He is the husband and we are the wife, the load of our having to produce is lifted. He produces; we, as a wife, bear what He produces. We are ready to really live now! No more stress—only rest.

Spontaneous Living

The believer now realizes the Father can trust him to live spontaneously, as though he had never had a problem in life. The union with Christ is so perfect that all that is done is done as unto and for Christ. This is how the fruit of the Spirit is borne. A knower knows that he has no virtue, love or faith of his own. He also knows that Christ is all these things to him, and with this fixed in his mind, he can go on living, knowing that all he does is Christ.

It is the same way with the gifts of the Spirit. The gifts are ministries of the Christ within and as the believer lives Christ, spontaneously, the ministries of Christ will come forth.

A word of caution is necessary concerning the believer's service. More than one knower has reverted over the issue of service and duty. The Christ in us wants to serve; a sense of duty only binds the believer. The majority of believers today are doers; their chief concern is to work for the Lord. Service is the emphasis of their lives and service requires promotion. Such promotion eventually becomes duty. Sooner or later, the result of every form of self-effort becomes nothing but a barren waste—a spiritual Death Valley. Our growth is bound to dry up when service is predominant. The service-centered believer has little concern for spiritual growth. This is especially so in the formative years. Conversely, when our growth in Christ is given first place, service never suffers. Furthermore, our life-work will be accomplished in His time and in His way—without physical, mental or spiritual breakdown.

The Blessings of Serving as Him

There is nothing more sickening to those who are seeking Christ's fullness than to see those who do nothing—no service, no works, no life. It would seem that a balance is needed between the two ideas. If we try to get a balance, it is still our efforts. It is not balance we need; it is Christ. We need to see Him as the worker, give ourselves to Him, and let Him be the doer.

It is error when any knower thinks the Christ within him ceases to do service so his rest will be unhindered. Rest comes from our no longer working to save ourselves or feeling that our doing will bring us more of Christ. We are free of this idea. Although we see our rest, we must also see Him alive in us, wanting to reach a lost world.

Paul was at rest in the Lord, but worked tirelessly to bring the gospel in his day. He never worked to earn what was already his by grace, and he never worked to become what he already was in Christ. It was the Christ in him that propelled him to the ends of the earth, through desperate circumstances, under every condition; yet he never left the rest that was his in Christ.

We must not confuse the issue. A knower will be a Christ-doer, an unceasing worker. We who are seeing Christ as our all and in all are laboring as never before. The difference is that Christ is the Laborer, the Giver, the Doer.

I cannot mention service without mentioning the Father's ultimate intention. It seems that when service takes hold of a believer, he tends to forget everything else. God's great purpose in our lives is to conform us to the image of Christ. We were not saved merely to stay out of hell; we were saved to come, eventually, as sons to the Father's house. Not even service pre-empts this.

Finally, the believer who comes to know who he is in Christ and what the Father's intention is for him has entered the same life and victory of the only begotten Son of God. What a declaration! This goes beyond all finite imagination. This carries the believer where God intended him to go. There is victory *now*.

In conclusion, let us look at some of the victories which belong, exclusively, to knowers.

1. Because you are a vessel of mercy and are being conformed to the image of His Son, your every action is preparing you further for the purpose of God in your life. *"For whom He did foreknow, He also did predestinate to be conformed to the image of His Son..."* (Romans 8:29).

2. Because you are no longer hindered by your sins, God's infinite power can work through you in service, in daily living, and in consecration. His power in you will keep you safe, for the blood still removes all guilt. *"And He is the propitiation for our sins..."* (I John 2:2).

3. Because God's love in you has freed you from the responsibility of trying to love and serve others (for you cannot love), He alone is the lover; and now, in victory, you can express His love to everyone.

4. Because you are the pleasure and the delight of God, you are freed from danger, Satan and sin. He will never suffer you to bear any more than He gives you strength to carry. You were given to Christ, and Christ has given you back to the Father (John 17:9,11).

5. All knowers know there is now—right now—no condemnation, for Christ has swallowed up from within any and all things that condemn. Furthermore, Christ is at the Father's side right now making intercession for us (Romans 8:1,34).

6. By your death and resurrection with Christ, your connection with Satan, his death-life and his lies, is broken forevermore. You are reborn, and you have a new Father. You are a brand new species upon this earth. You are eternally alive—literally raised from the dead (Colossians 2:13; Romans 6:13).

7. You and Christ are *one.* You have been baptized into Him; thus, we can no longer see separatism. You, in Him, are like a sock in the water. You cannot tell whether the sock is in the water or the water is in the sock. Union is perfect. As you see this and walk in it, you will live the life the Father intended for you to live from the beginning (John 1:13).

I believe that a knower cannot be defeated. The Father is putting together a great army right now that is seeing these things. He will not stop until He has all whom He chose from the beginning as His own.

Chapter 13

The Transforming
Power of Christ

The transforming, purging power of Christ is constantly brought out by the Christ-life message. We who have been taught by the Holy Spirit the marvelous truths of Christ in us believe that this is our only hope of glory. These truths are beyond all comprehension—transforming, purging and healing truths. Any honest student of the Christ-life will be absolutely purged by the Christ within him, for this Christ within him is the only cleansing truth there is and only in the Christ-truth is there victory. This victory will help any true believer, in his everyday life, to overcome the strife of daily living.

Obviously, there is a good fight that must be fought by those who keep the faith and finish their course. It is the true desire of every Christ-life believer to come to the end of his earthly days, even as Paul did, being able to declare, *"I have fought a good fight, I have finished my course, I have kept the faith"* (II Timothy 4:7). The fight must be fought by those who keep the faith and finish their course. This will require a thing that we shall call "mental purgation." Mental purgation *must* take place, for it has the power to accomplish at least three imperative things in the growing believer.

The Power of Mental Purgation

First, mental purgation promotes spiritual growth. Only as the mind is purged of the pollution coming from the carnal, the secular, the worldly and the material, can Christ have control of the whole life. As long as the mind is given only to the body and the world, and to the things concerning the body and the world, there can never be Christ-growth. It is only as the believer grows up in the Christ who is already in him that he will be able to rule over body and thus have the life which the Bible so clearly promises is ours.

Second, mental purgation means that the believer can reach the highest height of human endeavor. The average believer so often is held down by erroneous thinking and by the pollution of knowledge that comes from the world. The true believer can scale the heights of the highest mountain in the Christ-life only as his mind is purged and he is willing to exchange the lesser truths of man for the greater truths of the Christ-life.

Third, mental purgation causes the Christ-life believer to gain knowledge which otherwise could not be reached. As long as knowledge centers upon self, body and the world, and the believer's existence in and through these things, he shall never come to the place of having overcome sin. Even though the body, as Paul says in Romans 7 and in First Corinthians 15, might remain a body of sin, it does not and will not remain, to the growing believer, a sinning body. We must keep in mind that, although the body is made out of dirt and has *down motivation* in it and may even be called corruptible and a body of sin, still, if the mind is given to the Spirit of Christ, that believer does not succumb to a sinning body.

I repeat, *a body of sin does not have to be a sinning body.* Neither must a body of sin succumb to the judgments of that sin, for the believer, as Paul said, can bring the body under subjection to the Christ who is within.

The Knowledge of Sonship

What is a good definition of the Christ-life? Although there may be innumerable definitions, the one that most concerns the truth we speak now is that the Christ-life purges us of the sin that might be within and promotes our spiritual growth until Christ within rules over the whole man—especially the body.

True knowledge defines man's relationship with God as that of sonship. As the idea of sonship comes to the believer, he is able to see that the Christ within him is already God's perfect manifestation of *life, happiness, truth* and *health;* and, as the believer gives a mind to Christ within him, he is an equal expression of these virtues. This means that Christ can be ever present in human consciousness. The endeavor of the growing believer is that of coming to the place where this consciousness of Christ in him is spontaneous.

Glorious, wonderful provision has been made by God to every hungry believer that, in time, growth in Christ will cause him to be a spontaneous expresser of Christ within him, even as Christ, as Jesus of Nazareth, was a spontaneous expresser of God. It means that we are examples of Christ wherever we go. We are examples of Christ because we are birthed sons. We have been born again, taken out of Satan's fatherhood and placed in the Fatherhood of God by actually being birthed. We can rejoice with the Apostle John, who says, *"Beloved, now are we the sons of God"* (I John 3:2).

Coming to this *now* is the imperative of Christian endeavor. As we see Christ as our all and as our only life, He demonstrates true sonship through us. He exemplified sonship better than anyone who has ever lived, and at the same time, He clearly indicated that this truth of true sonship is available for all. By living and proving His spiritual sonship, believers are able to overcome sin, sickness and death, even as Jesus did. To know this is to understand and prove man's oneness and union with God.

The Error of the Adam Idea

Thomas asked Jesus about the way and how to find it. Jesus said, *"I am the way, the truth, and the life: no man cometh unto the Father, but by Me"* (John 14:6). Jesus understood His sonship with His Father God so clearly that He overcame the suggestion of a personal self and independent self in anything that He did. Everywhere Jesus went, He was quick to say, as a son, "There is birthed in Me, God the Father [Emmanuel—God with us], and the works that I do, the words that I say, and the life that I live are all of and by the Father." Jesus so much as said, "As far as My mortality is concerned, I do not live. I only live by spirit, by the God who is in Me." Therefore, the mortal Adam symbolizes the claim of an opposite to God-like man. The Adam idea (Satan's promotion of the knowledge of good and evil), which is so prevalent in the world and even in religion, suggests that man has somehow become mixed with matter and the material, so that sin, sickness and death are an ordinary and natural part of his existence. Now, there is no merit to this thought, as the Adam idea is not and does not rule over Spirit revelation; and the believer who has begun to be taught by the Holy Spirit that Christ is within him, becomes free of the Adam idea. Rather, the growing believer begins to see that the Christ in him has overcome sin, sickness and death, and that because He lives through us we can overcome them also. We begin to understand our true selfhood, freed from self-independence. We see that our real selfhood is a Christ-self and that we are indeed Christ-persons in action. We are purged and transformed and freed from the tangled, bewildering ideas of the mortal mind. We become free from the suppositional mind of Adam.

How and where does the Christ-life transform us? As we progressively understand our divine sonship—that we are birthed, born again and now the sons of God—we begin to see our true nature. The Apostle Peter says, in Second Peter 1:4, that we have literally become partakers of His divine nature. When the mind is transformed and we begin, by the teaching of the Holy Spirit, to see that we have been birthed with a new nature in us, then and only then are we freed from the illusions of the Adam idea. Jesus, with profound simplicity, said, *"If ye continue in My word, then are ye My disciples indeed; and ye shall know the truth, and the truth shall make you free"* (John 8:31,32). The Apostle Paul went further with this truth when he said that in Adam all die, but in Christ all are made alive (I Corinthians 15:22). We see that by the searching of the Scriptures, living in the Word, and by that Word coming to see Christ within us, we are able to enter into truth that sets us free—in body and in soul.

A New Race of People

Total deliverance for mankind comes from man's seeing that the Adam idea—the way he was naturally born—no longer holds any power over him, for by the new birth he has entered into a new life. He sees that he is one of a new race of people, no longer bound by the old race, created by the corruptible seed (I Peter 1:23). When the believer is able to drop this mortal sense of self-independence and perceive that Christ lives in him, he will cease to live his own life (Galatians 2:20). As Paul says, *"[I no longer live], but Christ liveth in me,"* so do we enter into a new existence of health and freedom. Seeing that we are now the sons of God, we replace the Adam idea of pride with Christ humility. We are freed from the Adam idea of self-will, self-independence and fear, and enter into the liberty of the Son of God (Galatians 5:1). As we move from the Adam idea of envy and insecurity, we begin to yield to the Christ-life truth that He who is within us is the true expression of God's love and that we not only will feel that love but express it also. The Adam idea of guilt, sin-burden and discouragement will be lifted as we grow into an unchanging expression of the Christ within. As we increasingly perceive that there is nothing real or true of our Christ individuality and identity except what God has said in His Word, we will be able to become who we are. To not see that Christ is our all is to be bound by selfhood and separated from Christ within us. Awakening to our true nature, our God-nature, and a consequent freeing from the

Adam idea that the material and worldly powers rule us only comes about as we become involved in the good fight Paul speaks of.

Patient persistence is involved in bringing about our actual oneness and likeness to God. It will take much renouncing of sense knowledge for us to enter into this transformation. The Apostle Paul says, in Romans 12:1-2, that we must cease our conforming to the world, which is Adam's idea in operation, and be transformed, even daily, by the Christ within us. The truth of our sonship with God enables us to understand our spiritual nature. Our freedom from the belief of having been born only by a corruptible seed (I Peter 1:23) gives way to the greater knowledge that an incorruptible seed has been placed within us. This comes about by our willingly and unerringly hearing *the message* of the renewed mind in the Scriptures.

The Need for Honesty

In daily life, the Holy Spirit will make us aware of the limitations that are in our flesh. It is by the Spirit's showing us these limitations that we shall be able to move into the higher calling of what is ours in Christ Jesus. To be able to accomplish that, we must become honest with ourselves. Honesty is required in this warfare with false belief. We must be willing to cease justifying or excusing ourselves in error and to look to God for what is true of ourselves and others. We need to firmly resist all that would oppose our understanding of our true spiritual nature. Much of the pollution of modern materialism, secularism and religion must be ignored to the extent that we cease to believe they hold any truth.

As we honestly strive to understand and to better express our true selfhood, we can confidently expect a transforming, healing effect on our everyday walk, on our health, and on our relationships with others. Jesus was an honest man. Therefore, in His honesty, He was a good carpenter, a good man. By this He was able to exemplify God in all ways. Likewise, the Apostle Paul was an absolutely honest man. This is shown especially in the Epistle to the Philippians, in Chapter 3, where he says that anything that makes him anybody by his own accomplishments, he lays aside and counts but dung for the excellency of this knowledge of Christ, his Lord. This sort of honesty is absolutely necessary to spiritual growth. Nevertheless, many times growing believers will encounter acute immediate struggles in their thinking between what they know of their true selfhood and the unhealed errors that are in the Adam dream.

Look at Jacob

This is borne out in the life of Jacob. Jacob's wrestling with error at Peniel illustrates such a situation. Jacob struggled mightily just before he was again to meet his brother, Esau, whose birthright and father's blessing he had robbed years earlier. Even though Jacob had grown much spiritually in the intervening years, he was gripped with fear as the meeting with Esau approached. As he prayed through the long night at Peniel, his growing perception of his relationship with God enabled him to persist courageously in wrestling with material fears and doubts that he had in his mind. He would not let go of the angel who had brought the message of truth to him. He would not let go until his mind and heart were healed. Then he was able to meet his brother with humility, love and fearlessness. So it is with the believer today; it may require a period of wrestling.

This means that so many of our preconceived ideas must give way to honesty. The believer may wrestle in his thinking, as did Jacob, until he comes to this point of knowing who he is and what God has birthed in him by the supernatural miracle of regeneration. The question then comes: How willing am I to fight the battle in my thinking between the Adam idea and the Christ-life—the battle between the errors that seem so real and man's true spiritual sonship? Sometimes we come to a crisis, as Jacob did that night. But the transforming power of Christ appears in our persistent efforts to think and to act as God's offspring, to demonstrate what we know of the Christ-life in the details of our daily affairs.

Satan's Offering

Mental purgation that accompanies the transforming action of Christ in individual consciousness often meets resistance from what Paul calls the carnal mind. The carnal mind is nothing but the false Adam consciousness that can be eliminated only by the Christ within us. Such opposition to this Christ within us takes many forms. There are at least four forms of which we must be warned.

1. Sometimes we are deceived by Satan in the belief that a magnetic personality—a very charismatic person—can take the place of the Christ within us. This belief in persons other than the Christ within only demoralizes the Spirit's work of revealing the true Christ, for the true Christ is revealed only by the Holy Spirit, and the true Christ is never revealed in other persons as our means of deliverance. The Holy Spirit reveals *only* the delivering Christ who is in us.

2. Another form that is often taken as opposition to Christ-life knowledge is the claim that flesh has power and that man is controlled and governed by his flesh. This is error. Flesh is only a manifestation when the mind is given to body demands. When the mind is given to the Christ within, then does man rule over his body. Also, there is no power that can control and govern man according to God's idea better than the Scriptures. By these Scriptures, as taught by the Holy Spirit, he learns what is in opposition to his happiness and health; he will be aware of all harmful aspects.

3. Opposition often comes in the form of temptation. By this Satan causes the believer to believe that he is a mixture of the immortal and mortal, of the temporal and eternal, and by such belief, causes him to be frustrated about Christ in him triumphing over all. However, we learn from the Apostle Paul and the Apostle James that such temptation is not grievous, for it is but a stepping stone to greater knowledge. The greater knowledge is, as John declares, that eternal life dwells in the believer *now,* and that as the believer fixes his mind upon this thought and as it becomes a conscious action in his life, he is freed from the opposition of the mortal and temporal pulls.

4. There is opposition from the flesh to be lustful and greedy. That which is of the flesh, the Apostle says, reproduces flesh. Never out of our mortal lives does there come spiritual truth or healing. It is only as we see God, the Creator, working in and through us that we can have happiness and health. The struggle from our flesh to be greedy has captivated mankind through the centuries; but now this trick of Satan has made knowing believers aware that there is no blessing from it and that the real blessing comes from the Christ within us, who is not greedy. Carnal knowledge would urge the believer to be a taker, but the Christ within, as a true manifestation of God's nature, is a giver. Only by our becoming givers and revealers of God's love, not minding what the cost to us is, are we able to enter into the life that is worth living.

The Allness of the Christ Within

Now the question may come: How do we triumph in the struggle within our thoughts, between the Christ-life and all that would oppose it? We do this daily by basing our reasoning on the allness of God and the perfection of God. We do this by understanding ourselves as His true offspring, with His divine nature operating through us. We do this by seeing that, in time, we can become incapable of responding to the suggestions of the carnal mind. Now, with the mind of Christ, we can become spontaneous "livers" of the life of God in us. Man's sonship with God is the active, living truth of our nature. There are three things to be said about this:

1. We can devote our thought to the prayerful contemplation of God and our relationship to Him daily and, though it may begin by self-effort, the Spirit of God within us will eventually bring us to a spontaneous living out of our true nature. In the meantime, we come to the living of this true nature within us by prayerfully waiting before God and daily contemplating what is our true relationship with God.

2. We can come to this understanding of our true nature as we have a hunger to know more about God. The Christ-life believer presses constantly deeper, not just to know about God or even to know the God that is outside of him, but rather, he strives to know the God Son within him, who has been birthed in him and who indeed *is* his life—his *only* life.

3. We can come to this knowledge of our true nature as we demand increasing evidence in our daily affairs of the truths that we are learning. This means that we literally will learn of the Holy Spirit, and by that learning will have the power to bring our whole bodies and souls under subjection to that truth and demand it daily in our lives. As we faithfully persist in waging the daily mental warfare, which often seems required to lift our thinking above the Adam idea to the immortal reality of being Him in our human form, we are transformed and purified. By doing so, we enhance our understanding and we demonstrate our true individuality as Christ-persons. We also increasingly cease to be deceived by the suggestions of a carnal mind that would accuse us of being mortals and of living in a temporal realm and an evil atmosphere. Because we have Christ as our very lives, we are lifted out of the mundaneness of temporal and material living into the glories of His divine purpose for our lives.

The Defeat of the Accuser

John the Revelator saw this great battle between good and evil in the individual as well as in the world. He perceived the eventual victory of God through Jesus Christ over all that would oppose and discredit the truth. He wrote of the victory of good over evil: *"And I heard a loud voice saying in heaven, Now is come salvation, and strength, and the kingdom of our God, and the power of His Christ: for the accuser of our brethren is cast down, which accused them before our God day and night"* (Revelation 12:10).

As we yield to the transforming energy of Christ within us, the victory over all that would oppose Christ is inevitable. Now, this is a *progressive* transformation. This transformation begins in our thought lives and grows until we become spontaneous thinkers of who and what we are in Christ. This transformation brings about a change for all mankind and is the very essence of the current move of God. By this move of God, disease, sin and death are overcome in the believer who is a knower. The Adam idea embraces such lies that the believer must be constantly over-whelmed and pressured by these enemies of daily living.

The Great Adventure of Paul

Paul began to experience this liberation from evil the moment he saw Christ as the Savior on the road to Damascus, in Acts 9. The immediate transforming effect of Christ in his life led him to cease the cruel persecution of Christians in which he had so mistakenly engaged. Then, later on in Galatians 1 when Paul had the revelation that this Christ he had met on the road to Damascus was literally in him as his only life, he came to the highest level of understanding, knowing that with Christ in him he could overcome all things. He was destined finally to say in Philippians 4 that he could do all things through Christ who strengthened him (v. 13). Paul prayerfully progressed in this new understanding that Christ was in him; and as he abandoned total sense of himself to a Christ-self, he became the greatest missionary the world has ever known. Because he yielded so completely to the Christ within, he was transformed into an individual able to make a contribution to mankind that to this day is the fullest explanation of godliness we know. He wrote to the Romans, *"There is there-fore now no condemnation to them which are in Christ Jesus, who walk not after the flesh, but after the Spirit. For the law of the Spirit of life in Christ Jesus hath made me free from the law of sin and death"* (Romans 8:1-2). To the Corinthians, Paul wrote, *"For as in Adam all die, even so in Christ shall all be made alive"* (I Corinthians 15:22). Paul also soundly declared what is freedom, stability and the abundant life. He has plainly unfolded to us in the Scriptures an experience, learned with transformation, that goes beyond man's comprehension.

Today, as we let the transforming power of Christ in us become our only thinking, we will find that this same Jesus will be manifested in our daily lives and not only will we be expressers of Him who is our life, but we also will enjoy the graces and the benefits of His abiding life within us.

BOOKS BY WARREN LITZMAN

Free at Last, Praise God, Free at Last

Nicodemus and The Mystery
of the Birthing

The Seven Crises of The Christ-Life

The Message in Seven Points

The Believer's Secret of Happiness

The Proper Distinction Between
Religion and the Gospel

Church Unity

Every Believer Must Have
a Revelation of Jesus Christ

The Shape of The Future Church

Christ-Life Healing for Body and Soul

Jesus Lost in The Church

Revelation Knowledge and
4th Dimensional Living

The Radical Change in God's
Plan at Pentecost

The Making of the Son

Order from:
CHRIST-LIFE PUBLISHING HOUSE
Warren & Robbie Litzman
P.O. Box 17307
Dallas, Texas 75217